Nadine Rosenthal is chair of the Learning Assistance Department at City College of San Francisco, and former director of the Center for Reading Improvement at San Francisco State University. She has taught, consulted, and written in the fields of reading, literacy, and study skills for fifteen years, and has authored two books relating to adult literacy, *Teach Someone to Read* and *Ten Career Readers*.

SPEAKING of READING

Other books by Nadine Rosenthal

Teach Someone to Read
Career Readers

SPEAKING of READING

Nadine Rosenthal

Heinemann
Portsmouth, NH

Heinemann
A division of Reed Elsevier Inc.
361 Hanover Street
Portsmouth, NH 03801-3912
Offices and agents throughout the world

We would like to thank those who have given their permission to
include material in this book. Every effort has been made to contact
the copyright holders for permission to reprint borrowed material where
necessary. We regret any oversights that may have occurred and would
be happy to rectify them in future printings of this work.

Grateful acknowledgment is made to the following publishers and authors for permission
to use copyrighted material:

Excerpt from Cynthia Heimel, *The New York Times Book Review, March 23, 1986.* Copyright, 1986 by The New York Times Company. Reprinted by·permission.

Jack Prelutsky: From *The New Kid on the Block* by Jack Prelutsky. Text copyright 1984 by
Jack Prelutsky by permission of Greenwillow Books, a division of William Morrow, Inc.

John Russell: From *The New York Times Book Review, April 10, 1986.* Copyright 1986 by
The New York Times Company. Reprinted by permission of the publisher.

Library of Congress Cataloging–in–Publication Data

Speaking of Reading/[compiled by] Nadine Rosenthal.
    p.   cm.
    Includes bibliographical references.
    ISBN 0-435-08119-5
    1. Books and reading.   2. Interviews.   I. Rosenthal, Nadine.
Z1003.S736   1995
028'.9—dc20
                                           95-5102
                                           CIP

Cover photograph: Peter Wrenn
Cover design: Diana Coe
Printed in the United States of America on acid-free paper
98 97 96 95   EB   1 2 3 4 5 6

For my sister
Carole Martin

◇

ACKNOWLEDGMENTS

I give my heartfelt gratitude to the men, women, and children whose poignant and lively recollections of their reading experiences form the essence of this book. My deepest thanks go to Lisa Heyer for crafting the transcribed interviews into absorbing essays without losing the originality of the narrators' voices, and for her extensive editorial advice. I appreciate Shelley Coleman for encouraging me to complete this book, and Corinne Brackenbury for providing me with so many helpful suggestions.

CONTENTS

On Reading

Your family sees you as a lazy lump lying on the couch, propping a book up on your stomach, never realizing that you are really in the midst of an African safari that has just been charged by elephants, or in the drawing room of a large English country house interrogating the butler about the body discovered on the Aubusson carpet.

Reading is an escape, an education, a delving into the brain of another human being on such an intimate level that every nuance of thought, every snapping of synapse, every slippery desire of the author is laid open before you like, well, a book.

Cynthia Heimel

Why are some people drawn into reading, pulled as if by magnetic force into distant worlds or intellectual explorations? And why are others repelled by reading, incapable of focusing their attention long enough to create vivid images in their minds or grasp complex concepts? Can those who read infrequently learn to enjoy reading from those who read avidly? These are the questions that planted the seeds for *Speaking of Reading,* a collection of both avid and infrequent readers' reading histories, patterns, and behaviors.

As my interview subjects revealed the intimate details of their reading experiences, I found myself especially affected by the stories of the frustrated readers. My heart saddened as they described battles with closing eyelids and thoughts that continually drifted to daydreams as they read. Some spoke in detail about how they are unable to concentrate for more than a few pages and become bored, then restless, anxious, and distressed, finally setting aside their reading material in favor of endeavors with a higher probability of success. One young man whom I interviewed for the chapter on frustrated readers said, "I just get tired and sleepy and my mind starts to wander somewhere out there in left field. I come back in and read a bit more, and then I go into this grey area and I'm back out in left field again. I say, 'Why am I doing this?' and I go do something else."

I identified with his story because I was also a frustrated reader well into adulthood. As I listened to his and other stories of minds closed to reading, the door to my own reading history cracked open, and I found myself facing memories I had long forgotten.

During my first reading class, the teacher sat us in a circle, handed out copies of *Dick and Jane,* and told the first child to read. That child read the first page; the second child read the next one. As my own turn approached, my anxiety began to rise until I started to cry uncontrollably and ran out of the room into the privacy of a stairwell. How were those other children doing it? I felt trapped by my own ignorance. I vowed then never to be embarrassed in this way again, and after that, worked diligently at my reading lessons and listened intently while my mother read to me at home. Fortunately my self-esteem didn't suffer too many blows before I caught up with my classmates. The teacher moved me up from the lowest reading circle to the highest one later that year.

I can only speculate on the reasons I had such difficulty learning to read and why, even after I could read, I remained an infrequent reader for so many years. My parents read to me when I was young, so why couldn't I read like those other children? Perhaps I was just a late bloomer as a child. Maybe I needed my parents to read to me even more than they had. Perhaps their joy of reading remained hidden from me, and so I had no models to emulate. Or perhaps my early attraction to a sport took my interest away from reading.

Unfortunately, I have no crystal ball to help me look into the past to solve the mysteries of childhood. In school, I had learned to read the words, but even as the years passed I rarely read voluntarily. Reading seemed like just another chore. Throughout my formal education I did my homework as assigned, and did it well, but I wasn't able to take real pleasure in reading until I entered adulthood.

The event that changed my relationship to reading occurred in my twenties when I happened to confide to a friend that I didn't read very much. This friend was an avid literature reader who told me stories from her childhood similar to those of the literature readers you will encounter in Chapter 1 and the voracious readers in Chapter 4. She reminisced about her mother's love of reading stories aloud to her with creative vocal renderings of characters' voices. She spoke passionately of the ways reading has enriched her life by giving her access to that special world of language found only in literature. She told me she still loved the delicious feeling of spending all day Sunday reading a novel while cuddling up at the end of her sofa. I wanted to experience such enthusiasm for reading myself and asked her to assist me.

This friend then became my reading mentor and set me on a program that ultimately helped me overcome my reading block. She began by helping me find an author and genre that interested me. She gave me two Toni Morrison novels, *The Bluest Eye* and *Sula,* and suggested I begin with those books for several reasons: they were short; the main characters were female; the stories they told were unusual and engaging. After I finished each one, she would take me out for coffee to discuss the books. In this way, she continued to encourage me. When Morrison's *Song of Solomon* came out, she gave it to me as a gift, and I read it eagerly; it became the first full-length novel I was able to have the experience of losing myself in. As its unpredictable characters and plot unfolded while I read, I caught a glimpse of life inside the covers of a book, of escape and adventure, and of my own ability to suspend disbelief. That one positive experience gave me confidence to read other authors of the same genre, including Maya Angelou, Alice Walker, and Gloria Naylor. From those books I learned something about growing up African-American in the United States that my history books had neglected to tell. I learned that there were books out there that interested me. I also found that the more I read, the easier it became to read.

I was now transforming myself from an infrequent and frustrated reader to an avid literature reader. As I read more and more, I continued to consider my past reading history. I realized it was no longer important to figure out why I hadn't enjoyed reading as a child—this didn't seem to matter now that I had become a reader.

I began to tutor adults in reading, an activity that eventually led me to study for a master's degree in reading. Through working with non-reading adults, I became acutely aware of how fortunate I was that I knew how to read at all. My literacy students told me about their often traumatic childhood reading histories, which made mine seem desirable by comparison. They told me their tales of cover-ups and deceptions, of avoidances, close calls, and missed opportunities. I was moved by their sophisticated coping mechanisms and felt angry that so many bright and competent people had not learned to read when they were young. I found it disquieting to hear stories of deep-seated pain that comes from having a reading disability. In Chapter 6, I share some of these stories with you in the interviews with adult new readers.

Throughout my twelve years as an adult literacy teacher, my students continually taught me about the multitude of ways in which reading affects every aspect of their lives. This led me to wonder just how reading affects the lives of all types of readers, and I began to ask my friends about their reading. To my suprise, many of them had been powerfully affected by their various reading experiences, and were often quite articulate when they described them. It became clear, however, that they had rarely thought about their reading before. "Why not?" I asked. It seems that no one had ever asked them.

Purpose

When I began interviewing readers for this book, I had in mind an audience of adults who are just learning to read and adults who are frustrated with their reading. However, as I began collecting interviews, *Speaking of Reading* developed into a book for those who spend a great deal of time engrossed in the pages of books. You are the passionate readers who will be naturally drawn to a book in which people recount their private reading lives, and who will appreciate this book for its candor and its insights into the lives of readers. It is my hope that you will share this book with someone who doesn't yet share your passion. Like my friend, perhaps you can serve as a reading mentor and enourage that person to begin reading more often.

Speaking of Reading will also make an excellent supplement to required textbooks in teacher-training courses that focus on reading in the secondary schools and adult education programs. In addition, community college reading instructors, adult literacy teachers and tutors, and English and special education teachers can use these narratives as material in their classes. Their students can read selected narratives and then perhaps write their own reading histories. I would enjoy reading any such stories that your students write, sent to me at Heinemann.

Those of us who read successfully find that reading gives us pleasure and enriches our lives immeasurably, and that it gives us options, control over our lives, and the ability to make informed decisions. I pose a challenge to avid readers: How will you initiate conversations with others about reading? How will you bring reading into the life of another human being so that both of your lives will be enriched? How will you develop a relationship with someone who needs the kind of mentorship my friend provided for me? I hope you will find some worthwhile suggestions in *Speaking of Reading*.

Chapter Contents

Although the narratives in this book fit into general categories of avid readers and infrequent readers, I divided them into more specific subcategories, which became the chapters in *Speaking of Reading*. In the book I present the chapters in an order that juxtaposes contrasting types of readers. Each chapter begins with an introduction that explores the particular nuances of its narratives, and the concluding chapter on reading mentorship gives you information on how to pass on your reading to someone else. For the moment, I would like to focus on the more general categories of avid and infrequent readers.

The category of avid readers branched into six chapters: in Chapter 1, I present the Literature Readers; in Chapter 3, you will encounter Those Influenced by Childhood Reading Experiences; Chapter 4 brings together the Voracious Readers, and in Chapter 5, you meet their close relatives, the Habitual Readers; Chapter 7 gives you the Information Readers, and finally, in Chapter 8, I have collected Those Aware of Their Reading Process.

In Chapter 1, literature readers describe their reading as a "time warp" experience in which they escape into the pleasures of beautifully written literature. Many read literature to savor the beauty and richness of written language.

Chapter 3 focuses on readers who highlighted their childhood reading experiences in their interviews. Although the majority of these experiences paved the way to a lifetime of satisfying reading, a couple of them led to a life sentence of reading difficulties.[1] In some of these interviews, children themselves voice their relationship to reading .

The voracious readers in Chapter 4 read for relaxation, entertainment, escape, and knowledge. Unlike literature readers, who are more selective about what they read, voracious readers will pick up anything and everything with print that enters their field of vision; they feel naked without a book in their hands.

Chapter 5 gathers together habitual readers, those voracious readers who describe themselves as compulsive, who often feel uncomfortable about their overpowering need to read.

The final two chapters of avid readers include narratives in which readers describe their reading process. The information readers in Chapter 7 read mostly nonfiction. They read widely in the journals, magazines, and technical manuals that compliment their interests, professions, and academic disciplines, compiling immense amounts of information as they read. Like those who describe their reading process in Chapter 8, a number of information readers can describe the techniques they employ to give meaning to print. Chapter 8 includes readers of both fiction and nonfiction who discuss the specific methods they use to collaborate with the author to give meaning to print. They are not only aware of how they read, but are able to articulate their reading process, a feat most people cannot achieve.

The category of infrequent readers branched into two chapters. The frustrated readers presented in Chapter 2 know *how* to read, but are reluctant to read more than is necessary for their jobs and daily living. They describe the difficulty of keeping their attention focused on written material, which makes comprehending the text laborious at best. Many also tell about particular situations from their childhood that led them into their present reading difficulties.

In Chapter 6, adult new readers who are attending adult literacy programs share the intimate and often poignant details of their lives without reading and their struggles to achieve reading skills. They openly discuss their stories of neglect, anger, courage, and resolution.

Most people in this chapter requested to be identified with a pseudonym because of their fear and shame at being publicly revealed.

In the concluding chapter, which discusses reading mentorship, I explain the process that avid readers can take to mentor their friends and relatives who read only infrequently. The chapter explains how active readers can develop an awareness of their own reading techniques, and learn to model these strategies for others. This chapter provides numerous suggestions for mentoring adults, children, and even preschoolers.

Suggestions for Reading this Book

Speaking of Reading is not a book that must be read from front to back cover. Skip around and explore in your own way the variety of remembrances found among these pages. You may want to go directly to the chapter that you identify with the most. If you find yourself relating to those who read for information—those nonfiction readers who strive for an understanding of complex phenomena—then go directly to Chapter 7, the information readers chapter. Or perhaps you're curious why some people find reading painfully difficult. In that case proceed to Chapter 2 on frustrated readers along with that chapter's introductions, then skip around to other chapters. You'll begin to understand a great deal about each particular aspect of reading after you've read the narratives of the chapter and the introduction that precedes them. If you believe that reading is your best and most reliable friend, be sure to read the concluding chapter regarding reading mentorship. In this chapter avid readers such as yourself will discover the underlying purpose of this book: to encourage you to become a reading mentor to a nonreading friend.

Although many narratives fit into two or three different chapters, I placed each one in the chapter where they seemed most at home. The people I interviewed spoke of many aspects of their reading, but the fascinating part of their story usually pertained to a particular aspect that ultimately placed them in one chapter more than another. You'll probably find that your own reading background would place you into several chapters as well.

Reading Defined

At this point, before you begin reading the actual interviews, I would like to introduce you briefly to some basic concepts of reading theory. In the past, reading theorists defined reading as an essentially passive process in which the reader found meaning inside the text itself. Reading was defined as the decoding of this meaning. Accordingly, reading teachers taught us how to read letters, words, syllables, sentences, and then whole paragraphs in preparation for comprehending the author's intended meaning.

In the early 1980s, reading researchers began changing their views of the process of reading. They defined it rather as a process of "constructing meaning" from print.[2] They began to look at reading as an active, creative process that takes place when we connect what we already know with what we read on the page.

In this process, readers rely on the prior knowledge of the world they have gained through their family history and culture, their values and beliefs, and their own experiences. To this background they add the related information they already know about the topic. Finally, they add their knowledge of language and their expectations of linguistic formations to construct their own meaning from the text they are reading.

For example, when we read a human interest story about a popular male entertainer, we bring with us some familiarity with the person, his music, or at least the genre of music, and perhaps we even know some details of his lifestyle. We probably hold some opinions about him and his music as well. As we read the article, we apply this prior knowledge to the new information in the article. We also read "between the lines," matching the new with the old, revising and fine-tuning our former assumptions, facts, and conclusions.

The product of this process, reading comprehension, occurs when our background knowledge interacts with what is written in the article to create meaning. For competent readers, such as literature, voracious, information, and habitual readers, this process works smoothly.

By contrast, frustrated readers and adults just learning to read tend to employ a passive, decoding-oriented process, which may be part of the reason they encounter difficulties as they attempt to comprehend the text. They often read as if they were sponges, soaking up words from the page without first weighing their relevancy. One such reader reported that she moves her eyes from words to sentences to paragraphs, and waits for the text to reveal its meaning to her. While she's waiting, she daydreams about what's for dinner rather than work with the text to create meaning. Another passive reader I interviewed summed up his reading: "I'm always vaguely confused when I read, but I don't do anything about it." Many frustrated readers remain infrequent readers because no one has taught them how to use active reading skills.

How do reading researchers view the difference between active and passive readers? They have developed theories and isolated numerous techniques that active readers employ to actually construct their own meaning from the printed text. Following is a summary of two reading theories, which will give you a brief overview of the reading process.

Metacognition means thinking about thinking, thinking about how we think. Metacognition theory describes how active readers monitor their thinking as they read. Active readers are aware of when they are understanding the content of what they are reading and when they have lost the thread of meaning. They also know how to regain a sense of meaning when they become confused.[3]

One of the strategies that active readers use to monitor and repair comprehension is to sift through the written material while making and confirming predictions about what will be written next.[4] Another strategy is to argue with the author. Some readers ask themselves questions such as: "What's this supposed to mean?" or even a simple "Huh?" Others make statements to themselves such as, "I don't get it," or "What I'm curious about is . . . ," or "OK, it's just like. . . ." Many active readers I interviewed weren't even aware that they engage in this complex process while they read. When asked what they do when they read, they said they "just read." Others were quite aware of their reading process, especially those who were voracious nonfiction readers.

While metacognition theory tells us that we must think when we read to give meaning to print, schema theory describes the background we need to engage actively in this thinking-reading process.

Schema theory tells us that we must have a schema, a sketch, an idea, a framework, or pattern for what we read to successfully give meaning to print. The greater our store of previously acquired knowledge on a topic and the more substance we have to connect new information to, the more we can read with fluency and a feeling of control over our reading. The same article about the popular entertainer would have a very different meaning for a recent immigrant who has not been exposed to American popular culture and therefore is lacking in the the necessary schema to fully understand the significance or nuances of the information contained in the article, even though she might be able to "decode" the words and sentences.

Again, reading is the construction of meaning from print; we rely heavily on our accumulated schemata during this construction process.[5] Our schemata create our world view, which we carry around with us in our minds and use to interpret what we read. What we bring to our reading is crucial because without a notion of or interest in the topic, deriving meaning from a text is difficult.

I assume if you have read this far, you do have an interest in the topic of reading. I hope the narratives you are about to read will broaden your perspective on reading, and enable you to see the numerous ways our reading abilities and interests determine so much of the course of our lives.

CHAPTER 1

Literature Readers

When I was little, I'd be walking down the street and my ears would be cold, but I didn't believe they were as cold as the cold described in books.

Adair Lara

Spellbound by the emotional depths of characters, the intricacies of plots and the sound of well-written prose, literature readers relish reading much as gourmets savor gastronomic delicacies. An evening at home with a good book pleases literature readers as an epicurean feast would please a lover of food. Literature frees its readers from their own lives by propelling them into distant worlds peopled with characters they wouldn't have otherwise met, into imagined worlds that reach back to extinct civilizations and previous centuries, or deep into the inner worlds of characters with emotional conflicts that bridge the gap of time.

A common theme among the literature readers I've spoken with is the belief that their understanding of the human condition has significantly expanded from their experiences with the myriad complex characters they have encountered through books. The characters inhabiting the novels they read provide them with experiences and insights, and attitudes and beliefs which they might not have developed if left to their own devices. One woman described how she found ways to cope with her own personal problems from reading about characters who cope with difficult situations similar to her own.

Many literature readers read simply for aesthetic pleasure. They relish the sound and structure of the language, the artistry of well-crafted sentences. Sure, they might also read page-turners and mysteries, but while those types of books can amuse them, such books don't truly satisfy the hunger for artistry desired by most literature readers. And while many literature readers also read nonfiction books and articles as well as novels, literature is their passion, and it is this passion that differentiates them from the voracious and habitual readers in other chapters.

Literature readers tend to spend focused, enthusiastic attention on their reading. Some create pictures, visualize scenes, and imagine characters, while others hear sounds and feel feelings while their eyes move across the pages. Most become so lost in their mental imagery that they become unaware of their surroundings and unable to hear or respond to people speaking to them. One literature reader described letting the stories "wash over" her. She can read page-long sentences by allowing the prose to sweep her away without focusing on each detail of sentence structure or content. Another woman told me that she spends much of her reading time drawing connections between the story and her own insights.[6] She often stops to ponder a character's motives and actions for hours before continuing on with the story.

When deprived of the beauty, subtlety, and inspiration found in literature, many of these readers feel constricted, bound by the limits of their own lives. Without reading they lose the opportunity to transcend themselves and drift into the complex emotions, motives, morals, and deeds of characters living lives different from their own. I interviewed an avid literature reader who imagines a life without reading literature to be pale, void of depth or color. His viewpoint contrasts greatly with that of an infrequent reader who looks at avid readers in bewilderment, and asks, "Why do they persist in missing out on living life to its fullest and instead choose to sit alone with a book in their hands?"

A large number of literature readers I interviewed vividly recall their mother's voice as she read children's stories to them, adapting her accent and creating vocal flourishes to dramatize characters and events. A distinct culture of books and reading thrived in many of their childhood homes. Some fondly remember the high regard their families placed on books, the titles of special books they once received as gifts, and weekly treks to the library. Others established their own library of storybooks in a bookcase in their bedroom even before they entered school. Books enabled certain literature readers to escape their family stresses. More than one realized that reading was an acceptable excuse for not completing household chores.

How did this childhood enchantment with children's stories affect them? Most were exposed to the plots of hundreds, perhaps thousands of stories before they even entered school. They learned early the descriptive vocabulary and complex syntax of the English language found only in books. Far ahead of other children who entered school with them, they had a good chance of moving ahead in reading as the years progressed, an accomplishment which increased their self-confidence even further. Apparently they acquired the ability to visualize naturally without requiring specific instruction in comprehension techniques. Most importantly, they developed an ease and comfort with reading; they learned to take pleasure in reading which continues to profoundly affect their existence still today.

But not all adult literature readers grew up in a household full of books. One woman whose parents were not readers described an illness and the time spent in bed recovering as the initiating event which brought her to read literature as a child. Another subject spoke fondly of a grandmother who provided the necessary role modeling by spending time transmitting her own love of literature to him.

The narratives in this chapter bring you into the lives of those who are fed by the literature they embrace.

ISABEL ALLENDE

Chilean author Isabel Allende speaks emotionally of the importance of reading in her own life, and of the illiteracy of so many Latin American people. Her words seem to originate in the deepest part of her soul, swirl around her heart, and flow through her lips with poetic clarity. One of the few widely distributed Latin American woman writers, she has achieved worldwide acclaim for her novels, which include The House of the Spirits, *which was made into a movie, and* Eva Luna.

Reading is like looking through several windows which open to an infinite landscape. I abandon myself to the pleasure of the journey. How could I know about other people, how could I know about the history of the world, how could my mind expand and grow if I could not read? I began to read when I was very small; I learned to read and write practically when I was a baby. For me, life without reading would be like being in prison, it would be as if my spirit were in a straitjacket; life would be a very dark and narrow place.

I was brought up in a house full of books. It was a big, strange, somber house, the house of my grandparents. My uncle, who lived in the house, had a lot of books—he collected them like holy relics. His room held a ton of books. Few newspapers were allowed in that house because my grandfather was a very patriarchal, conservative man who thought that newspapers, as well as the radio, were full of vulgar ideas (at that time we didn't have TV), so the only contact I had with the world, really, was through my uncle's books. No one censored or guided my reading; I read anything I wanted.

I began reading Shakespeare when I was nine, not because of the language or the beauty, but because of the plot and the great characters. I have always been interested in adventure, plot, strong characters, history, animals. As a child, I read children's books, most of the Russian literature, many French authors, and later, Latin American writers. I think I belong to the first generation of writers in Latin America who were brought up reading Latin American literature; earlier generations read European and North American literature. Our books were very badly distributed.

Books allow me to see my feelings put into words. After I read the feminist authors from North America, I could finally find words for the anger that I had all my life. I was brought up in a male chauvinist society and I had accumulated much anger, yet I couldn't express it. I could only be angry and do crazy things, but I couldn't put my anger into words and use it in a rational, articulate way. After I read those books, things became clearer to me, I could talk about that anger and express it in a more positive way.

The same thing happened with politics. I was aware of injustice and misery and political violence, but I couldn't express my feelings until I read about those issues and realized that other people had been dealing with them for centuries, and had already invented the words to express what I was feeling.

I have often been separated from my mother, whom I love very much. She now lives in Chile and we write a letter to each other every day. We talk about what we've read or what we are writing. I do it the first thing every morning of my life, even when I'm traveling. It's as if I were writing a journal. It's like having a long conversation with her; we are connected with a strong bond. This same bond also connects me with my daughter, who is living in Spain, because when I write the letter to my mother, I make a copy that goes to my daughter, and they do the same. This is becoming a very strange network of letters.

My mother is a much better reader than I. My reading is very fast, hectic, disorganized, and impatient. If I'm not caught in the first pages I abandon the book. My mother, however, is very patient and goes very slowly. She is the only person who reads my manuscripts, helping me to edit, revise, and correct them. She has a strong sense of poetry and such good taste. She's very well informed, very cultivated, very sensitive, and loves reading.

I have tried to give my children the love of books. My daughter is a good reader. She's a psychologist and has to read a lot of professional books, but she loves novels, short stories, poetry. My son, however, doesn't read any fiction. He's a scientific person with a mathematical mentality. I've tried to imagine how his mind and heart work, without nourishment from books, but I can't. He's a great boy, but how can he do it? I don't know.

My uncle, Salvador Allende, who was President of Chile before he was assassinated during the military coup, hardly affected my life. I liked him and loved him, but only as I do other relatives. He was the best man at my wedding. I was never involved in politics, and never participated in his government. (I became interested in politics only after the coup.) He was not a very strong reader of fiction, actually. He was always reading reports, essays, books about politics, sociology, economy, etc. He was a very well-informed person and he read very fast, his eyes practically skimming across the page to get the necessary information, but when he wanted to relax, he would rather watch a movie than read.

During the three years of Allende's government, any Chilean could buy books of "Quimantu," the state publishing house, for very little money, the equivalent of two newspapers. In this way he hoped to promote culture. His goal was that every single Chilean could read and write and be able to buy as many books as he or she wanted by the end of his term.

My own experience of life, my biography, my feelings, my self as a person, affect my reading. The writer puts out half of the book, but then I read the book in my own unique manner. This is why reading is so interesting; we as readers don't have passive roles, but very active ones. We must integrate into the text our own experiences of life and our own feelings. While reading a book, we are constantly applying our own knowledge.

Our backgrounds determine our strengths and interests as readers. Many themes that are extremely popular in North America are impossible for me to read because they aren't part of my culture—I just don't care about them. For example, I can't relate to those books by daughters who write against their mothers. But if I read a book by Toni Morrison or Louise Erdrich that deals with being a woman and part of an ethnic minority, I can relate to its content. Also, I like Latin American authors very much, especially Jorge Amado, Garcia Marquez, Mario Vargas Llosa, Juan Rulfo, Jorge Luis Borges, and many others. There are a few Latin American women writers that I enjoy as well, but they have been badly distributed and poorly reviewed. Latin American literature has been an exclusively male club, to say the least.

I have met many people, including well-informed, educated people, who actually take pride in the fact that they haven't read anything by a woman. Recently, I received a clipping from a newspaper in Chile. It was a public letter to me from a Chilean entertainer apologizing that he had never before read any of my books because I am a woman. He wrote that he never read literature written by women. After he made a special effort to read my books, he felt he must apologize to me and say that I could actually write.

I will always be interested in programs of illiteracy because it is such a common problem in my continent: 50 percent of the population of Latin America cannot read or write, and of those who can, only a few can afford books or have the habit of reading. To me, not reading is like having the spirit imprisoned.

ROBERT MACNEIL

In his memoir, Wordstruck, *Robert MacNeil affirms his lifelong passion for words, describing himself as ". . . crazy about the sound of words, the look of words, the taste of words, the feelings for words on the tongue and in the mind." Co-anchor and executive editor of the award-winning* "MacNeil-Lehrer NewsHour" *on the PBS television network, he played a major role in the creation of the nine-part television series* "The Story of English" *and co-authored the book of the same title.*

As I wrote in *Wordstruck,* the foundations for my becoming an avid reader were laid down from my very earliest years. I was read to extensively from the time I was a tiny child; it started younger than I can remember. I suppose it began with nursery rhymes, and then continued on with wonderful stories, or amusing or dramatic poems.

Mostly it was my mother who read to us; she did it simply because reading is a good thing to do with children, not as a conscious attempt to develop our love of books. She took it for granted that children are read to, though I don't think she herself was read to a great deal as a child. When she read us Louisa May Alcott's *Little Men* and *Little Women,* and Dickens' novels, I think she was reading them all for the first time herself. She was a lonely woman—her husband was away at sea a good deal of the time—and I believe reading to us was entertainment for her, as well as for us.

My parents read all the time and had books around as a matter of course. They demonstrated unconsciously, just by their demeanor, the pleasure, absorption, and escape that may be found in books. My father sat for hours at a time turning the pages of a book; I knew he was not paying attention to me, but rather to something else that was deeply interesting to him. Like a collector, he talked lovingly about books. He showed his affection for them by the pride he took in their bindings, by showing me what a good book was and how it was made.

I didn't read extensively for myself until I was about ten because I had been continually read to. By that time I had developed a taste for quite good books: Stevenson's *Treasure Island,* for example. I think it is extremely important that parents, grandparents, or aunts, whoever is reading to a small child, do not stop reading to him when he goes to school. A child between five and ten years is capable of understanding and appreciating all sorts of great books if they are read to him, books that he won't be capable of reading to himself for years. Many parents cut off a child from reading because they assume that since he's going to school he is learning to read for himself. I think this is sad because it will be years before he can read anything as complex as what he's capable of understanding.

Some kids go to school and come back bitterly disappointed. They go to school and what are they given to read? *Dick and Jane* for years. They thought they were going to learn to read all kinds of neat stories like *Alice in Wonderland.* They know what is waiting for them when they get through *Dick and Jane;* they know what wonderful pleasure exists inside the covers of books, and are reminded every night as their parents read to them.

Take as a parallel a child who grows up in a musical family and is exposed to a great deal of classical music. The chances are, that by the time he's grown up, his ear will have been shaped to appreciate classical music, and that he will enjoy it for the rest of his life.

Fiction is too lightweight and dismissive a word for what is actually some of the great thought of the world, such thought as may be found in an author's expression of the human experience and his understanding of human psychology. I have been immeasurably enriched by reading great and even not-so-great fiction. Reading fiction is a way of finding out about other people—of being with an enormous variety of people in all kinds of circumstances. If you haven't read Dostoevski you haven't been into his strange part of the human soul and I think you're somewhat deprived. Reading is as good as traveling and meeting people; I can't imagine cutting myself off from the experience it provides.

I'm dismayed when I run into people who say they have no time to read. They don't know where I find the time to do it. How can one not find the time to read? There's no other substitute for finding out about the human condition. You can go to plays and movies and you can travel, but nothing else gives you, in such a concentrated and economical way, both in terms of time and money, the rich exposure to the human condition that reading does. Your soul is very much smaller if you don't read.

I read good fiction slowly because I want to savor the words. If I find myself reading very quickly and turning over the pages rapidly it's because the material is very boring. I've never wanted to take a speed reading course because I don't want to read more quickly than I must. I'm not convinced that speed reading courses really enable readers to absorb or digest or retain the material. Certainly they don't help them get any aesthetic pleasure out of their reading.

The more I read, the more I understand of what I read. The wider my cultural background, the more anything I pick up and read fits into a context. Having read previous books by an author, as well as other books written in the same country and at the same time, gives me a context from which to understand that author more thoroughly.

I have to read a lot of material I wouldn't choose to read if I weren't a news anchor. I absolutely have to read a number of nonfiction books and articles every day, so I learned to read them very quickly and to skim. I also have staff who digest things and point out what is important for me to read. But this hasn't changed my reading of fiction or literature. I still read for enjoyment in the evenings, and on weekends and holidays.

If I'm reading something I've got to understand and remember for a while, I try to read without distraction, and to concentrate totally. I say to myself, "Okay, for this hour you've got to sit down and master this material." While I read I make little tick marks, and at the end of the book I note the page number and a word or two that will remind me of what it was I wanted to remember at each tick. If I'm writing a speech or an article, I'll go back and number the ticks and code them into categories related to the outline I'm pursuing, then make the outline. I never make extensive notes; I've found it's just a waste of time to write everything down.

Doing research on the series "The Story of English" made me a great deal more tolerant of speakers of nonstandard English. I was a language snob going into the project. I was both intolerant and ignorant of the origins and importance of nonstandard forms, and the last thing the world needs is another reason for snobbishness and putting people down. So now I'm more interested in encouraging young people to enjoy and take pleasure in language, rather than blasting them for the way they use it.

I would encourage a speaker of nonstandard English to read by saying what the black superintendent of schools in Philadelphia said to his students in our series, "The Story of English": "Look, your speech is an honorable way of speaking that links you to your family and other people like you. It has deep historical roots and is something you can be proud of speaking all your life when you're at home and when you're relaxed. It's your language. But you need to speak another language in order to get on in this world. You need standard English to get promoted and be successful on the career path."

CHRIS HAIGHT

The walls of Chris Haight's house are lined with thousands of books, revealing his passion for literature. Unlike most literature readers, however, he did not develop an interest in reading until adulthood. Before this time he says he was "the biggest intellectual slouch of all time."

I learned to read in school with *Dick and Jane* and it was tedious. I didn't take any pleasure in reading except when I was sick and could stay home. At those times, I read books for boys about heroic sports figures. It's comical now because I don't like sports at all. By the time I got to the eighth grade I had probably read only two dozen books.

I didn't like fiction because I thought, "What's the point of reading something that's not true?" If it really happened, then I might be impressed, maybe. I read Jack London's biography. I was impressed that he had to shovel coal for a living, and I even remember how he learned vocabulary. He would look up words and write them on pieces of paper and stick them up all over the place in his crummy little room. When he learned the words he would take them down and put up new ones. It never occurred to me to do the same thing, and it never occurred to me to read any of his fiction. Jack London was the same kind of guy as Roger Bannister, whom I also read about in high school. He had been burned in an accident as a kid and they thought he would never walk again, but he went on to break the four-minute mile. I liked that both these guys worked hard and had self-discipline.

When I was in my twenties, I got myself a subscription to *Time* magazine, but when each issue arrived, I put it aside and said, "Oh, I'll read it later." Pretty soon I had a whole stack of unread magazines lying there in perfect condition. Then I realized what a complete and utter fake I was. I was lying to myself that I would read them. I had become really good at faking that I read—I could pick up the gist of a conversation by listening intently and then I'd get into the conversation and act like I had read the book they were talking about. I used to say to myself, "Someday I'll read that book."

I only seriously started reading in my mid-twenties and I began in response to an emotional crisis. I had what I now realize was a nervous breakdown that had to do with breaking up with a girlfriend. I saw my "faking it" pattern in the relationship, too. I started going through a depression and began reading self-help and pop psychology books.

But I also somehow read a book called *The Romantic Agony* by Mario Praz. It was about the romantic poets and their tragic lives and it was the most difficult book I had read up to that time. It had a lot of quotes from Byron and Shelley and Keats. I was so intent on reading about the poets' tendencies toward depression and this tragic sense they had, and also the humorous sense they had of over-dramatizing themselves, of being self-absorbed and melancholy. There was also a lot in that book about wildness and recklessness which I liked because I was very composed. The romantic poets lived and died romantically and tragically and young. Anyone who lived to be over thirty-five was somehow not really living. But here I was—a person who didn't smoke or drink or do anything that would jeopardize his chances of living to be a hundred, so I suddenly felt, "What's the point? I'm so boring. I don't even read my *Time* magazines. I don't really do anything. I'm such a fake."

That book led me into poetry, which I had never had a taste for before. Poetry offers something that is beautiful in itself—the right words in the right order—but it also gives insights beyond the words. Then I began reading literature because I discovered that fiction writers could also give me a lot of insight into psychology. I read Kafka.

I suddenly realized what people got out of fiction—I began to see that fiction has its own beauty. And then I realized that libraries have all sorts of books just waiting to be read. It was just amazing. Suddenly I started making lists of books and plans for reading. I wanted to read everything. I was twenty-four at the time.

After I began reading, I discovered that my grandmother was a reader and that I could talk with her about what I was reading. Until that point, she had just been a grandma who had money, who gave me gifts, and who I had to go see as an obligation. Then during one visit I realized that this woman was really interesting. She read Mann and Proust and Joyce. If it weren't for my grandmother, I don't know that I would have gotten into the writers I did. She gave me the confidence I needed to believe I could understand them. I just looked at her shelves and I knew she had read that stuff, and if she could do it, so could I. I realized how carefully she selected the books on her shelves. Her husband was raised a cowboy and didn't share her interest in reading at all. Her books were for herself, for her own pleasure, for this private life she had.

My grandmother had tried to encourage me before. One year she gave me a Bible, the King James version. At the time I thought, "Gee, thanks," and set it aside. But when I got into reading the classics, I wanted to read the Bible, and I wanted to read the best Bible, and I had a copy right there. I realized she gave it to me as a work of literature. I took it with me on a trip out of the country and read it like a novel. I was completely bowled over by it. I had a really strong response to some of those stories, especially Saul. I think about Saul being chosen—not wanting to be chosen, yet being thrust into the position and then trying to do the right thing. The poor guy. He was thrust into this difficult position and he reacted to the strain. He was inflicted with an evil spirit. Well, that's what I felt like when I was in my depression. I could relate to him. A character can be both good and bad. I couldn't close the book, I was so amazed.

I started going to the library every Saturday and checking out whole bunches of books. I also checked out records of Shakespeare, Byron, Shelley, Keats, readings of poetry. I would make tapes of the records and listen to them over and over. I became completely steeped in the stuff. I would go out for long walks at night and the poetry would be going through my head, just lines of poetry rolling through my mind getting mixed in with the night smells of the sweet night-blooming flowers. I was enveloped in the world of the senses, with the poetry and the literature all mixed in. It was overwhelmingly beautiful. It created a whole mood and atmosphere.

And all this pleasure was available to me for free! All I had to do was to open up to books. I had never had much self-esteem as a student, but suddenly I had motivation to take these books, to consume them and make them part of me. Reading is an act of will and I willed these ideas into my consciousness. I just gave myself over to the authors and became completely immersed in what they could give me.

I had always been passive in my relationships and here I was actively applying my intellect to these works. I recreated myself through literature and started to become who I am today. Before that depression, I didn't really have a personality. I had fragments of a personality, tendencies to be certain ways. But suddenly I had opinions and complex feelings about things. My opinions meant something. I could even argue with a writer while I read the book. What I decided to take in from what I read helped to create me. My reading has been a triumph of desire over education.

JULIE HARRIS

Throughout her illustrious stage, screen, and television career, Julie Harris has shown a deep understanding of the many characters she has portrayed. She speaks here about the worlds of experience that lie within the covers of the books she reads, and how she shares those worlds with her audiences by bringing them to the stage. Ms. Harris made her Broadway debut while still a child in 1945, and has since won five Tony Awards. She has also been nominated for an Academy Award, as well as nine Emmy Awards of which she has won two.

I find reading to be very stimulating—through it I discover the confirmation of being alive distilled into a story. Books express the experiences of loving, of losing, of marching through life the way we all have to do. The book form is very appealing to me. Reading one book leads to reading another so that I believe I'll never get to the end of them all. On my deathbed I'll say, "No, I just want to read that one more play." I really will. Gertrude Stein said that her only regret in life was that she wouldn't have time to read all the books she wanted to. I feel like that too; I read while I work, when I eat, and even while I talk.

The poems of Emily Dickinson were thrilling to me when I first read them, and eighteen years later I did a play about her. I recently did another play, *Charlotte Brontë*—I've always loved reading the Brontës and I carried this love through to the theater since that is where my work is. These lives are so dramatic that they lend themselves to being told out loud. When I read I get emotionally involved with the characters. Within the pages of a book lies a whole world of experience, a whole lifetime's worth of experience, that I can share and inspire others by when I bring that experience to the stage.

In order to make substance from something I read, I read it over and over. The same is true with music and art. I'm now listening to a concerto by Mozart once or twice a day. I have an entirely different feeling about it now that I know it so well. I go through a similar process with painting also. If I see a painting that really appeals to me I'll go back and look at it. Then I'll read about the artist's life, and go back and look at it yet again.

I found Shakespeare very difficult to read in the beginning, but developed a love for him by seeing his plays, and gradually became aware that they were mighty works. In *Romeo and Juliet,* Juliet says, "Romeo, Romeo, wherefore art thou, Romeo? Deny thy father and refuse thy name." For years I had it wrong. It's not, "Where are you, Romeo?" It's "Why are you named Romeo? Why do you have to have that name?" Being cast as Juliet and working with a fabulous director helped me understand it. Shakespeare takes a lot of work to read, partly because he wrote in a different age, four hundred years ago.

Reading silently is like digesting food; no one can do it for you. When I'm digesting a book, the words go directly into my psyche. Sometimes I'll come to a passage that moves me or that I like the sound of, and I'll read it over twice so I won't forget it. Reading aloud, however, is a little like performing. I've read aloud to many different people in my life and have always found it to be very rewarding, very exciting, because we are sharing the material. I love to share my reading with other people. I'm like an evangelist if somebody doesn't know the Brontës, for instance. When I tell somebody about a book it rekindles my own enthusiasm for it all over again.

When I have to memorize the lines for a part I don't read the script much before rehearsals begin. When they do start I work eight hours a day; it's very intensive while I am memorizing the lines, one by one. I'm not a very quick study; I don't have a photographic memory, so I just have to knuckle down and go over and over it. I keep repeating the lines until I get them right. I don't think about the ideas until I've memorized all the lines and have them in my head so that when I come to speak them, they're part of me.

I never try to memorize books when I read them. I read every word, I don't skim any parts, and I read from start to finish. Since I don't have big lumps of time and am only able to read a little at a time, I sometimes have to go back and reread a part to refresh my memory. I've always been a thorough reader; when I was a student I was told to read every word, so that's what I do.

Everything interests me; I'm very curious, just like my father was. My older brother is gone now, but my younger brother is also a great reader—he's the only Ph.D. in the family. Our parents gave us a love of books. They were avid readers; there were hundreds of books in the house. Mom said, "No matter how terrible things get, as long as I can read a book, I'm all right."

Reading has greatly influenced my life because it has helped me to look beyond myself. I am very moved whenever I read about people like Mother Teresa or Ghandhi. Spiritual quests and the idea that life is more worthwhile when one does something for someone else move me tremendously. If I hadn't read about others' spiritual ideas, I wouldn't be where I am, surely. My life wouldn't be nearly as interesting as it is.

SUSAN SCHULTER

For Susan Schulter, who has been blind since birth, books provide an important way of experiencing the world. She says, "Reading is my photography. When I read, I feel the way I imagine people feel when they look at pictures. I become transported to wherever it is that I'm reading about. Reading is my bridge between me and everywhere." She is a poet, a writer, and a university English instructor.

I had a very rich childhood. I was read to and sung to a zillion times. My mother constantly read bedtime stories to us, even news articles that pertained to children. One of my first experiences with literacy was when we wrote a letter to Santa Claus before I could actually write. I told my mother what I wanted to say and she wrote it down. Around that same period, my mother took me and my siblings to the library, where we got library cards. It was a rainy day and I remember feeling the sacredness of the library because we whispered. We came home and I told my father about it.

We had lots of books around the house and general encyclopedias, *National Geographic,* and *Sunset*—reading material that invited discovery. My mother was very neat, but there was always a book open somewhere. She'd say, "That's OK, a book should be open because it is asking you to enter it."

I went to a preschool for children with visual impairments. It is the only special school I went to because after that I was mainstreamed in public schools. At the preschool, I had my first introduction to braille. We learned to write our own names on a little Dyno labeler. I remember that day—I held the little plastic with the tape on the back in my hand and I went over and over it saying, "That's me!"

When I was in kindergarten, I began receiving talking books for the blind. There's a whole studio in the Library of Congress that records books on disc, record, and tape for people who can't see. Those books gave me my first introduction to E.B. White's *Stuart Little* and *Charlotte's Web*—they were talking books read by a male narrator. Later, in second grade, when my teacher was reading *Charlotte's Web*, I had some difficulty because she didn't voice things the way he had. I already had certain characterizations in mind, and had to make adjustments because her reading was different. Only later did I realize I could put my own voice to those characters.

So my earliest reading experiences were quite auditory, then they became tactile, especially in the first grade. When I went to public schools we had a resource program for the ten blind youngsters in the district. We had a special resource teacher who taught us our braille skills as well as phonics and math—everything our peers were learning, but in braille. We spent most of our day with her. Then, in the mainstream classroom, she would provide the materials in braille, we would do our work in braille, and she would transcribe it.

In the sixth grade I read a book called *Road to Volograd* about a Hindu boy in India whose younger sister is going blind. He walks her from their village all the way to the city of Vogra to see a doctor there. The book is full of the exotic. They go down a well to sleep, then wake up because they hear a cobra scratching its scales over the rocks as it moves. He talks about wrapping food up in banana leaves and about the smell of elephants and burning cow dung. All that was so foreign to my experience, yet I had had experiences with bananas, if not banana leaves, and I knew what other manure smells like when it's burning, so I made the connections. As long as the experience was sensory, I could make a connection. I once petted an elephant at a zoo, and I once heard an elephant scream at the circus, so when I read that book, I was able to connect with it. If I have to make up too much, I usually don't like the book. But then, that's probably true for anybody.

There's a passage in *The Wind in the Willows* where the mole, who has been away from home for about a year, is out on a winter day running with the rat, and all of a sudden he falls over on his haunches and says, "Oh no, oh dear, oh dear." He starts sobbing and crying. He says, "It's my home. I smell it." They go tunneling around under the snow and find his home. I've had that experience myself. I went to church one time and the smell of the wood was identical to the smell of a church that was near a cabin we used to go to when I was a little girl. It was the smell of sun on boards and firewood smoke. I walked into that church and instantly remembered that passage from *The Wind in the Willows*, and I said, "Yeah, that's what smell does."

Science fiction is all the same unless there is something human, universal, about what's happening to a character. I liked Robert Heinlein's *Stranger in a Strange Land* because Valentine Michael Smith wanted to learn how to love—he wanted to learn what sexual and sensual and emotional closeness was. There was a funny word for that, grocking. It was a human experience I could relate to. There's also a Ray Bradbury story, "All Summer in a Day," about a little girl on the planet Venus, where it rains all the time except for once every seven years when the sun comes out. She remembers the sun from when she lived on Earth, so she tells her class how much they are going to love it. She talks about jungles and steam and the smell of wet plants and how they feel springing under your feet. These are things I know. The other children don't believe her, so they lock her in the school linen closet. The sun comes out and they all go outside to play and forget her. Then it starts to rain again and they remember her and let her out.

I also very much like the way language sounds. That's why I like to read and write poetry. The connection between poetry and music is constantly going on for me. Poetry goes back to music. The first poetry I remember well is *Child's Garden of Verses* by Robert Louis Stevenson. I had a recording of it when I was little. I really liked the way the lines rhymed with each other. I can still remember falling in love with the sound of Robert Frost's reading voice because he sounded like my grandfather. One of my school projects as a child was taking Frost's poem, "Birches," and gathering little branches from the birch trees in the front yard and setting them up in Styrofoam and varnishing them so they would look snowed on. To me all this was reading, all of it was making books come alive for me.

When I read, I hear it and I see it in braille. When I read a book, like *Paradise Lost,* for instance, I can see the way the dots look in my head. It's a tactile image, but it's there. I use the word *see* because it's so common. Now I also have a reading machine which runs like a scanner. It provides everything in auditory feedback. I find I remember text auditorily in chunks, and I can reconstruct a whole block at a time, whereas the documents I experience in braille I remember more linearly, sentence by sentence.

I also find that I'm a very bad speller, although I'm getting better. This has to do with being an auditory reader. I have a braille computer that I can connect to the scanner which can give me a braille readout of anything I'm listening to, and I find that if I see a word with my fingertips, I remember how to spell it. It has a completely different character than if I hear it. I can't say I like one form better than the other—I like putting them together.

I teach freshman composition courses. My students type their papers and my optical scanner scans them and reads the papers aloud to me. I listen to the paper once through first from beginning to end, trying not to let myself stop along the way. I jot down my overall impressions of the content on my little braille word processor. Then I listen through again, stopping quite a bit to write down specific notes on certain sentences that read ungrammatically. The scanner mispronounces misspelled words, so I can catch them too. Sometimes I copy down whole sentences to decide what kind of recommendation to make, a transition that doesn't seem to be working, or paragraphing that needs work. All of this is rather tedious. Sighted instructors would probably circle or underline or write arrows and notes. Next I must decide how I want to respond to that paper. I usually compose a letter in response to the student on my word processor. My students get their own work back and my letter stapled to it rather than red marks on their paper. They have told me they like their own text coming back untarnished.

Before I got the scanner, they taped their papers and I listened to the tapes, and spoke my remarks back into the tape. The students with very good auditory skills like that, but the more visual students prefer the letter. If the students do handwritten work in class, I have my teaching assistant read the papers to me and I tell her what I want her to write on the paper.

I remember the names of the authors and the characters of the books I've read quite well. It's my math, it's my orientation pattern. It helps me know where I am in time and space to be able to remember them all. I get a real warm pleasure when I recall books I have read, like seeing somebody that I love after I haven't seen her or him for a few years. I get a sense of belonging when I can do that. It's a nice reminder that there really was a past, and that there is a sense of the future. It's a wonderful, grounding experience to have a record, a documentation that lives have existed before our own. I've always thought that writing and music have the power to say, "Yes, this confirms it—so-and-so was here before." I need that connection. I think it would be frightening to live only in the present.

JoAnn Ybarra

JoAnn Ybarra is a first-generation Mexican American who, after a rebellious youth, started a company that provides banks with electronic security.

Here she relates how her close relationship to literature has been her "life-saver." She now devotes her energy to studying art history and working with a cancer resource center.

My father was a southern Baptist minister and my family was very religious. My grandmother taught me to read the Bible in Spanish when I was six and I was utterly terrified by the stories. For example, "Jonah and the Whale"—here you are in the stomach of a whale and it is up to God to decide if you're going to be saved or not. He is testing your faith and I knew as a kid that I didn't have the kind of faith it took to get out of anybody's stomach. I accepted that I was damned.

When I got to school I had a very hard time thinking in English. I simply didn't think in English, I didn't understand it well, so I ended up in the remedial classes. I was reading pretty well in Spanish, though. It wasn't until I had a Latin teacher in fourth grade who told my mother that I was bright, that I could do everything they wanted me to, but I could only do it in Spanish, that I was moved out of remedial classes. But I still had a problem thinking in English. I would think something out in Spanish first, so I read slowly. I still do this at times.

A minister's kid is supposed to set an example, which I couldn't do, so I became very rebellious and ran away. I couldn't see living with my father and all his dogma. I ended up in juvenile hall. This wasn't so bad because there were a lot of books that people donated through charity, and being a loner anyway, I read a lot. I read Homer because my counselors told me he was good and that it was the oldest book around besides the Bible. They liked it when I read—when I tried to be smart I got attention. I felt validated. Of course, I didn't understand Homer until much later, but it was interesting to read about gods who got mad and heroes who came home only to die at the hands of their wife's lover. The stories were similar to those I had read in the Bible, so it felt familiar. I also read Anne Frank's *The Diary of a Young Girl* while I was locked up. Again, I really didn't understand the story because I knew nothing about the Holocaust, but I could relate to it since she couldn't get out and neither could I.

I kept reading, searching for some group to identify with. At a very early age I was reading Dante, trying to understand my own dilemma. Later, I started picking up books by authors who were pretty depressed. I have much inside that I want to express and I look for role models in my reading. In the last two weeks I've read three books and they're all different, but I suppose they do have a common theme: pain.

One of the novels I read is Joyce Carol Oates' book, *Black Water,* about the Chappaquiddick incident with Edward Kennedy. Reading the book made me understand how the Kopechne family must have felt about having their twenty-six-year-old daughter drowned in the mud while Kennedy got away. Here you have a family in tremendous pain.

I read *After Henry* by Joan Didion last week also. I love her—she's an idol of mine. *After Henry* is a book of short stories about the Reagan administration. Henry was Didion's first publisher and she writes a story about his death. There's a line in the book that says that childhood was when nobody died.

I also read Marguerite Duras' book, *Hard Rain,* about a very poor family with two very brilliant children. The brother and sister are in love with each other so there's that taboo, even though they don't actually have an affair. People in the town think they were abused, and by our standards, I guess they were. Reading the book made me feel that life and its depth and pain is OK. I see Duras as a person in angst and pain herself. I see her as someone who has been completely out of control but uses writing to study herself and express how she is feeling in this insanity she has been born into.

Duras is also one of the few writers I've read in English who affects me the way that those who write in Spanish do. Spanish is somehow more traumatic than English. If someone is sad, they're very sad. If they're happy, they're very happy. There's something in the Spanish language that brings out emotions. I have a strong emotional and cultural draw to Spanish. In English, I can often remove myself emotionally.

The main authors in my life are depressive, but I wouldn't call myself depressive. I'm attracted to these authors because I seek out their hard experiences. Maybe this is because, according to every one of the probation officers I've had, I should have been dead by the time I was eighteen. And my doctors told me two years ago that I was going to die of stomach cancer. Duras should have been dead, too. Didion should not have made it as a writer because she's so political, but she did. I have a living relationship with these writers. I care what they say and what they think. They're a barometer of whether or not I'm still alive in my mind and in my heart. With these authors, I seek out the strength of having survived something. I seek out their experiences and tell myself, "JoAnn, you've had a hard life, but so have other people." My reading has been my lifesaver.

Barbara Cymrot

Barbara Cymrot's introduction to American literature came when, as an adolescent, she wrote to detective writer Ross McDonald, who sent back to her a list of the books she should be reading instead of his.

I had a really funny experience when I was fourteen: I wanted to read a dirty book, so I found one with a picture of a man and a woman in a suggestive position on the cover, and I bought it for a quarter. The author was a detective writer named Ross McDonald. I read the whole thing, but there wasn't one sex scene in the entire book. I was so furious, I wrote the author a letter. I said, "How could you do this? You put this picture on the cover, but there's no lovemaking or romance anywhere in the book." My parents didn't know I wrote the letter. Eight months later I got a reply. It was probably the first time I ever got anything addressed to me. My mother flipped out that I got a letter from a man. "Who is this McDonald person?" she asked me.

I opened the envelope and inside was a two-page letter. He apologized and said he had no control over the cover. He said he always wanted to be a great writer, but he didn't think he was. He told me he made a lot of money from his books and that he lived really well, and he said that I seemed to be a really intelligent young girl. But, he said, I shouldn't be reading his books. Then he wrote a list of all the people I should read. It included all the great American writers. I read the books starting with Faulkner. Thomas Wolfe's *Look Homeward, Angel* was the first book on the list that made me realize that what I experience is not the end of what may be experienced in this world, that there are some things way beyond me. I discovered that through reading, I could go to a totally different world than I'd ever been in before. I was taken away.

I have read *Jane Eyre* eight times by now; it always moves me. It's just like a friend. The story is the same every time I read it, but I still get surprised. The beginning always gets me because in it, she is alone and reading. This book helped me to see myself as being very much alone on earth, but also not alone, because I am part of nature. I have a spiritual feeling about this book—that somehow I am this book.

Reading helps me to understand that there are other viewpoints, other realities in a way that TV can't. Television is like bad literature. It dumps information on me and then tries to structure my thought processes to tell me what to think about it. It takes my brain, maneuvers it, manipulates it, and then, when the show's over, drops it. This leaves me with a very stale and tired feeling. Television, and bad literature, for that matter, don't allow me the possibility of self-discovery.

Sometimes I need time to think about a book, to let it settle in, like a good meal. When I read a good book, I actually feel whatever it's about. The best writers don't give away their whole treasure in the beginning, but give me feelings, environment, texture. They give me clues, bits, reactions. They make me so hungry to fill in the spaces that I have to use my own inward knowledge, experiences, self, to complete the picture. I work along with the author to create the characters. I like books in which people change. I like to see the characters meet a force that is impossible to overcome unless they change something in themselves. Maybe this means they will just have to accept the impossibility of the situation. I like to see the characters renewed through their experiences. This is what I want in my own life.

LISA HEYER

Lisa Heyer relishes the artistry of a well-written novel and attributes much of her understanding and empathy for others to her exposure to so many different characters in the literature she has read since she was a child. She tries to bring her love of literature to the students in her university classes for non-native speakers of English. Her quality editing brought Speaking of Reading *to life.*

I remember the first time as a child that I stayed in bed all day Saturday reading a novel. It was a delicious feeling to go into the world the book created, and be cozy and warm in bed at the same time. I have the same experience to this day with books—I get into bed and pull the covers up around me and enter the world of the book.

Another great reading time in my life was when my son was a little baby and I would nurse him, with a book in my hand. I spent hours this way, rocking and reading. Then, when he got to be three and four, I'd say to him, "I'm going to read now, and I'll either read my book out loud to you or you can lay down and look at your own book while I read to myself." One time I was reading *Richard II* for a class on Shakespeare, and when I got to the beheading scene, Brendan jumped up and said, "Why'd they cut off his head? Why'd they cut off his head?" I was amazed that he could figure out what was happening in spite of the unfamiliar language and the fact that he was only three.

I love to eavesdrop and hear stories about people I don't know—that's one of the reasons I like to read fiction. The spark that propels my life is other people, my interest in them, my curiosity about them, and I don't need to be in a relationship with them personally to get something out of knowing about them. The insight authors can bring to the portrayal of their characters becomes my insight, which carries over to the next person I meet, the next book I read. Each author has his or her own way of looking at the world, and if they're good, they will get me to see it, too. Just by moving over that one step into somebody else's reality, my own outlook becomes broader.

A character in *To Kill a Mockingbird* said that you never know a person until you've walked around inside their shoes. That's what a good novel will do—it will enable me to walk around inside, not only the shoes of the characters, but the shoes of the author, since I am in fact getting their perspective on people through their characters. By reading, I can develop empathy; I can learn to understand that everybody is valuable. I can broaden my view of the people in the world and learn more tolerance for them, as well as have more interest in them. If I didn't read, I'd probably be more rigid in my assumptions about how other people are in the world. Reading makes my world more intimate, and more expansive at the same time.

For me, a really good novel has good characters, good character development, and interesting interaction among the characters. Plot is less important than characters by far. As long as an author presents a character in great depth and with great insight, I'll find the book interesting. I even like books in which nothing happens except people talking to each other. I'll definitely read the character descriptions with more interest than the descriptions of place, which I almost skim.

I've been reading Toni Morrison lately, and she is a great example of an author who produces strong characters. It's the people in her plots, how they make the plot happen, and the effect that being next to these people has on me as a reader that is important. I see the world through the eyes of the characters in a novel like *Beloved* for a long time after I read it. I'll actually live the book while I'm reading it, but then it goes deeper into me and becomes part of my whole outlook. I internalize it so it becomes part of me and remains inside forever. I am a product of my experiences, my background, and my reading.

Over years of reading, I've also become interested in the actual words and the way they're used in the writing—the style, the language. Sometimes while I'm enjoying the characters in a book with my right brain, I'll also be reading with my left brain, looking at the language and how it's achieving its effect. Or, maybe some part of the language will hit me and I'll stop and just look at it and say, "Wow!" It might be a wonderful little turn of phrase, just two particular words together, or it might be a whole sentence or paragraph that is put together in a special way. I love the artistry of writing, the part that no one else can do except the person who wrote it.

On the other hand, if I am reading something that is not so well written I let my eyes just skim over the page because I'm not interested in how it's put together. I won't notice the language unless it bugs me in some way; I'll just read for the gist of the story. I don't pay attention to words when they're in predictable order. When they fall predictably, I don't need to read carefully because I know essentially what the next phrase is going to be.

Toni Morrison is also a good example of an author who uses words in a totally original way. Everything she writes is being written for the first time. In *Beloved,* the subject and the emotional context of the story seems to have determined how she wrote the book. It's about ghostly feelings and people and how the past is intertwined with the present, and the style is misty and hard to pin down. I found myself being propelled very quickly through the book by its compelling nature and I had to force myself to slow down because I wanted to savor the wonderful way she uses language.

Another fascinating author who comes to mind is Jean Rhys. She wrote in the '30s and '40s in Paris and London. Her own story is as interesting as her novels, and in fact they are more or less autobiographical. Anyway, my mother gave me this volume that contained her four novels and I was just gripped by them. They're the most depressing, most devastating stories, but they're also some of the most beautiful prose I've ever read. I was totally involved with every page, with what she was saying and how she said it. Yet something in me was resisting at the same time because she is so painful to read. I read them cover to cover, hardly doing anything else until I am finished. My son was two then and I remember sitting in the rocking chair in his room reading this book while he fell asleep, and then staying there, stuck to the chair for hours afterwards because I couldn't put it down.

I usually read novels a sentence at a time, but some authors write such complicated sentences that I am forced to change my tactic. William Faulkner, for instance, writes in these three-page sentences and with books of his I have to let go of trying to control the experience and let him do it for me. I just read and don't try to understand every sentence or even every paragraph. With this kind of reading the meaning comes in through the back. I keep reading, taking in what I can, collecting the little bits of information that I hope will eventually come together. I'm aware, as I read, of picking up these bits and waiting for a place for them to all make sense, but I don't try to put order to them. It becomes an intuitive process and one of trusting that the author has a controlling idea for his or her work that will eventually become clear.

I get panicked when I don't have something to read. It's like a habit—if I don't have something to read I get really nervous, and if I don't have something good to read I get frustrated and can't wait to go to the bookstore or the library to get a book because until I do there's something wrong in my life. Something is not right when I'm not having an interaction with a book that excites me, stimulates me, gives me pleasure, makes me feel sad.

I can't imagine what my life would be like without books. I would be a different person, I know that. I would know so much less about the world. Reading creates a context for events and people of the world, past and present. The exposure to the world and all its different aspects that comes from reading creates an interest in these things, which then stimulates the desire for more knowledge, which in turn provokes the desire to read more. So you see, reading is at the heart of an incredible cycle.

CHAPTER 2

Frustrated Readers

Maybe [my friends] read because they weren't as gifted mechanically as I was and couldn't do things with their hands.

Todd Martin

When frustrated readers sit down with a novel in their lap opened to the first chapter, they typically read a few pages and then proceed either to drift, daydream, or fall asleep. Perhaps they wake up feeling embarrassed and uncomfortable, even disgusted and angry that they were once again unable to concentrate long enough to develop an interest in the characters, the plot, or the topic. They may reach for the newspaper, a magazine with short articles, or a lifestyle improvement book in the hopes of finding material brief enough to hold their attention. Frustrated readers are *able* to read, but can't seem to concentrate long enough for their minds to engage with the words to create meaning.

They are reluctant readers discouraged by their slow pace, poor attention span, comprehension failures, and inability to focus. One woman told me she reads each word separately and slowly, and feels depressed by the experience. "Why?" I wondered. Many excellent readers read slowly so they can think about the words. After talking with her I understood that she subvocalizes as she reads, saying each word aloud under her breath, and that she makes many regressions while she reads—she will read five to ten words and then go back to read them again. Both subvocalizing and regression slow down reading and can result in comprehension failures because such readers are unable to develop enough momentum to establish an uninterrupted train of thought.

In addition to being slow readers, frustrated readers tend to be passive readers as well. I've seldom heard frustrated readers describe their reading to me as an active process in which they are engaged in constructing meaning from print. Rather, they begin with the first word and progress through the text slowly, one word at a time, until they finish, whether or not they understand or follow the content. They are generally unaware of the metacognitive reading strategies active readers employ, such as stopping purposefully at the end of a segment of material to ponder and digest its meaning, arguing with the author after reading a particular point, or asking questions of themselves to determine if the meaning was clear.

A large portion of adult frustrated readers were read to only sporadically, if at all, as preschool children. As a result, they lost out on that early opportunity to learn to read with ease and fluency. For them, reading never became a natural part of life, like walking or talking. Instead, they learned the motions of reading without really connecting with what they read.

When preschool children sit for hours listening to the fantastic stories their parents read to them in the descriptive prose found only in children's books, they often develop a love for words and a sense of comfort in books. If parents continue reading to their children as they move beyond the preschool years and well into their childhood, they are even more fortunate because then they can listen to stories with complex characters and plots which they can understand, but which they are still unable to read on their own because of the sophisticated linguistic structures and vocabulary.

By contrast, the first reading experiences of many frustrated readers often occurred in elementary school, where they read short and simple books such as *Dick and Jane* that stimulated neither their imagination nor interest. One adult frustrated reader told me he has deep regrets that he wasn't inspired as a child to find joy in reading. By the time he was in fifth grade, when he was cognitively capable of reading imaginative, engaging stories on his own, he was already bored by reading. Since he had found no past pleasure in books, he saw little value to be gained from the seemingly immense time and effort it took to sit down and read a book. He hadn't developed the concentration and comprehension skills of those who were frequently read to because he simply had not been stimulated to connect to the process of reading.

Without support from parents or other adults outside of school, reading in school can become a boring and tedious experience. Instead of reading interesting literature that is relevant to their lives or stimulating to their imaginations, they complete workbooks, fill in phonics work sheets, and read from books with simple words and plots which invite little curiosity. Again, they see little reason to learn to read.[7] Many adults who were frustrated readers as children report that their poor reading affected their overall classroom behavior. One such reader remembers the fear of being called on to read aloud in class and stumbling over the words, and so "hid out" in his classroom by avoiding eye contact with his teachers. Another created diversions in the form of disruptive behavior to avoid being called on to read. Yet another compensated for her poor reading by developing better listening skills so she could pick up the general content of a text simply by listening to the teacher and students discuss it.

(Fortunately, today's elementary schools tend to use the whole language method of teaching reading which, among other things, provides students with authentic literature rather than stories with controlled or simplified words and sentences. Teachers now surround their students with literature and encourage them to pick out and read on their own books on topics that interest them. Traditional phonics lessons have not been abandoned, but are now derived from the contexts of the books the children choose.)

When adult frustrated readers find themselves among avid readers, they easily become self-conscious. They are often embarrassed by their lack of reading skills and they tend to lose much of their self-confidence even though they themselves may posess accomplishments in other areas.[8] And yet, many frustrated readers would welcome mentors who would take the time to encourage them in their reading efforts. One such person confided in me, "Nobody's ever cared much if I could read well or not. My parents even wanted me to quit school so I could add to the family's income." Many frustrated readers would like to know successful readers who would not judge them for their reading difficulties, but would lead them step-by-step into the world of reading. Frustrated readers, like those inhabiting this chapter, need "book-nurturing" by people who enjoy reading. They need mentors to guide them toward a fully-engaged reading experience. It is my hope that the avid readers among you might recognize a friend or relative in the pages of this chapter whom you might agree to "book-nurture" yourself.

JANICE STRASSHEIM

Janice Strassheim has been diagnosed as having minor learning disabilities, and is making slow but steady progress toward her goal of becoming a stronger reader. She uses her skills as a magician to entertain and delight children of all ages, and is a special education teacher for the blind.

Until I was nine years old, I loved comic books—my favorite was *Richie Rich*—but I loved *Superman* and *Archie* and the *Zap* comics, too. Then, around that time, I started reading books on Buddhism and witchcraft. I don't remember how I got my hands on them, or what interested me in those topics, but I became fascinated by anything spiritual. My mother got really upset. She didn't like the witchcraft or the fact that I was reading anything about other religions. I remember reading a book that I got from my middle sister called *Oversexed*, about a five-year-old nymphomaniac, and it was OK with my mother if I read that, but the witchcraft really got to her. Finally we had a huge fight and she ripped up all my books. That fight was a turning point for me because afterwards I hated books and I hated to read. After that, I only read if I had to for school.

I was very numb during junior high and high school. I don't remember anything from those years. I listened to a lot of music and did drugs. How can you read when you're on drugs? Mostly, I just spaced out. I did read a book I loved about Janice Joplin. She was a heroine to me. I loved her music and I loved her style. She was very adventurous, very self-destructive. Nothing was boring for her. Every single day she tried to pack so much into her life. She did it all to the max and then burned out. I also read about Judy Garland. And somehow I also read enough to get through college.

Books are slowly coming back into my life. I got really interested in Anne Rice's vampire books, and some Twilight Zone type books. I don't like the kind of science fiction that has the action taking place on another planet, but I do like the more believable kind where the character is driving in a car and all of a sudden goes through a time warp. I've tried to branch out from science fiction, so I've gotten into mysteries, but they're definitely not the same. It takes me a long time to sit down and give a book a chance because I'm still very resistant to reading. If a book doesn't grab me in the first five pages, I don't get to the middle. I wish I could say that reading helps me learn new things, but that's not the kind of books I read. Like right now I'm learning about vampires. I really like vampires. I'd like to grow up to be one. But that's not really learning anything useful about myself.

Recently I had to study for the state exam you have to take to be a teacher. This was hard for me because I kept thinking I was stupid, but I knew I needed to get through it to go back to school to be a teacher. I failed it at least twice. It was really hard to keep studying for it. I had a difficult time reading the selections and comprehending what they wanted me to comprehend, understanding what they were looking for, being able to interpret the way they wanted me to. I realized I needed help, so I asked for it. I even read those yellow practice books to find out what they mean on the test when they say, "What does the author mean when he says. . . ?"

When I finally took the exam, I had so much test anxiety, I couldn't relax. My heart was beating very fast. I had my favorite candy bar with me and I just had to trust that I would know how to pass. Every time I got stuck, I would breathe and try to relax, and not worry about the time ticking away. I understood everything they were asking, basically, but for the life of me I couldn't make sense of the little three-sentence paragraphs they wanted us to read on some political concept or another. Everything they asked about them made me feel as if they were written in a different language. If I was interested in a topic, I could get a perfect score, but if it was something I didn't relate to, I just couldn't focus on it. It was really hard on me when I failed the test over and over again before I finally passed the thing.

Not being a reader has been very painful. I feel I'm not articulate, and that my vocabulary is limited. It was hard to trust myself enough to go back to school. My friends are very much into books, and ask me if I've read this book or that book, and it makes me feel strange not to have anything to say. I can talk about soap operas because I watch them all the time, but television is depressing because I don't grow in any way when I watch it. I think TV is the worst invention. If it wasn't around I think people would read a lot more.

When I do read, I hate to read fast; I read one word at a time. I don't skip anything because I'm afraid I'll miss something. It's like not falling asleep in the car—I have to know what's going on outside the window even if I'm a passenger. With books, I'm afraid of missing something because I don't want to get cheated out of the book.

I feel I have such a long way to go, even though I'm reading more now. I wish that I could just soak up all the great books, that in one night I could read a whole library filled with all those books I feel I should have read, like *War and Peace*. I wish I could just put them all in my head and have them inside of me. I would if I could.

MICHELE OLDMAN

After a lifetime of living with an "inner critic" who told her she couldn't read, Michele Oldman finally discovered the pleasures of reading, partly with the help of her friend and reading mentor, Maggie McBride, whose own story is in Chapter 5.

I remember my first-grade classroom, the teacher, and even where I sat though it has been thirty-five years. Why? The image is so clear because my friends were laughing at me and I wanted to cry—I was reading out loud in a circle of students and I could not pronounce some of the words. I just wanted everyone to go away so I could practice. No such luck. I was a public failure. I hated the book and hated the idea of reading. From then on, I spent most of reading group trying to figure out which line would be mine so I could practice ahead of time. I did not pay attention to the content; all I cared about was if I was ready when my turn came. Reading was not fun and certainly not a way to learn.

I had other negative connotations about reading. I got the message early on that "reading" meant being thrown into a room by myself—banished. Somebody was going to close the door and say, "Don't bother me. I don't want to talk to you. Here, read something. Leave me alone." You had to do it by yourself. Nobody was going to talk to you. Nobody was there.

Fortunately for me, and I'm not sure why, I was able to compensate for my reading in other subject areas and go on to be successful in school. In most cases, I was able to learn enough by listening in class. One day I was working on math and the boy sitting next to me was way ahead in the math workbook. I asked him what he was doing and he said, "Well, you know, you might as well just do as much as you can. It's more fun to go ahead instead of just sitting around." I thought, "What a great idea." And so we both had a good time racing through the math book. I became very interested in math—it was easier than reading and I could do it at my own pace. Nobody was listening to me stumbling along.

For years, whenever an activity involving reading came up at school or at home, a voice inside me would say, "Oh, you won't be able to do that," or "How can you escape this?"

A while ago I walked into a store to buy a book for a long airplane ride. I knew I probably wouldn't read it, but I thought I should have a book just in case. Well, for some reason, I started the book and I actually enjoyed it. In fact, I loved the book and read all four hundred pages. I kept thinking, "You're reading a book and liking it. What happened?" Then I picked out another book all by myself and read that one. Wow! I liked to read! I discovered the adventure of being in someone else's shoes and following their thought process. It was fun. I could put all my own issues to rest and step into another's mind and see how they handled things. So after thirty-five years of hating reading, something happened. I am not sure what, but now I like to read. This doesn't mean I'm a great reader, but a whole new world has opened up to me.

Around that same time, my friend Maggie gave me a book to read, Wallace Stegner's *Crossing to Safety*. For some reason I got right into it. I looked forward to coming home from work every day and reading the book. It was like coming home to see a friend. The book got into characters' minds and showed what they were thinking and how they were making decisions. Now I finally get why people say reading is their best friend. You don't need anybody else to talk to when you read.

Maggie even went with me to see Wallace Stegner read to an audience after I got into that book and other books of his. She has continued to give me more books and keeps asking me, "Well, did you read this yet?" She was the one who turned me on to reading. She still gives me books for Christmas, birthdays, anytime. I couldn't possibly read all the books she gives me, but we do talk about the ones I read.

Recently I read an article by Matthew Ignoffo entitled, "Improve Reading by Overcoming the Inner Critic." This article made me stop and think about why I hated reading. I just thought that I couldn't read, but I never allowed myself to think about why. The main point of the article is that many people hate to read because they have a negative self-image as readers. His approach to helping students revolves around creating self-esteem. First, he helps you discover that you have an inner critic and what it sounds like. Then, he helps you turn off the inner critic and allow yourself to read.

RICH CLARKE

Rich Clarke's reading was a labor to him until ten years ago when an opportunity to read aloud to a class of second graders unexpectedly released him from the emotional barriers to reading he previously felt. He is a former school psychologist who is now a program administrator for a foster children's educational support program. An outdoorsman, gardener, photographer, and cook, he is also the father of Kevin Clarke, whose interiew follows his.

My early childhood was traumatic. I was sexually abused before the age of four, and also sent off to my grandmother's to live for a year before age six. Shortly after I came back, my brother died. When I came back to first grade I was in the bottom reading group, even though I had started out in the middle or top, and I stayed down there all the way through my school career. I'm sure there was an emotional component to my reading problem; other areas of my development were also delayed, like my teeth came in late and my coordination was poor.

I felt very frustrated with my reading and envied the kids who could read, the kids who could take written material and make something of it, who could follow directions to make a model, for instance, because I couldn't do it myself. I didn't have confidence that I could get information off a page. In cub scouts we had to read the cub scout manual together, and I remember the shame of not being able to read out loud. I would bumble my way along until somebody couldn't stand it and took over the reading.

I soon developed adaptive skills to protect myself so I wouldn't feel the embarrassment and shame of not reading. For instance, I'd do something "accidentally" in class to turn the attention from the reading so I wouldn't have to continue feeling the bad feelings it gave me.

My seventh-grade reading teacher had a celebration for me when I read my first book, *Thirty Seconds Over Tokyo*. Reading it was a big deal; my parents celebrated, my English teacher was ecstatic, and I, too, was overjoyed. But I didn't follow it up with another book. Later, while repeating ninth grade in a boarding school, I had a horrendous problem in a literature class. I just could not figure out abstract symbolism, what everybody else was talking about, and I felt shame all the way through that class. My teacher nicknamed me 'pinhead' because of my limited ability to excel in his class.

My grades and SAT scores were decent enough to get into college, though the first time I took it, my English score was low. You see, college was part of the 'program.' As my parents' son I was going to college; it wasn't an option for me not to go. But I was never into the academic side of college, I went there to play—to party, hunt, fish, and backpack. I took tests after college that indicated I was reading at the ninth-grade level.

I was an economics major because it was a field that required little reading, and few language skills. It mostly required math skills and the ability to read graphs. I learned certain phrases that I could put down on my exams to make it sound like I knew what I was talking about. I had no real idea what "marginal efficiency of this," and "elasticity of that" were about, but I learned the phrases and sounded as if I knew what I was talking about.

I even managed to get a graduate degree, but reading was not my primary mode of learning. I used other adaptive skills, such as taping lectures, listening to outside speakers who were talking on the subjects I needed to know about, or talking to somebody else who had read the information.

The turning point in my attitude about reading came some years ago when I was a school psychologist. A second-grade teacher asked me to come to her class and lead a discussion group about kids' issues, and try to raise questions that could lead to some feeling-oriented discussions. Her idea was to read some stories to the kids, and then talk about them. I thought it sounded interesting, so I tried it. Suddenly I found myself very nervous about reading out loud to second graders. Here I was, a thirty-five-year-old man going through the fear I had had in second grade about reading out loud before the class. I hadn't realized how difficult reading out loud really was for me until I tried to read that book. But I got up there and read and I discovered that I liked the sound of my voice, the sound of the language as it came out, the lightness in my voice, and the response I got from the kids—they wanted more. I came home and talked about the experience with my family, and fit together the pieces of my developmental problems as I had never done before. The little kid in me was finally able to feel a sense of mastery over reading. It was a breakthrough experience for me actually to read that children's book to those kids.

After that I started reading out loud to other kids. I read one story by Ken Kesey at a kids' camp, and at home, and even to a few adults. I find that when I read out loud to kids I'm able to act out the different voices and it becomes more of a theatrical performance. It's all very new and exciting to me.

Sometimes I still have difficulty comprehending what I'm reading, though, so I'll have to read it over and over. It may be the linguistic style that creates the problem, or that too many concepts are introduced in too short a span of time. If I don't quite understand the first concept, then the next one that's linked to it will be fuzzier still, until pretty soon I won't be able to digest anything further down the page.

But the real issue is that I hit an internal mechanism that says, "By God, I'm not going to be able to understand this. I've gone through it two and three times, and I'm not going to try to decipher it anymore, it's just too frustrating." The adolescent is rekindled in me, and I just bail out. Whatever I am reading today becomes a chain to the past; it's as weighted with past history as it is with the present.

The act of reading has always been emotionally charged for me. Until the incident ten years ago, I didn't read at all unless I had to for school or work. I just would not read. Now I'm addicted to certain authors. A friend of mine turned me on to Tony Hillerman. He writes mysteries with Navaho cops as main characters who solve crimes on a reservation. Although he's an Anglo, he's a real champion of Native American culture. He grew up in Oklahoma near a reservation my grandfather grew up on, and rode a bus to school with reservation kids, and was discriminated against by the city folks right along with them. His mysteries integrate Navaho, Hopi, and Zuni cultural knowledge into the crime solving. These two Navaho cops go out and pursue a criminal on a reservation, differentiating between one clan and another by the behavior patterns revealed in the crime. I've even gone to listen to Hillerman talk a few times, and really enjoyed him.

I guess I'm an intensely emotional person. When I read, the emotion on the page is what registers most to me. What turned me off before was the emotion connected to the event of reading. I had enough bad stuff going on in my life when I was a kid, so I avoided whatever I could that was uncomfortable, including reading.

KEVIN CLARKE

High school sophomore Kevin Clarke is frustrated by his inability to concentrate while reading novels and textbooks, and admits it is finally time to come to grips with his reading difficulties. He is active in many sports, including water polo, volleyball, swimming, and weight lifting. He is Rich Clarke's son.

My fourth-grade teacher was really horrible. She called me stupid when I didn't understand something. She'd just scream at me when I asked questions and make me feel like I was the stupidest person on earth. I wanted to learn the stuff, too. That was back when it wasn't cool to be the screw-off in class like it was in seventh grade. It was sheer frustration. My parents wanted me to read, but I just wasn't doing it. I wasn't passing any of the tests either, only cheating on them. I didn't understand the reading and I didn't like it. I had the feeling of being the supremely dumbest kid around. All the other kids seemed to be able to read. There was one girl in my class who was reading *Gone with the Wind*. I hate her still.

When I was in fifth grade I read a book called *The Lemon Meringue Dog*. It was the only book I ever enjoyed reading. My mother even took a picture of me reading it which is still tacked to the kitchen cabinet. My parents made me read it. They said, "You have to read something for fun, damn it. If you don't read something for fun, we're going to ground you." So I read it for fun and actually enjoyed it. Then they suggested I should read another one, but I couldn't. I was too afraid I wouldn't be able to understand another book. The fact that I understood that one was a mystery to me.

I went to a small island in Maine with my friend and his parents during the summer between eighth and ninth grade. We'd go boating and take short swims in the freezing water, and just kick around. I felt kind of uncomfortable because all three of them were reading a lot of the time and I'd be doing something else like walking around the island or something. The only books they had were some really old ones and a few supermarket novels. My friend started reading a book about some insurance fraud thing. It was OK for him, but the print was too fine for me to read. I think they were uncomfortable that I wasn't reading. Maybe they thought I was stupid or something, so they said, "How about a book?" I froze up but I said, "OK." They found a book for me called *Wifey*, by Judy Blume, but written for adults. They read some of the explicit pages to me and that got my teenage self interested. It was about this housewife who had this asshole of a husband, really not a cool guy, you know? He wouldn't even let her mourn the death of Kennedy because he voted for the other guy. I liked the story, but when it got into what she was thinking and all that, I just couldn't understand it, so I quit. Reading is a waste of time for me unless I understand the book, which is rare.

I guess people who read all the time must get something out of it that I just haven't experienced. They must take in the material and really understand it. I don't know whether they force themselves to read or not. I'm sure there are a lot of people who don't want to read, but at least they can if they have to. I think good readers must be interested in whatever they're reading about, or they must find interesting things in a book after they start reading. They must, how else could they read if they weren't interested? I know I can't. If I'm not interested in a book it becomes completely boring; it's just impossible for me to keep reading.

I recently read some of *Brave New World*, but only after it was assigned to us a second time. The first time I didn't read any of it; I didn't like it, I was not turned on to it. I didn't understand the first page. One character would be talking and then someone else would be talking—it was too complicated. I thought it was the same person and I got confused and angry. Why were they making me read this? It didn't make any sense to me, but it did make sense to some of the other guys.

I don't hear the voices of the characters in books, but I do try to envision what I'm reading. When I was reading *Brave New World*, I pictured the main character as this guy I know who is thin and wiry and wears glasses. I always relate characters to people I've seen before because I can't make up somebody I've never seen. Places are hard to imagine, too. I have to borrow a place I've already seen.

I saw this movie that was a play of *A Tale of Two Cities*. We read the book beforehand in class, and I bought the Cliff Notes. But when I saw the movie, the people and scenes were much different than I had envisioned them. There was one character, a woman who I expected to be old, feeble, and crotched over, but in the movie she wasn't like this at all. I assumed I was wrong and the movie was right, because the people who made the movie are smarter than I am and so they understood the book better. I don't trust myself to read it right.

When I got into the eighth, ninth, and tenth grades, reading became a really difficult process because I had to read a lot for school. Each night I might have to read fifteen pages in a biology book, ten pages in an English book, and fifteen more for history. That's an immense amount for me. I start to read, and I get down the first line, OK, second line, OK, third line, OK, but I just can't concentrate after that. I'm reading but my mind is trying to distract me from the book. It's the most frustrating feeling. I say, "OK, think," and slap myself on the face, and go back to the beginning. Or I ask myself, "What have I just read?" and I know nothing about what I just read. I might have read six pages and I know nothing.

I get totally uncomfortable when I try to read, and there are always other things I'd rather be doing than making myself uncomfortable and straining myself. I get embarrassed when I read, not because there's someone else around, but because I embarrass myself when I can't do it. I say, "Jeez, you're fifteen and you can't read a whole book, or even a chapter." Why should I put myself in this kind of discomfort on purpose? Sure, I have to do school work, but I can call up a friend to brief me on the chapter, or if I have to answer questions from the reading, I can skim, looking for the important words and write out the answers. I'm definitely smart in a lot of other subjects, but when it gets down to reading, there I am, in the thirteenth percentile.

I've known about my reading problem for a while now, and I'm starting to hit hard on it. I realize it's not something I can just work more on and have it go away. I really have to come out of the closet with my reading problem.

DONALD HILL

Donald Hill has worked as a carpenter for many years and recently began preparing taxes for his friends in his spare time. He is now pushing past a long-time reading comprehension block in order to study for the Internal Revenue Service's enrolled agent exam.

I never did enjoy pleasure reading. I just get tired and sleepy and my mind gets to wandering somewhere out there in left field. I come back in and read a bit more, and then I go into this grey area and I'm back out in left field again. I get tired. I say, "Why am I doing this?" and I go do something else.

I have to read for a purpose, a reason. I'll read the sports pages because I used to be an athlete, and I'll read about taxes because I'm a tax preparer, but I can't just read books. I think I only read one whole book all the way through in high school, *The Ox-Bow Incident.* It was one of those classic cowboy stories about a small hick town where three men had robbed a bank and killed somebody. Then the people in the town picked up three innocent men and hung them by mistake. I still remember it as if I read it yesterday because I read so few books in high school. In junior college I had to write a report about a book and get up in class to speak about it so I picked *The Pony Express* because it was a small book and easy to read. I did it because it was homework for a class, but if the teacher had said, "Here's a few good books. How 'bout picking one out and reading it in your spare time?" I might have picked one up, but I'd never have read it.

Television is a big mistake for people like me. I got hooked on television when it came in and got away from reading. That messed me up quite a bit. My mother tried to make me read, but I could only apply myself to a book for a little while, and then I had to go out and run the streets with the other kids. Even today, I might get interested in reading something, but there'll be something on TV that I want to watch, and so the reading goes.

When I was in school, I never cut classes. I'd attend every one because I found out I could get by just by going to class. Whenever an exam would be coming up, I'd wait for the teacher to tell us what it was about and then that was the time to study. I always passed the exams; I never got an F. I did what I had to do. I liked math courses though, because they took me away from reading. I was a math freak—I got all the way to trigonometry.

I had a cousin who was straight A's all the way. He was always reading out of the books for excellent students, and as a student I was somewhere in the middle, bordering on poor. We got into an argument one time—I said, "I'm tired of you getting A's and me getting C's. Next time I'm going to beat you out—I'm going to get the A." I studied and studied and we both got A's. He couldn't believe it but I proved I could do it. I showed I could apply myself when I had a competitive goal, and I loved it, but then I just let it go.

Another time we had a spelling bee and it was a challenge to beat all the girls out. The teachers gave us a whole bunch of words to study and I won the bee because I crammed for those particular words. It was a challenge, and that gave me an interest and a purpose so I got involved until I was really good. But for some reason it just didn't register that if I had an interest to do well in all of school, I would also have the ability to carry it off.

A lot of people in my union can't read and write. Myself, I bluff it. They all think I'm very intelligent. They come to me to solve their problems. They say, "Go ask Don," when somebody wants some forms filled in for them. They don't know I'm bluffing it because I do help them out quite a bit.

I can read tax stuff with no problem—I run through a tax book just like that. I can pronounce the words and I know what they mean. It's exciting to me and I know exactly what's what. I can read tax books because I read them for a reason.

I have my state license to prepare taxes, but now I want to get my federal license, but that involves passing an exam. I know the material—it's not really that hard—but the reading comprehension part of the test throws me off. I have a problem focusing when I try to read too fast.

I'm finding myself beginning to read more lately. I'm starting to pick out the words I can't pronounce—I want to learn how to spell them and know what they mean. I'm starting to keep my own vocabulary lists and I want to change my lifelong habit of getting tired and bored when I read. I'm working on it.

CAROLE MARTIN

Having had few positive childhood reading experiences, Carole Martin still finds it difficult to concentrate when she reads. But even with her concentration difficulties, one of her hobbies is buying used books at garage sales. She is a merchandiser for department stores, and the mother of two adult children, including Todd Martin, whose interview follows hers.

What I remember about learning to read is that they split us up into groups and we learned to read in sentences, not words. Phonics wasn't used. I had a hard time because we were supposed to read the whole sentence all at once, not just the words, and I got very confused. Some of us got it and others didn't. I didn't like it that I couldn't read. I always wanted to be in the top group, but I couldn't be because I didn't know how to read. I was always behind in elementary school. Only as an adult have I realized how far behind I was; I never really knew at the time. Most of my friends were nonreaders, too. As I got a little older I read *Pippy Longstocking* and some Nancy Drew stories to myself, but I don't remember reading very much.

When I went to junior college, I read the books that were assigned, but my comprehension wasn't good then, and it still isn't. I daydream when I read. I'll start reading and all of a sudden I'm down to the bottom of the page, and I don't remember a thing I've read between here and there. These days I do read the newspaper, though. It plays an important role in my life: I come home from work and I sit down and read it—it's a way for me to relax and change from work mode to home mode. But I still daydream, even on newspaper articles; if it's two or three pages, I space out. Usually, I try to read articles from the beginning to the end, but sometimes I skip around. If I want to get the gist of what's going on in the article, I'll read the first sentence in each paragraph because a teacher once told me the first sentence is the most important.

I like to read magazine articles also, and lately I enjoy the *East West Journal* and *Computer Age Magazine*. They are interesting to me because they're about the new age and what's happening in the future. They have stories about psychics and stuff like that, about how to eat better, how to live your life better. I buy *Better Homes and Gardens* and *Cosmopolitan* too; I'm fascinated by self-help magazine articles and I'd like to incorporate what they say into my life, but I usually don't. I don't see doing something like that as a part of reading.

I read one article lately on why people choose to have negative attitudes about life. It gave me some ideas on how to be more positive; I even practiced the ideas for a little bit. A more positive person, a person who doesn't have the problems that the article described, would probably just skim over it and not even be interested, but I read most of the words.

I love books, I collect books, but I don't read them. I don't know why. I buy them at garage sales. I collect all kinds: mysteries, self-help books, romance novels, best-sellers, even textbooks. Sometimes I buy them with the intention of reading them myself, sometimes I buy them to give to someone else. What I buy on any given day depends on my mood—if I'm in the self-help track or not. But if I can't find the kind of book I want, I just buy what's there. Most of the books I find at yard sales are about families and how they've struggled, or about women who are divorced, that kind of stuff. I don't go in for the romance novels much. I like the classics, but I don't buy them because I don't feel I would understand them.

I don't read novels much even when I do buy them. They take a lot of time and I have to concentrate on what's going on. I would want to sit down and read most of the book and I don't want to take the time; I have other things to do, like put dinner on the table, wash and iron, so it's better not to get involved in a book at all. When I do pick up a novel, I read about ten pages and all of a sudden I'll find I'm someplace else and I don't even remember what I've read. I need glasses, so it's hard to see the print.

I find it easier to concentrate on reading when the TV is going. When I come in the house and nobody is there, I have to have noise, so I turn on the stereo or the TV. It makes me feel like there's something going on. Another part of the problem with reading is that we don't have good lighting in our living room. The lighting we do have is not conducive to good reading at all.

If I could do it all over, I would pick a teacher who would really teach me how to read. I would pick somebody who, by reading to me, would show me her own exuberance for reading, show me that reading is a positive experience, and that I could gain important knowledge through books. If I read more, I'd know more about how other people live their lives, and how to live my own life another way if I wanted to. Reading keeps people abreast of what's going on in the world. It helps them make decisions based on real information so they don't get left behind. I don't want to be a sixty-year-old bag lady. I probably wouldn't make it through the first winter.

TODD MARTIN

Todd Martin is a quiet and organized young tractor mechanic who enjoys taking apart and reassembling cars, motorcycles, and bicycles in his spare time. For Todd to be able to concentrate on reading, the topic must be directly related to his interests. He is Carole Martin's son.

I'm into my work: engines. I read a lot about engines at the tractor dealership where I work—there are books there about the equipment, and I read them on my own because it helps my career. Some days, if I'm working on a certain part of the engine and have no clue how it works, I'll come home and read the service manuals. I usually go to the part of the manual I'm interested in the most. Sometimes I daydream though, especially if I'm reading about a boring part of the tractor.

One of the mechanics I work with doesn't read because he didn't finish high school, but he's been working on tractors all his life, so he's the type of person who will tear something apart and then put it back together; that's how he's learned. The other mechanic went to school and does basically the same thing, but he'll go and read the manual, then go back to the project. Even though I'm around two guys who know a lot, I want to learn it on my own. I'm going to school to help myself in certain areas, like right now I'm taking a course in hydraulics. I don't tend to daydream when I read material for school.

In the first grade, I cried because I had to stay after school, me and a group of other kids, and I didn't know why. Then I found out we were all having a hard time learning to read. We stayed after school an extra hour every day and read out of these tall, skinny books about some little man. Eventually we got to write our own little books. I won a fifty-cent award for my first book, called *My Motorcycle and the Dinosaurs*. Winning that award helped my self-esteem; the book is still in the school library.

The crowd I hung around with in high school were all very intelligent people, 4.0 students. I was the jock, and they accepted me for who I was. I got average grades, 3.0 and above, but they were all very high mentally. I guess they all liked to read a lot. I couldn't figure it out. Maybe they read because they weren't as gifted mechanically as I was and couldn't do things with their hands. I've always been good with my hands. Maybe they read because although they couldn't do something else really well, they could be good readers.

I think I should read more, but that's probably just an insecurity. Maybe being able to say I read a lot would help me fit into different crowds better. I don't like being an outsider; I would feel more confident about myself if, when somebody came up and asked me if I read, I could say yes.

I don't read novels, I never have. I tell myself I could be spending my time doing something else. I don't know why, but somehow I feel I'm wasting my time when I read. I wish I didn't feel this way. I would like to be more of a reader instead of sitting and watching television or going out and working on something. Many people have told me that reading would make me a much smarter person and I believe it's true. My younger brother was always slow at learning things until he started reading. By the time he was in junior high he was reading

Dungeons and Dragons, and he got better grades than I did all through high school.

I have a bad tendency to daydream when I read. I'll be into it at first, and then I'll just start daydreaming or skipping sentences. My eyes will travel. I'll read down to the end of the page and not know what I've read. When I was in school and we had a reading assignment, I'd start thinking of how I'd run in the race after school. I was always into sports, and spent a lot of time thinking about how I was going to perform better that day. Now I do a lot of bicycle road racing; some races are a hundred miles long. This is my first year of racing so I've only done three of these. I used to ride twenty miles a day, and fifty on the weekends, before I got into my work so much. I like competition, it makes me feel good. To me, racing and finishing are part of the same feeling. It's maybe like what finishing a book might be to another person.

My mom reads the newspaper constantly, and I'm starting to look at articles in it too, because when I come home from work and sit down on the couch next to her, the newspaper will just happen to be there. I've always looked through the sports, but sometimes I go through the rest of the paper, and an article will pop up that interests me, oh maybe about a person going to Europe, or a project that somebody's working on.

When I was a kid, reading was forced on me so I would get good grades. Now I read for my own benefit, to make myself a better person. I read now so I will be more knowledgeable about my job. I've always been into self-improvement.

GEORGE ISMAEL

George Ismael plays center on a college football team, but the discipline and drive he has learned from football doesn't seem to carry over into his reading, except when he is reading about the topic he is most interested in—serial killers and murderers. He wonders, "How can they kill like that?"

I wasn't read to as a child because my mother worked long hours, but she always pushed me to read and do my homework, and I always came out as one of the top students in my elementary school classes. There was this other kid and from kindergarten to fifth grade, and whether it was math or reading, we would always race each other. It was fun. We got everything perfect. We would always compete to see who would come out on top. If I lost on one assignment, I knew I would get him on the next one. It was a motivation to get me to read, but when he went to another school in sixth grade my motivation was gone. There wasn't anybody to compete against. That's when I began slacking off. I just lost interest.

Now the only kind of books that capture my attention are books on serial killers and murderers. I try to put myself into their shoes: How can they kill like that? Why did they kill? Why is it so hard to catch them? What are the patterns in their killing? These things fascinate me. Some just live a normal life in their youth, and then something happens. For example, one woman I was reading about, she got married and that put a lot of stress on her, and so she snapped one day. She ended up killing two of her kids and tried to blame it on some mystery man that jumped out in front of a car. What do they think about, that's what gets me. How can someone kill a little ten-year-old? How can someone rape a young girl and then kill her afterwards? Do they actually know what they're doing, or are they in a different state? Does something take over their mind? Probably—look at Charles Manson and the Zodiac killer. I also want to find out what happens to them in the end, if they're captured or are they still on the loose.

No, I'm not going to turn into a serial killer just because I like to read about them. But sometimes I think, "What if one tried to kill me?" There's so much anger inside me I think they wouldn't be able to. I'd put up a good fight, but who knows? I wouldn't want my younger brother or anyone in my family, my mother, to come across one of them. My mother still teaches me right from wrong and keeps me in line when I'm out of center.

I'm the kind of person who, if I see someone being jumped on the street or an old lady getting her purse snatched, I have to step in. I even wrote a paper once after I saw this little kid being jumped by two bigger kids. The little kid had his watch taken, and his wallet. Everyone was watching but no one stepped in to stop them, so I had to. The little kid felt secure that finally somebody big was on his side. When I looked at him I saw my little brother. I'd want somebody else to stop a fight if my brother were involved. I think that's why I want to become a cop.

I can read about serial killers, but if I read a story that's assigned to me as part of a college class, it dulls me out because I'm not interested in it. I'm in an English composition class now and we have this book of short stories and I have to read a few every week. I'm just not interested in them. I get bored. I can read, but I'm just bored.

When I read a story that's assigned to me, I get easily distracted. If there's a TV, I turn it on. If I hear somebody outside my room, I put the book down and go talk to them. Just anything can distract me. I don't know what it is, I'm just not focused on a story I have to read. I think, "Why am I reading this story?" Or I think about something else: What am I going to do tomorrow? What's on TV? My eyes are looking at each line, each word, but my mind is thinking about something else. I couldn't even tell you what the story was about if you asked. Usually, I fall asleep. I have to be up and walking around to stay awake.

I know if I don't read I'm not exercising my mind or learning new things and I'm just staying on the same level. I don't know how I'm going to get through without reading and knowing what I'm reading about. I know that reading is important, but I'm still not doing anything to help myself. I should read, but I don't. I just don't know why not. I can find the motivation to exercise because I can look at myself in the mirror and see that I'm not getting fat. I can't seem to find that motivation in reading. Maybe this interview will motivate me to read more.

NANCY JAICKS

Nancy Jaicks is a trauma, grief, and hospice consultant who works with people facing life-threatening illnesses, their care givers, prisoners with AIDS, and abused women. She is staff to the internationally respected leader in the field of death and dying, Dr. Elisabeth Kubler-Ross. Here she compares her exceptional abilities to listen to her clients with her frustrating attempts to comprehend words on a page.

I can still see the illustrations in a book of nursery poems that was read to me at age four as though it were yesterday. The drawings were very sensitive and romantic, made with light colors. The girls had hooped dresses, pantaloons, and pointy slippers. There were little tiny dogs in the pictures, like miniature poodles, and boys playing with hoops and sticks. I have this memory, but I know my reading was traumatized early on.

In first grade the teacher used a machine, a tachistoscope, that ran sentences in front of us at a certain rate. Now I was a premature baby, and back in those days very little was known about how much oxygen should be put in the incubator; if they made it too strong, it would burn the tissue in the eyes. I'm very lucky not to be blind, but I've always felt there is a lot of tension in my eyes as a result. I can still remember the anxiety of trying to read with that tachistoscope, the competition in the class, and me looking over at the other students to see if I was doing it the right way.

I stuttered and bit my nails when I was young. Although I had a superb education, I felt totally inadequate, so consequently, I was a very poor student. Now that I am older, I know I have a good mind and a high I.Q, but that still doesn't help me with my reading.

Even today I am a very slow reader, and I sometimes have difficulty comprehending or retaining what I read. If there's any kind of stress or pressure involved in understanding the information, or if I feel I have to get the information quickly, I become very aware of my eyes. I feel that my eyes stutter—I'm not able to see the words fast enough, smooth enough. As a childhood stutterer, I couldn't get information out. As a reader, I can't get information in, in a fluid, effortless way.

I start books, yet very seldom do I finish them, even if I love them. There are maybe twenty-five books here on my bookshelf that I've read in total. My emotional side is the most evolved and productive because it doesn't involve reading. What I do professionally involves working with people's feelings, and I'm very, very good at it. But my intellectual side? I feel I never measure up.

My reading comprehension is especially bad under stress. To be on Elisabeth Kubler-Ross's staff as a trainee I had to go to several of her workshops on death and dying. During the workshops, when somebody would give me instructions, I sometimes was too panicked inside to be able to hear them. I simply froze up, and the information couldn't come in. It's the same with my reading—it's hard for me to concentrate or stick with something when I'm under pressure. I feel very scattered, and I have a sense of not being grounded, not being focused.

When I listen to a client I'm very focused, however. I've trained myself so that if I don't know what a client is talking about I can allow my not knowing to be OK, to let my understanding evolve. I can do that easily in an emotional situation, but not in a reading situation.

I do not have a college degree. I left college in the middle of my sophomore year because of family pressures. I'm terrified to go back because I feel there's no way I could do the job. The mere thought of even taking a class, much less getting a degree, fills me with such panic that I put it right out of my mind. If I went back, I would put such pressure on myself, so much internal pressure, that I wouldn't enjoy it. It's too, too scary.

JESSICA ROBLE

Although Jessica Roble began as a strong student in elementary and middle school, her personal life in high school had a profound effect on her studies—and her reading. Now she is building a new life, which includes getting back to reading.

I was what they call a "latchkey" kid. As early as second grade, I had to do everything on my own. After school every day, I was by myself at home until the evening when my parents came home, and even then they didn't help me with my homework. I could do what I wanted. There was no authority. They would ask, "Did you do your homework?" and I would say, "Yeah." I didn't have a parent who spent the time to read to me.

You would never think he is, but my father is an alcoholic. When I was young, I never understood—I just thought he was drinking soda all the time. That man couldn't go anywhere without bringing a cooler with him.

My reading in elementary school was very positive. I did so well in sixth grade that I skipped seventh grade. In my eighth-grade English class, I was the TA, the teaching assistant. In those years I was very academic. I played clarinet and I worked for the counselors. I did all the things that would get teachers to notice me.

Then, when I was fourteen, I started going out with somebody who was three or so years older than me. What drew me to him was that he was musically inclined and artistic. But it was a very bad relationship. He did alcohol and drugs and had problems left and right and I believed I could help him. I felt there was nothing wrong with me, but there was something wrong with him and I could help him. I got into his family and his problems more than my own. I got drawn out of my own life—he was my life. He was also a person who didn't like to read.

As soon as I began that relationship, everything in my life changed. I started cutting school and my reading went down and I became pretty illiterate. I didn't have the drive or desire to read. I'm just going to tell you the truth: I cheated my way through English classes. My girlfriends and other people around me helped me out. I was very popular and had a lot of friends. I didn't perceive myself as a person who needed to cheat, but it was so easy because the teachers didn't get really involved with the kids. I passed through my freshman year cheating the whole way and they never knew. I did it right in front of their faces.

Even the lowest level of reading became overwhelming for me. I did not have even a broad understanding of what I read. I couldn't focus on reading or on school. I didn't want to go to school. I hated school.

In my sophomore year, I dropped out. I decided to go to the continuation high school instead because my boyfriend was there and that gave me much more time to deal with his problems and help him out. At that school, I could walk out of the room anytime I wanted, but I had to learn to be independent, to stay and do the work and get the credits. I was reading at a low level, but I didn't let anyone know except one teacher. He spent more time with me than the teachers at the regular high school and he actually helped me. I told him about my reading and he helped me get through. I made my last credit on the day of graduation.

I drew away from my family during those five years—we didn't have a very good relationship while I was with that boyfriend because they knew that I was hurting and they didn't want to see it. They wanted me to get away from him, but I couldn't. I moved out from my family when I was sixteen. Then I went back home for a while, and moved out again when I was eighteen.

Now I'm glad I went through all that because it made me grow up as a result. A psychologist advised me to read a book called *Women Who Love Too Much*. This book really got me to understand why I am who I am and why I do the things I do. I like reading about relationships, about why we are the way we are. Right now I'm reading a prenatal book because I'm pregnant. I can read and understand this book because I want to learn about it so much.

I don't speak "streetwise" anymore; instead, I speak much more formally. It's my choice now. I've become an independent person and I've met somebody that I'm getting married to who is totally the opposite from my other boyfriend. He does not drink; he does not do drugs. He has supported me and helped me. We support each other—it's back and forth together as a team. And my relationship with my family has turned around. They always wanted to give me support, but I didn't want it because I knew they couldn't really support me when I was with that other person—the wrong person. But now I'm with the right person and they can see that I'm much happier.

My whole life has changed. I've worked in the department store for just one year and I'm up to almost a management position. Of course, I hide my reading difficulty from them. I cover it up with my professionalism. I work fabulous with people. But when it comes down to reading, it's still hard for me to understand things sometimes.

I have a lot of friends who are very intelligent and know a lot of things, and I don't, so I feel embarrassed and hide it. My time is so pressed that I don't read hardly at all on my own. I work full-time and go to school full-time. My extra time is spent on my fiancé. But I know I've got to work on my reading and I'm ready to do it. It was only in my college reading class that I began to realize that I don't have to read every single word. Now I look for the meaning around the words instead of in the exact word itself. I'm a little better, but I still don't read unless it's something very interesting to me.

One day it will all come together. I'm starting out at the bottom again, but with this ladder I'm on, I hope I can achieve everything I need to know.

TITUS WATTS

Like many other young children who have trouble learning to read, Titus Watts was put in special education classes, where he stayed through high school. Even though he still has difficulty reading, he is the only one at his work who has been able to figure out how to use the computer that diagnoses automobile transmissions.

My dad and his whole family can't read worth a dime. My uncle is the only one who graduated from high school and went on to college. He's the only one, and he's a halfbrother to my dad. My mother is the only one in her family who went to college; she has a B.A. in accounting. But my mother's brother is a pastor at the Church of Pentecost, and he even wrote a Christian book that's pretty easy to read. When I was young, my mother would sit there on the bed and read a novel to herself, but I don't remember her reading to us. She taught my dad how to read the newspaper.

When I was in grammar school, I couldn't keep up with the other students. The teachers noticed I didn't have good reading so they put me into a special ed. program and I stayed there until I graduated from high school. The program didn't really advance me at all. You just stay at the same point in a special ed. class. I had a hard time learning to sound out words, but I could get good grades by doing the work they asked, which wasn't much and the teachers would just pass me on. It wasn't hard enough to make you really put out. It's bogus, but that's what happens. Honestly, I read only one book in all of high school, and I don't even remember the name of it.

I always had troubles with "b's" and "d's." The teacher would say the words and I would go over them and keep practicing. Also, my spelling is bad. I hear a word and I just write down what I hear, not what it really is. I can't seem to visualize words like *read,* that's r-e-a-d, right? I go, "Huh, should it be r-a-e-d?" I confuse the letters and sounds. I still today cannot get *girl* right. Is it g-e-r-d? I took classes for learning how to spell, but I still get lost.

I want to read, but I start and then I get lost and have to go back. I get stuck or lost or forget what I just read. I have to read things over and over. Sometimes I read and I get stuck on all the words I don't know. Or I read the paragraph real slow to try to remember what I just read, but I can't. Then I lose my focus. Or I'll read a second paragraph, but while I'm reading it, I'm still thinking about the first one and what was going on in it. I get frustrated; it just drags on and on.

I keep trying to think of ways to understand a paragraph better because I'm tired of getting stuck all the time. I tend to focus so much on the words that I don't pick up on the whole content. Recently what I've been trying to do is to read and visualize what's going on, and try to read faster and concentrate and not worry about remembering everything, and that works out better. When I try to remember everything, my mind just gets lost. So I try to get the whole big picture. My comprehension is better that way. But I still have to re-read every paragraph anyway.

If only I could read something every day, maybe ten minutes here and five minutes there, then maybe it would be a lot better. But I don't do it. I just can't force myself to read even though I know I should. Last week I actually picked up the book my uncle wrote and read, maybe not the whole book, but a bit of it. When I get home from work I think maybe I should read, but then I watch TV instead. It's even harder to get myself to read before I go to bed. I haven't hooked up an extension cord to the light that goes beside my bed. And that's what it comes down to: If I wasn't so lazy, I would get that extension cord and I know I would read. Sometimes I think I'll hook it up soon, but I never do.

I'm the only one who knows how to use the computer at work. I do diagnostics on transmissions with the computer, and to do that I have to read through the books and search for the information that I need about the transmissions. I get stuck on certain words sometimes, so I have to go over them to make sure I've got it right. The computer works with you so nothing bad is going to happen. It just says that it needs more information or something. My boss doesn't know I can't read, but I can use the computer at work because I can figure it out.

Probably people who read are more aware of what's going on than I am. Maybe their minds are focused on different things. At work my mind focuses on just getting to lunch. Maybe their minds focus on other things. Without reading, I'm limited in what I think about and what I can do, what kind of job I can get. I need to learn how to read better because I want to get somewhere in my life.

◊ CHAPTER 3 ◊

Those Influenced by Childhood Reading Experiences

Comic books opened up my imagination and gave me a large vocabulary, too. What other six-year-old would know what a serum was? Or invulnerability? Or radar?

Sharon Cho

Both routine occurrences and fleeting encounters can have profound effects on a child's future life. The individuals who speak out in this chapter met up with remarkable influences when they were young—influences that were often dramatic, sometimes traumatic—influences that affected their early reading abilities, and significantly contributed to the quality of their adult lives. Sometimes it was the reading itself that changed the narrator's life, while other times it was the people or events that surrounded the books that affected them so profoundly.

Most of the subjects in this chapter relate childhood reading stories that positively molded their adult reading lives. One man I spoke with recalled the rare books in his uncle's study that he was forbidden to touch. He would set his alarm for 3:00 A.M. and tiptoe downstairs for a view into this secret world. He testified that he would never have developed an interest in books if they hadn't been forbidden. A woman told me about her fifth-grade teacher, who recognized the difficulties she was having during the time her father was on trial for burglarizing a store in order to put food on the table. This teacher took a personal interest in her and fed her book after book to help her through her family crisis. That was how she became a reader.

In a couple of cases, childhood encounters and events led to later difficulties in reading. One woman told me that as a young child she read fluently and was even her teacher's pet. However, when she entered high school, she became involved with an older boy who didn't read at all and whose numerous personal problems became the focus of her energies. Her ability to read decreased dramatically as a result of this

51

involvement. Another woman reported how her mother tore up her books because she did not approve of the subject matter. Although this woman had been an avid reader as a child, after her mother's rampage, she developed a reading disability as an adolescent.

Many of this chapter's interviews have much in common with those of some of the other types of readers I present elsewhere. Yet there is something so compelling about each of these subject's particular experiences with reading during childhood that I was persuaded to create a separate chapter for those whose stories so clearly emphasized this aspect of their reading history.

SHARON CHO

Sharon Cho's childhood passion for comic books has extended into her adult life. Like one of her beloved superheroes, Sharon tries to do right by the people she encounters, including the many comic book artists whose careers she manages.

I grew up in Singapore speaking Chinese at home and English in school, but English is my primary reading and writing language. As a young child, I read everything I could get my hands on, especially comic books. My mother says I'm so nearsighted because I used to read under the bedspread with a flashlight. I was very sick between the ages of four and twelve and was bedridden a lot. I was only in school about 30 percent of the time, so reading was my main form of entertainment.

Reading comic books gave me a sense of being special. I always wanted to be a superhero, and I still do. I probably had ten to fifteen stacks of comic books about two feet high each. Most of them were hand-me-downs from a friend who gave them to my sister first, who then handed them down to me. The others I bought myself. Comic books opened up my imagination and gave me a large vocabulary, too. What other six-year-old would know what a serum was? Or invulnerability? Or radar? I picked up so many things in comic books having to do with super powers and stuff like that. As a result, my English became a lot better. My mother didn't care what I read, as long as I kept out of trouble, but she did finally make a rule that I couldn't bring comic books to the dinner table.

I'm one of the few females I know who grew up on superheroes and really took them to heart. Only a few of the superheroes were women, and it was very hard to find them. There was Supergirl and Batgirl, and later there was Miss Marvel and Spiderwoman and a few others that aren't worth mentioning. I wanted to be Supergirl. She was the innocent one, the pure of heart, the one that never questioned what she did, she just did it. She was a teenager, and for a few years we were the same age. About ten years ago, she died and I sobbed. Now there's a new Supergirl, but I can't stand the new one.

Comics instilled in me a very profound sense of "truth, justice, and the American way." Ha, ha. They gave me the belief that one person *can* make a difference. There's one phrase that came out of *Spiderman*: "With great power comes great responsibility." And Superman would never, never stoop to the level of the villains. He was above that. There was always a real difference between a good guy and a bad guy in the old comic books. Good guys always found a way to defeat the bad guys, and used honorable methods to do it.

I really don't like the ways heroes are portrayed in comic books these days. There's no longer any clear line between heroes and villains. Heroes kill people and don't care. Today's superheroes still believe in what they do, but they don't question—they just go ahead and kill. That really sickens me. But some of the new comic books are adult oriented and have darker themes, which I do like. Those heroes are very confused most of the time, which is more like reality.

Comic books are like American myths. I also loved the Greek myths—reading about Hercules is like reading a comic book—here is another hero who is able to do super fantastic things, but still has human failings. I loved the Greek myths, but not the Roman myths. I always felt the Romans were cheap rip-offs. In fact, whenever I hear somebody calling a god or goddess by his or her Roman name, I still get angry. Artemis is *not* Diana. Diana is a watered-down version of Artemis. Artemis and Apollo were my two favorites—Apollo because he was god of the light and Artemis, who was his twin sister, was the goddess of the Moon. Of all the other Greek goddesses, Athena was too cold, Aphrodite was too lusty, and Hera was too jealous. Artemis was just the strong, silent one, the one with passion. She was more of a superhero.

I had a huge set of Bible stories that my aunt sent from the States. I absorbed those Bible stories in the same way I absorbed comic books and Greek myths. I saw Christ as a superior. He died for the good of mankind. He was so good that nobody could understand him. He was perfect. He was the son of God. The prophets were much the same. I see Mohammed and Buddha in the same light also, because they achieved enlightenment. Yes, there are definite parallels between the Bible stories and the superhero comic books that I read.

Reading about superheroes gave me delusions of grandeur. I'd like to think I am grand, but I have many friends who would tell you I've done stupid things thinking I was a superhero. For example, I chased down four men into a tough section of town because they sideswiped my car. I didn't care what happened to me; what I cared about was that they apologize, that they do something about my car, that justice be carried out.

When I turned thirty last year, I made a promise to myself that I was going to try and make sure that every action I did was something admirable. I still want to be a superhero and I'm very, very tough on myself. I can't stand it when I feel I'm using or manipulating people, or anything that I feel isn't heroic in some sense of the word. I've tried to take what I read and put it into my life in some way. I'm an idealist in my heart and believe that somehow if people listened more and took the experiences around them more to heart, maybe the world would be a nicer place.

My family doesn't understand that my value system comes from superheroes. It tears my heart out when I see homeless people on the street and I've befriended a few of them. I wish I could do more. My family sees that as the irresponsible part of me. They see me give away my money. One of the conditions of my family helping me to buy my condo is that I'm not allowed to shelter anyone. They see it as foolishness when I take people in and give them a place to stay.

I don't know who I would be if I hadn't read comic books as a kid. Comic books influenced me to be a good person, a hero in my own way.

ED UDELL

As a child Ed Udell had trouble speaking. Reading became his escape from the ridicule of the other children, as well as his eventual cure. He grew up on a farm, spent many years working odd jobs, and then took nineteen years to complete his master's degree.

As a child I couldn't speak very well—even members of my family made fun of me—so I hated to speak at all. In the first grade I went to a rural school where the teacher made us read out loud every day. I hated it because even though I could read the words, some of them were just hard for me to say. The harder I tried, the more I stumbled over the words, and then the other kids would start laughing. Some folks said I was retarded. Forty years ago, if you didn't speak clearly and stuttered, people looked at you very strangely.

Mom told me I wasn't retarded, that I just had a speech problem, and I could improve. She kept saying, "You can speak, and you can read." Around the fifth grade she said, "I want you to read to me every

Saturday." I used to hate Saturdays because I'd wake up knowing that after breakfast I had to read to Mom. I thought, "I've always messed up, I will always mess up, so why try?" Mom would just say, "You ready Ed? OK, find something and read to me." I thought it was a stupid thing to do, and that it wouldn't do any good. I even cried about it. I mean, everyone told me I couldn't speak, how was reading going to help?

I did read to her, and when I said a word wrong, she'd stop me and say, "What's that word again?" I'd say, "I can't say it Mom." She'd say, "Sure you can. Breathe real deep. I'm not going to hit you or get mad, and you can do it." I would say to myself, "She's so stupid, trying to tell me that I can speak when I know I can't. Everyone says I can't but her."

In the end, I always had to accept my mother's prodding. She told me how, when she was in school, she also couldn't speak well and stuttered. She told me how folks also made fun of her because her mouth was twisted to one side due to severely burning her face on a stove, which contributed to her stammering. Her whole body was twisted as well, due to an unknown childhood malady, and she said she almost never slept at night because of the pain, so she retreated into books, reading while everybody else was asleep.

During my elementary school years I, too, retreated into books because the books wouldn't laugh at me. Books became my friends. I imagined I was the characters in them, whether it was Paul Bunyan, or Roy Rogers, or Washington Carver, or someone from Mark Twain. I took a long time to read a book because I would read a bit, then I'd stop and imagine what was happening. If a book described tall, green, luscious grass, I could see it. It was exciting to imagine things from books as if they were really happening.

I read the Bible in church, and I always wondered, "Who wrote this? Why these words?" I started to question folks in church, asking them, "Why do you believe this?" They said everyone was supposed to. I asked, "Why? Who was Jesus? Where did he come from? Who made God?" They'd say it wasn't important. Later I began asking, "Why was Jesus white if he was from the Middle East? Why don't Christians like Jews since Jesus was a Jew?" Mom finally said that she didn't know the answers to all my questions, but that they were all in books somewhere, and that by reading I could know everything. I said, "But some books are hard to read; I can't do it." "What did you say?" she'd ask? "Don't say you can't." I had forgotten, never say can't in front of Mom. And so I started going to the library for my answers. I also started asking my grandfather because although he only had a third-grade education, he seemed to know everything, even math and science, since he was very curious and read all the time.

I kept reading when I got to college, but it was forced reading from lists of required books. Once I raised my hand and said, "Excuse me, Sir, why are we reading these books?" The answer: "Because they are required." I was doing very poorly in history, and hated the history books since the only reason I could see for reading them was to pass the tests. Then finally someone I could relate to, an African-American track star, became my study-tutor and showed me how little I actually studied. He said, "Start disciplining yourself to sit down and concentrate even though you don't like the subject. You have to study it anyway." So I started to study because I respected him.

Then I went to a college where I could design my own education and get a degree through regular classes and study. I found out there were books available on any given subject, I learned research techniques and how to use the library. I discovered I could find answers to any question I had on a subject in ten, fifteen books, and at least three magazine articles. I thought, "Books are great."

When my first son was in the third grade, I got a note from his reading teacher that said, "Ed cannot read well. He won't read. We need to have a conference with you and his mother." I hadn't even noticed he couldn't read. I hadn't read to him when he was a young child because I was working and trying to get back to college. It took years for me to finally finish my college education, so later, when my son was in the fifth grade, I got another letter from his teacher saying the same thing. I threatened to take away his sports until my mom said to me, "You're going to take away what he's good at to make him read? That's not good. Don't take away what he loves. Use it as a carrot." We tried that, and Mom started reading to him every evening after school. Later, when he was flunking tenth grade, I realized it was partly my fault; I hadn't spent the time with him. I started telling him about my mom's life, my life, and my speaking problems. I started doing for him what Mom had done for me. Now he's reading better. He sees that to get the good jobs he needs good reading skills, so now he's reading in order to make money. Whatever his reason, as long as he reads, it's good enough for me.

VIRGINIA HARRIS

By the time Virginia Harris reached graduate school, she had "pretty much assimilated" into white society. She was able do to this because, as a child, and all the way through college, she was exposed mostly to writing by whites, from children's fairy tales to the New York Times. She eventually left a career as a chemist, and with it the pursuit of the "American dream," to search for who she really is as an African-American woman, and to become a writer and quilter.

For the first twenty-one years of my life I lived in a totally black world in the South. White people were on the periphery. My parents' friends were professionals and were making it in the black middle class. I lived among the black intellectuals; their conversations were about what was going on in the world, and they were very well-read. Even though I had lots of conversations with my father about current events and history, and he encouraged me to read and talk about these things, he also tried to protect me from what was going on in the outside world. We were part of a black intellectual society that tried to protect its kids from racism while trying to teach us who black people were at the same time.

Even though I grew up in a totally black environment, almost everything I read was written by white people. From early on, black people knew a lot about white people. We have to know a lot about them in order to survive. Although I never had a very clear image of who I was when I was growing up, I did have an image of who I was supposed to be in order to be acceptable. I knew the white worldview and aspired to assimilate into it.

I got this from reading, and the books I read as a kid were by and about whites. I got *Grimm's Fairy Tales* when I was eight, I read my mother's popular novels, and I read the classics—Charles Dickens, Robert Louis Stevenson, Shakespeare, and Chaucer. At school we recited the poetry of Paul Laurence Dunbar and Langston Hughes during "Negro History Week," but the writings of Negro women got no exposure—women writers like Zora Neale Hurston, Margaret Walker, and Ann Petry were lost to me. When I think of who I read back then, it's no wonder I didn't know who I was as a black woman.

Black identification with whites was pervasive, even in college. I once took a literature class from J. Saunders Redding, a black writer and one of the premier black thinkers. *One hundred percent* of what I read in his course was by white folks. Our book had people like the Brownings, Poe, and others I have no reason to remember. Those are the people I was required to read by Negro teachers!

When I was twenty-one years old, I went to graduate school in Ohio, and earned a master's in chemistry. I went there because they offered me the most money. It never crossed my mind that I would be the only black woman in graduate school. It was the first time I was a minority. I was terrified. When I went there, I had a southern accent. By the time I came home in December, I didn't. I don't remember being conscious of changing it.

In my second year at the university I lived with three white women. We always got the Sunday *New York Times* and faithfully watched the "Huntley-Brinkley Report." I was in a white mind-set when I discussed the news and just about everything else. The whiter I came across, the better, since that was the worldview I was aspiring to have. It wasn't that I wanted to negate black people, but there was very little news to read about us.

When I graduated, the sit-ins and freedom rides were going on. Up until then, black people had been absent from the news, but now it seemed we were the only news. Every time I went on a job interview I was asked what I thought about what was going on. This put me into a fury, as much with the black people as with the white people. I felt black people put me in a position of having to take a stand. It was a major conflict for me. I agreed with what the students were doing, and I was furious because I couldn't do it too. I was trying to be this other person; I had chosen to assimilate. That was the most conflicted time of my life.

I went to New York after graduate school and I had a terrible time getting a job. One man threw my thesis in my face and told me it was impossible for me to have done it. But eventually I got a job as a chemist and married another black chemist. I had done it: I achieved the "American dream." I had a house, two cars, a boat, three vacations a year, a fur coat in the closet, and a different outfit for every day of the month. And I was miserable.

I worked in the corporate world as a professional. And I was black and female, so the civil rights movement and the women's movement had everything, and yet nothing to do with me since I was living every day all the things that black people and women were trying to become. But it began to hit home that what I read in the *New York Times* was not what was really going on, that there was another perspective.

Then Nixon was elected; the war in Vietnam was the evening news; crackdowns on campuses became violent; there was an uprising at Attica; and the Black Panthers were systematically annihilated. I began to change. One of my first acts was to stop straightening my hair. Over a weekend I became a "militant black" to the people I worked with and one of my coworkers wouldn't speak to me.

I read about World War II, and I especially remember reading *Inside the Third Reich* by Albert Speer. I got hooked on Nazi Germany, especially the similarities to what was going on in the United States. Reading about Nazi Germany gave me the words to talk about my experiences in the United States. When Stokely Carmichael and H. Rap

Brown talked about concentration camps here in the United States, I was not able to sit back and say, "Huh-uh, they wouldn't do that." Why should I think the U.S. was any different? After all, Richard Nixon was essentially quoting Adolf Hitler.

Then came the women's movement. The '70s and '80s were decades of learning who I was—not as a woman or as a black, but as a black woman. I read feminist literature, but my experiences were sorely missing. Many white women were saying the same things as white men had been saying about race—or saying nothing at all. Then black women's books became more accessible. I read African-American women authors and this certainly gave me a more rounded sense of who I was, these books made me more visible to myself. I began to know that there is value in my experience.

Reading has helped bring the far-flung and often buried parts of myself together, just as reading helped to fragment me in the first place. Maybe through my own writing, some girl-child will be able to see herself reflected in what she reads. I hope so because I see so many twenty-year-olds doing the same things I did. It's as if the last thirty years never happened. Now it really boggles my mind that anybody would *want* to assimilate into the dominant culture.

LE LY HAYSLIP

Born into a peasant family in Central Vietnam, Le Ly Hayslip survived the war that devastated her village and country, eventually escaping the violence in 1970 when she married an American and moved to the United States. Her first book, When Heaven and Earth Changed Places, *chronicles her youth in war-torn Vietnam and her 1986 reunion with surviving members of her family, and her second book,* Child of War, Woman of Peace, *continues her story in the United States. Together the books have been adapted into the film "Heaven and Earth." She is founder of the East Meets West Foundation, a humanitarian relief organization that provides services to the poorest people of Vietnam.*

I went to school from 1956 to 1960. In those years our village was still in one piece. Most of my school time was during lunchtime because in the countryside, people work from six in the morning to twelve, then come home and have lunch and go back to work from two to six or seven. So I went to school between twelve and two. That is how I learned to read in Vietnamese.

In Vietnam we didn't have any books to read. In the third grade we had only one book. When your teacher asked you to read to him, you couldn't read from the book—you had to read from your heart and your mind. We stayed up all night to memorize everything so the next morning we could close the book and read to the teacher.

I'm fortunate because among my Vietnamese friends growing up, most of them couldn't read or write. I'm the youngest daughter of six children, so my sister and brothers helped to take care of the family while I went to school. Most of my friends only had one or two children in their families because their mother got killed in the war or their father went off to war, so these children had to support the family even though they were only five or ten years old. They didn't have the time to go to school, but some of them were very, very smart.

As I grew older, reading and writing helped me a lot. It helped when I had to fill out papers, which helped me get work and keep it. For example, when I sold black market goods, I had to fill in forms, like how much whiskey or whatever to buy. I practiced it and memorized the words. I was also able to fill in the paperwork when my husband and I wanted to get married. At that time, I had to read and fill in so many applications. Of course, my husband, who was an American, helped out a lot.

I've been in the United States for twenty years now, and I have three children who have grown up over here. They hardly know what survival is all about.

When you watch nature and see all the little insects, and one tries to kill the other for meat, the other will run and run and run any which way just to survive. Survival is inside of you. When you are in a life-and-death situation, you always take a risk. Nobody wants to die. You make a decision that you have to stay alive to take care of your husband, your wife, your children, your father, your mother. You also have to stay alive to pay the obligation that you came here to do, whatever it may be.

In the United States you don't have this kind of survival. Here, survival is paying your bills and being responsible for your parking tickets. Here you have your doctors and your counseling and everything else to help you. And here reading is a much bigger part of survival than in Vietnam. In this country, it's reading and writing that give people opportunities to become what they want to become.

I regret that I don't have more time to read. If I could, I would read more about the spiritual world, and through this reading, I would learn how to become human. I am most interested in becoming a human being because to be able to understand the world around me, I must understand myself first. Where did I come from? Why am I here? What should I do while I'm here? Those are the three basic questions for understanding who I am. Without answers to these questions, I cannot do my work, I cannot accomplish what I need to do.

I read a lot of books on life after death, diaries from the other side. I read Ramm Dass, Shirley MacLaine. To a Westerner, a Christian, these ideas are probably odd. But in the Buddhist religion, they are common. Over here you call it New Age religion; over there it isn't New Age at all.

I used to read a lot of Buddhist material in both Vietnamese and English, which helped me to understand how the Western mind thinks because the English books put it in terms that the Western mind can understand. So reading like this has become very valuable to me. And my Buddhism roots also help me to read about spiritualism. When I read such books, I read about me, about who I am. I find out more about why I'm here. I want to improve myself, I want to make myself better than I was yesterday. I have read much about investments and have made a lot of money, but that didn't make me happy. My spiritualism makes me happy and working to make other people's lives better makes me happy.

LINDA THOMPSON

Linda Thompson's formal education ended in third grade when she chose to work in the sugar cane and rice fields rather than continue going to school where an insensitive teacher made her feel "like nothing." She continued to read nevertheless, and after a working life as a waitress, a nanny, and most recently a nurse's aide, she is spending her retirement passing on her love of reading the Bible to her Sunday school classes.

When I first went to school I was put in the chart class to learn my numbers and letters, but my mother had already taught them to me. When the teacher asked me to say my ABC's and count, I did it so she said, "I'm going to put you up into the primer class." That's how I skipped up from that grade to the next. I had a very good teacher at that time who was good to me, but when I got to the third grade I had to go to another room. Now this was in New Orleans where we have people of all colors and all mixes. This teacher was small and had long hair and a light complexion. She was black, but she didn't care too much for dark children, and I was black so she would snub over me. Whenever it was time to read she'd say to me, "You shouldn't be doing that!" and I would have to sit there while everybody else did their reading and writing. She would play with the lighter children but paid no attention to the darker ones. Honestly, I don't know what she had against us—I never did find out.

I cried and cried every day when I had to go to school. That teacher made me feel like I was nothing, but I just couldn't tell my parents about it. She made me feel so little and I just couldn't go back. My parents knew little things didn't bother me, so they figured if I kept crying it must be something really getting to me. Finally, my father said, "Well, if she doesn't want to go, then don't send her." (At that time people didn't go to talk with teachers.) "Let's wait awhile and maybe she'll want to go back. If we send her and she doesn't want to go, she'll just go somewhere else and get into trouble." That's what my father had done when he was young—he would leave home with the rest of the children in the morning, but then he'd go over to the train tracks and play in the ditches until the other children were coming home from school.

I was too embarrassed to go back to school when I got old enough to be in another teacher's class. I thought the older children would laugh at me. I think my whole self-concept was set by then. I kept saying to myself, "Who wants to be the only dummy in the class?" Time passed and I kept putting off going back. It burns me up now.

I guess I taught myself to read, though, because during that time I'd read my older brothers' books. I would read their books and do their spelling. They said, "We'll help you," but I was helping them. Somehow reading just came to me.

Every night I would read until I fell asleep in bed and my mother would take the books out of my hand. She'd tell me, "Your eyes will go bad," but I loved reading so well at that time of my life, I didn't care. Besides my brothers' school books, I also read magazines that the boy next door would buy. He wanted me to read them and tell him the stories and I was happy to do it because I was learning a lot of things I didn't know.

I never did go back to school until I was about twelve. By then we'd moved to another area and I went to an adult school where this lady was teaching adults, but even if you were younger, she would teach you, too. She was very nice and taught for nothing two days a week during the summers.

I also became a Christian when I was twelve. I didn't read the Bible too much then, but I prayed and asked the Lord to tell me what I should do as a Christian. I do believe that God revealed to me that I should teach women and children, which is what I'm doing now in my retirement.

These days, I read the Bible first thing every morning when my eyes come open. I read it prayerfully to understand it—the real meaning doesn't come through otherwise. Sometimes, if I don't really understand something, I'll get another Bible and that one might break it down a little bit better. The prayers are what really get to me.

If I'm not reading the Bible itself, I'm reading other little books that people have written about it. These books are about faith and how to live. I've been reading this one book about what God says about faith for about two months now. I read so slow that it all takes time. I used to read faster as a child; maybe I'm just slowing down now.

Reading the Bible makes me closer to the people in my church and to people in general. It makes me love the Lord and other people. It gives me peace of mind. It gives me strength as a Christian lady. I'm not afraid of lots of things that other people are afraid of.

I've taught Sunday school for the last few years to young women and children. We read out of a chapter book about the Bible, but I tell my students, "Read out of your Bible more because it's a more important book. The Bible is God's word, but this other book is just somebody's idea about it. To be a strong Christian, you have to read the Bible." We read the verses and talk about them. Usually, I've read and read the verses ahead of time so I know what they mean. My students say I explain things very well, but whatever I do in my lesson, I do from my heart. I'm a deeply Christian lady and nothing in this world is more important to me than my Bible and my church and my family. I don't know what I would do without reading my Bible. And I feel just wonderful to be educating others in what I educated myself in. This is my life and I love it and I would put nothing else before it.

JUSTIN AND JASON REED

Talented and charismatic twelve-year-old twins Justin and Jason Reed have won numerous awards and prizes for their folktale story telling. Their secret, they confide, is to adapt the stories for each new audience, rather than telling them word for word as they appear in books.

Jason: I want to tell you a story about a word the devil made up. They say a long time ago, Satan sat in his underworld and looked around, thinking. He didn't see enough angels, so he decided to go get some. He jumped out of his chair, and swarmed all over the earth. He looked into one cloud and saw a bunch of delinquent angels smoking and drinking booze and doing crack so he took one thousand of them under one arm and one thousand of them under the other arm and five thousand in his mouth, and swarmed back over the earth. Then, as he flew by Florida, he came across a young slave by the name of Aunt Nancy. She looked up and said, "Hey Satan, you fixen to take some more angels down there?" "Uh huh," said Satan, and when he did, all five thousand angels flew out of his mouth. When he reached out to get them, a thousand flew out from under one arm, and when he reached for them, the last of the angels flew away. So when any of your friends go, "Uh huh," tell them that's the word the devil made up.

Justin: My teacher had entered me into the annual story telling contest. He gave us all these story telling books and let us choose which one we wanted to tell. I took them home, read them, memorized them, and won the contest. Then my brother got into it, too. We told stories at libraries, and soon they took us to the Hyatt Regency to perform in front of the black mayors. Then we started performing at places where they paid us money. The rest is history. Jason wasn't interested in story telling at first, until the first time I got paid twenty-five dollars for three minutes.

Jason: Reading and story telling are two different things. We began with reading a long time ago and the story telling didn't come until just now. We were two when our older sister started teaching us how to read. She was our baby-sitter much of the time, and she read stories by Mark Twain to us because there was nothing else to do.

Justin: When we were little our dad would be home in the morning while Mom was at work, and at night he would be at work while our mom was at home, but in between times there would be nothing to do so my sister would teach us how to read.

Jason: At first, my mother didn't even believe we could read until one time we were in the bank and we read a sign. After that, we used to hate going to our auntie's house because they'd sit us up on a chair and say, "Read this. Now read this. Now this."

Justin: We do African folktales about slavery times. We get our stories from books like *Bantu Folklore* and *Knee-High Man*. We also tell tales about Brer Rabbit and Brer Fox from the *Uncle Remus* books. Those were tales told by the slaves to communicate to each other in a way the masters wouldn't understand. They were really saying, "We know that so-and-so is hiding, looking for the underground railroad. We need to get help to him," but they would tell it in a story so the master wouldn't know what was going on. Books about these times were passed all over the world.

Jason: *Aesop's Fables* are different. They're about animals and have morals to them. Let's see, one story is about a tortoise and a snake and it goes something like this: The tortoise needed some salt so he went and got a whole bag of it and he tied it to his tail. He had to walk for miles and miles to get back home. The snake came by and thought the bag of salt was just sitting around because the tortoise was moving so slow. So the snake grabbed the bag, and the tortoise watched him run off with it. They went to the high council. The snake claimed it was his bag because he had found it lying on the ground. The council agreed it should be cut in half. Later, the tortoise decided to strike back at the snake. He saw the snake resting and he said, "You're my snake now because I saw you just lying around." Then he went to the council again, and the council decided they should cut the snake in half, which they did. The snake had his end, which had the head on it, and the tortoise had his end with the tail part. The moral of this story is that you shouldn't try and cheat people or it will turn right back on you. That's a kind of Aesop's tale right there.

Justin: I've learned a lot from the folktales. Reading them has helped me better understand other things I read. I used to have a hard time reading complicated stories—I didn't really understand what they were about. I'd just read a story and say, "I've read it," but I wouldn't understand it. Now I find it really easy to understand what I read. Every story has a moral that teaches you something. The more stories I read, the more information I have for doing other reading and for handling situations in life.

Jason: Right. Now I'm my friends' psychiatrist. It seems like everyone always has a problem and reading stories helps me be able to solve them. The morals of the stories help me give my friends the right answer. I help them do the right thing. Both me and Justin were chosen by our classes to be peer leaders.

Justin: I'm the person they always come to to answer their questions. They come to me and ask, "What is this word?" or "Do you know how to do this math problem?" Being able to give them answers comes from reading and telling stories.

Jason: I read a folktale in order to understand it, but I don't tell it word for word—I just say it the way I think it should be said. The writers of the books probably didn't tell it just like they heard it, either. They wrote their own version, the way they thought it should be. Each story stays the same as long as the moral doesn't change.

Justin: All I have to know is what the story is about, and then I can add anything I want to make it more fun, more serious. Most of the time I adapt the story to my audience.

Jason: When I perform before an older audience, I make the story a lot more complex because they're sure to understand it, but with a younger audience, I make it real simple.

Justin: There are a lot of things to understand when it comes to story telling. Most kids read a story and the only way they think about telling it is word for word. They don't want to learn the ideas. But when I read a story, I look for the funny parts or for things I can make funny. I discover what the moral of the story is, and then the story is mine to reshape. So whenever I tell a story, it will be different from the time before—I keep changing it around. This makes the story a lot better.

Jason: One time my teacher gave me a twenty-one page story and he said, "I want you to learn this word for word—the audience will love it." I got to reading it, looking for the funny part that might get the crowd laughing or get them to give me a standing ovation, anything like that, but by page ten nothing had come up. I thought it stinked.

Justin: One kid in the first contest memorized a thirteen-page story word for word and when he told it, it seemed like thirteen pages, too. That's why he only won second place.

Justin: We mostly each tell our own stories, but we do have two tandems where we tell them together.

Jason: I like tandems, but Justin doesn't. Our first one, "W.E.B. and Booker T.," shows how the characters fight a lot, how they quarrel. Our second one is about a landlord and a tenant and how they fight.

Justin: The reason I don't like to do tandems is that we have different ways of telling stories. If I tell a story a different way from Jason, he'll look at me like I'm crazy right on stage, just because it isn't his way. OK, I guess we could do a tandem for you.

Justin: Landlord, landlord, my roof has sprung a leak. Don't you remember I told you 'bout it way last week? Landlord, landlord, these steps are broken down. It's a wonder that when you come up yourself, you don't fall right back down. Ten bucks you say I owe you? Ten bucks you say is due? Huh. That's ten more bucks than I'll pay you till you fix this house up new. What? You gonna get me an eviction order? You gonna cut off my heat? You gonna take my furniture and throw it out into the street? Huh! You're talking high and mighty. Talk until you're through, but you won't be able to say a word if I land my fist on you!

Jason: Help! Police! Come and arrest this man. He's trying to ruin the government and overturn the land. Coppers—whistle! Patrolmen—arrest!

Justin and Jason: Headlines in the press: Extra! Extra! Read all about it! Tenant threatens landlord. Tenant has no bail. Judge gives Negro ninety days in the county jail.

JENNIFER BIEHN

Jennifer Biehn fondly remembers her father's devotion to books. She describes how she had to wash her hands before she could touch the limited editions that he received every month in the mail. She is now an administrator who uses books to "open her mind" to the world and other people.

My father read a tremendous amount. He eventually collected about three thousand books, and knew each one from cover to cover. He collected favorite books and favorite authors. He used to say, "A book is a great treasure, particularly after it's been read again and again. It becomes a part of you, so that merely by looking at the bookshelf you can recall the glowing hours of previous reading."

At age thirty he joined the Limited Editions Book Club and bought a limited edition book each month instead of spending the money on frivolous items, and he continued to buy them until he was fifty-five. When the new book came in the mail, it was always a big event in the house. We had to wait for Dad to come home and open the big red box. Included with each limited edition was a letter, signed by the author and illustrator if they were still living, that included their autobiographies and a description of the publishing and printing process. These books contained gorgeous illustrations and were all hand numbered; they only printed two thousand copies of each. The whole family would look them over, but my father was the only one who read them all. The rest of us didn't, perhaps because they were so precious that in order to read them, we'd have to wash our hands, take them carefully off the shelf, and then put them carefully back into their binders when we were done.

I remember the limited edition of *The Call of the Wild* perfectly. It was bound in the green and black plaid wool of those heavy outdoor sweaters that people wear, which highlighted the spirit of the book, and had really beautiful paper and printing, all enhancing the book itself.

My sisters and I also belonged to a book club in high school. My dad would have the whole club over to our house to show off his books. We'd be so proud of him and his knowledge of books, it was part of the family in that way. My father was a doctor, but books were not only his hobby, they were his life.

My parents shared their love of reading with me and I loved to read from a very early age. When I was nine, all I wanted for Christmas were books about science and astronomy—books about life, among the stars, on land, under the sea. I got just what I wanted: wonderful science books with lots of pictures that told me all about the world. I was so proud and happy with those books. It was a very significant Christmas for me.

I adored books until I was in the seventh or eighth grade when I no longer had any choice in what I read. Instead I had to read the books that were assigned by the teachers. They had us read these ridiculous, boring books that must have been in the curriculum for twenty or thirty years. We didn't read anything current. I hardly read any books of my choice at all in those days. From high school through college, and for the first ten to fifteen years after college, I didn't read much, maybe only a book every two months or so.

Now I read quite a bit. I often read historical novels because I'm interested in learning about a time period, but I don't want to read the straight historical account the way I did in college. I've read novels about the civil war in Spain, and about China; I've read a novel about the fall of Troy, and another about the Second World War and the Resistance. For pure pleasure I read mysteries, fantasies, science fiction. I have been reading every night before I go to bed for the last year and a half. There are so many good books that I want to read; I always have a list of at least ten that I'm interested in reading, so there's hardly a dull night.

Bookstores are my favorite places to shop. I would like to get into the habit of going to a library and checking out books, but if I love a book, I want it on the shelf at home so I can give it to a friend. Almost all my closest friends and I share books—we give each other books whenever we see each other. One friend of mine wasn't a reader but became one because I kept sharing books I'd read and suggesting them to her. I also love to read out loud with my friends. I adore having somebody read me an inspiring short story or poem. Unfortunately, I think reading out loud is becoming a lost art.

I became quite dogmatic during those years when I didn't read a lot. Since then, I have opened up my mind to all kinds of things through reading. It has helped me to be more enlightened, more mindful of the world, more tolerant of other people's opinions. It's made me more open to my own growth and change. I can definitely say my reading has helped to bring an inner peace to my life.

DAN GONZALEZ

Asian-American studies professor Dan Gonzalez learned to read and write before he was four and here reveals how his early childhood reading affected his life both as a child and as an adult.

Filipinos see English as one of the great benefits of the somewhat colonial relationship between the United States and the Philippines. They see themselves as distinctly different from other Asians, especially in the American context, because most other Asians are non-English speaking. This relationship had a great influence on my mother, who taught me to read at a very young age. My parents were both immigrants from the Philippines. My mother was well-read and made an intentional decision to stay home and teach me to read. Before I was three I could write my name. That was a big thing with my mother. Soon she had me reading words, then phrases and whole sentences out of books. She used a combination of story telling from books complemented by records with the voices of Walter Cronkite and Edward R. Murrow, who had perfect diction. She also had Walt Disney records and Mother Goose rhymes. When I got tired of one record, she gave me others. She was very accent conscious. She was convinced that accent was one of the few negative marks of being an immigrant that you could change.

She started me at school before I was four. I refused to play house, but instead sat in a corner and read. The teacher noticed that the other kids would take a book off the shelf and ask me, "What does this say?" and I would tell them. I wasn't showing off; I simply had been taught to help other people out. One day the teacher asked my father to stay for a conference when he picked me up. I stood on the porch of the school listening to them. She told my father that they were having a problem with me. She said, "He's a liar." Of course my father did not take this well. He asked her what exactly I was lying about. She said, "When he's supposed to be playing house, he pretends to read instead, so the other children come up to him and ask him to read, and he pretends to read to them out of their books." My father asked her just what she thought I was doing. She said, "He probably has some similar books at home, and knows the words that go with the pictures." My father took a newspaper from under his arm, called me over, and told me to read it to him, which

I did. It was about the Korean War. The teacher paled. He said, "If this is what you think of my son, if you're willing to call him a liar rather than to find out if he knows how to read, then my son doesn't need this school." I never did go back there. From then on I went to Catholic schools. Never again did I look at teachers as the infallible authority figures that my parents had told me they were.

After my first two years in grade school, my parents became less involved in my schooling, but they were still with me in my spelling. They would sit up for half an hour every night and run me through spelling drills. As a result, I did well in spelling bees, but I felt like the teachers were putting me on display, which made me very uncomfortable. I knew even then that the teachers were taking the credit for my spelling when they didn't deserve any of the credit. Reality was reality.

Between the ages of seven and eleven, I was a latchkey kid. Since my parents didn't get home from work until 6:30 in the evening, I went to the local library. I became interested in poetry, and started reading it more and more. There was a poem we read in my English class called "The Falconer." In it, the falconer releases the bird and the bird starts to fly, ever higher in an ever-widening gyre. I thought, "Wow, that's great stuff." The teacher asked the class what we thought it meant, the symbolism and all. I said, "Well, I think it's about free will." It blew them away. Yet I couldn't understand how the other students in the classroom couldn't see it. They were out of the discussion. That's when I realized there was a really big difference between the way I looked at the world and the way others did. And that outlook was born from my early reading experiences.

My reading enabled me to develop a larger worldview, much less constrained than my peers. The other students saw me simply as a kiss-ass. They didn't see me as being excited about learning. I certainly couldn't get their acceptance, so it's true, I did strive to get the acceptance of my teachers. I was an outcast from many of the students. I was seen by the bullies as an easy pick, and got beat up quite a bit.

Because of my reading, I began stepping over boundaries. I read a lot about the civil rights struggle, and watched it on TV, and I knew that I identified with it more than I should. My parents, like so many Filipinos, still saw themselves as entirely different from other people of color and so did not identify at all with the civil rights movement. They felt people were asking for freebees rather than working hard for a living like they did.

Reading gave me a sense of what was possible, but in those days there wasn't any positive literature on Filipinos. I read of no one with my background, or even Asian or Mexican, making it. There was nothing there. I knew I could be the smartest son-of-a-bitch in the world and never be allowed to make it because of all the racial barriers. I always had a rebellious streak, but during the civil rights period, it really began to surface.

MOLLIE KATZEN

Mollie Katzen's much-loved Moosewood Cookbook *grew out of the illustrated journal entries she made about food and recipes while working as a cook in a small restaurant. Her combination of creative talents has produced three more cookbooks,* The Enchanted Broccoli Forest, Still Life With Menu, *and* Pretend Soup and Other Real Recipes, *a cookbook for children that she co-authored and illustrated. Fascinated by the process of making books from an early age, she still hand-letters the revisions to her early cookbooks.*

My mother was the major influence on my childhood reading. She had a special canvas library bag and took it every Thursday to the library. Library day was a part of my life growing up. Each week, for a very long time, I took out a Dr. Seuss book. I especially loved *Horton Hears a Who.* That book is one of the most profound things I've ever read. If you haven't read it, you must go out and get it.

We rarely bought books—I only had about five books, which I shared with my brothers, except for one particular book that my mother saved for me from her childhood. Her own mother had given it to her when she was nine years old. It was a little book called *The Magic Pawn Shop* by Rachel Field. She wrote her name in it when she was nine, and then I wrote my name in it when I was nine. I'm saving it for my daughter when she turns nine.

One of my fondest memories is of my mother reading the entire *Heidi* to me. She had a lot of other kids and could only spend ten minutes a night reading it to me. The reading went on for a couple of years, but we got through the book before I saw the Shirley Temple movie version. To tell you the truth, I loved the movie version, but I didn't recognize it as the same story. It was just a different story called *Heidi.* It wasn't the same as I had envisioned while my mother read.

My mother passed on her love of books to me, but even with all this attention to books as a child, I didn't become a tremendously serious reader. If I had a quiet hour, I would go to my piano, or go to my desk and draw. Reading children's books definitely made me want to write, though. I have liked to write poetry and stories from my absolute earliest childhood—practically from before I was literate.

I developed an early love of cookbooks without ever thinking I would eventually write one. Food was a big topic for me as a young teenager. I was a normal weight child and have never been overweight, but my mother was, and she was worried that she'd have an overweight daughter. So, she started dieting me when I was seven years old. She'd bake things for my brothers, and they'd get cocoa at night, but I'd get skim milk. By the time I was a teenager, I had some food deprivation problems. I wasn't food obsessed, but I hadn't had enough food enjoyment as a child and so I sublimated my desire for pleasure in food into an interest in cookbooks. When I was fourteen years old and started babysitting, I would go directly to the cookbook shelf as soon as the kids were asleep. I would sit and look at the cookbooks all night.

My mother didn't have a lot of cookbooks, but she did have a big recipe file. She wasn't a "non-cook," she was just a 1950s cook—a lot of instant stuff. Every once in a while my father would ask my mother to make some dishes like his own mother made—he wanted to hold on to his memories of his mother. Whenever she succeeded, he would be tremendously moved and she would be excited that she had gotten it right.

People are transformed by food. It definitely moves people and gives them memories, just like my father's memories of his mother. Food and smell does that for many, many people. On a hot day you can smell pine needles, and suddenly you can close your eyes and you're twelve years old and at summer camp, because the smell is so evocative.

I don't think of myself as somebody who writes books, but as somebody who *makes* books. From a very early age, I had a strong drive to make books and that includes writing, illustrating, designing, and binding. I made my first book when I was nine years old. I loved the entire physical entity of it. It was a little novel in chapters and I illustrated it and bound it and made a cover. To me all of those parts were as important as writing it.

I'm still doing that today. I still hand-letter the revisions to *Moosewood* and *Enchanted Broccoli Forest*, but it's so impractical. It hurts my hand. *Moosewood* grew out of my first journal; that's why it has such an informal feel to it. I was an avid keeper of journals and I illustrated them all. When I was in art school, I was cooking with a restaurant to support myself, and I started writing food ideas and recipes, how I thought dishes should be made, right in my journal. When people would ask me for recipes, I would jot them down and put some drawings and diagrams with them. I had no clue that the audience for my recipes would be any larger than the people I knew, friends and relatives.

My next career goal is to write children's literature. I want to write about young girls who have deep and complex emotional lives. I want to write the kind of literature I looked for in the library when I was a child, but never found, like my father searching for lost memories through food. I want to write and illustrate books about strong little girls who are adventurers and seekers and pioneers. I want them to be brave, but not foolhardy. Before a brave act has panned out, people call it foolish; if it's a success, it's called brave.

My own childhood reading gave me a vision of what I could do, what I could make for the world. I think for me there's been an interplay between being a reader and being a doer.

TARA CONYERS

Ten-year-old Tara Conyers has a well-developed sense of herself as a reader, but she has other interests as well, including dancing, building science experiments, and playing with her three-year-old brother. Her mother is Susan Petrowich, whose story appears in Chapter 7.

If somebody doesn't read to you when you're little, then you don't really know what reading is when you get into kindergarten. My mother reads to my three-year-old brother every night. After she reads the story he reads it back to her by looking at the pictures and making up the story from what he remembers. Sometimes I sit next to him and watch my mom read to him, so she's kind of reading to me too.

I read when I have time, usually when I'm in bed. I've got my own room at my dad's, but my little brother shares a room with me at my mom's, and he has to have the lights out, so I can't read in bed there. My mother and father used to read to me a lot. I heard that if you watch while your parents read to you, you can learn words better, so I did that. I remember when my dad read *The Hobbit* to me, I tried to read along, but I didn't understand some of the words because the book had real small writing and was very complicated. It was also a really old book and fell apart. I think I learned a lot from reading it with him, though. Now he's reading *Treasure Island* to me, and I read along with him, and when he makes a mistake I correct him. He doesn't make mistakes on purpose; he just misses a word or puts words in different places. We read at night before I go to bed.

My mother reads books about real estate and single parents— books about how to set up and control your life. Sometimes my mom shares what she reads with me. She just started reading this book about how to deal with divorce and she says she's going to read it to me when we have the time because I might be doing a report on the subject or something. She'll go through it with me then if I want her to.

One book I've read to myself lately is called *There's a Boy in the Girl's Bathroom.* I don't know why they called it that. It's about a boy named Bradley, and in one small part of the book he accidentally goes into the girl's bathroom. But the book is really about how he says things like, "Gimmie a dollar or I'll spit on you," and doesn't do his homework, and messes up all the papers the teacher gives him. You see, the kids thought he was a monster, so he acted like one. Then he decided to ignore them, and tried to start acting nice, and after a while they stopped calling him a monster. It worked!

I read the first one hundred pages at school, then I came home on Friday night and read the rest on my own. In the beginning, I didn't really like the book, but I just kept on reading, and in the end I did like it. I gave it an eight and one-half on my book report. I don't do that very often, but this was a really good book. It was also the first time I read a book in only two days. Now I can pass it on to someone else to read.

Sometimes I have to go to the library for a school assignment. First, I figure out where my area is, where the books for my age are, and then I look in the card file and find some books. When I first open a book, I look at the contents and pick out a chapter that looks interesting. Then I read the chapter and see if it's got the information I need, and if it doesn't I go to a different chapter. That way, I don't check out a book that doesn't have the information that I want. I learned how to do this by watching my dad, not from my teacher; he does those things and I thought it would be a neat way for me to do it too.

My mom's a real estate agent and she highlights words a lot, so now I do it too, that is if I'm reading a book that's mine. If I'm reading and I come across a word I don't know, I read the sentence over again and try to figure out what it means. I usually remember the meaning of a word after I figure it out. I learned that from my teacher.

I like nonfiction best because I like to read about animals. I like reading the books from science class, and I also have safari cards about animals. I just pick out an animal that looks interesting, like say an armadillo, and then read about it on the card. Or I read books about girls going through puberty. I just got one that my friends and I read together when they come over to my house.

If I didn't like to read, I probably would have different friends since I mostly met the ones I have in my reading classes. If I couldn't read, I probably wouldn't even be in the fifth grade.

EILEEN TURNER

An administrator and technical specialist for a large health care organization, Eileen Turner is adept at reading and translating often obscure government regulations. Yet in the privacy of her home, she prefers to give herself over to the lure of romance novels.

I had a lot of people around me as I grew up: seven sisters and brothers, my parents, my aunt and uncle, my grandmother. The older generation worked in the shipyards and the post office, and weren't readers. My father always read the newspaper, but never a book. We were the only black family in an all-white neighborhood. The public school I went to was great. I was in a February class, an off-season class, so I went through elementary school with only fifteen students in my classes. I had very high self-esteem because my family gave me so much attention, so I didn't want anybody to do better than me in school. I read more than the other kids and worked real hard. But one day in junior high, the teacher asked me to stand up in front of class and read from a textbook and I stumbled through every word. I don't know why because I could read well by that time, but the teacher said I should practice on my own so I could read out loud better. That's when I started reading *Secret* and *True Romance* magazines because I knew they had short, easy-to-read stories. I read them all the time, but I never told anybody. It never dawned on me to get a real book. After two or three years of reading the magazines, I could stand up and read in front of anybody.

Reading those magazines messed me up for years, though, because they were so ridiculous and unreal. When I got married I was looking for romance; I believed some wonderful man would come and sweep me off my feet, and it would go on and on for the rest of my life. What reason did I have to doubt it? I was very naive. Reality set in when I was about twenty-four and I realized, oh my God, life wasn't like that at all. Then I set out to protect myself.

I'm no longer a romantic person. It's hard to get close to me because I'm not affectionate either. I still read that romantic stuff, but now it's Danielle Steele and Sidney Sheldon. I enjoy reading their books; I don't care about the characters, I just want them all to have happy endings so I won't feel depressed. Sidney Sheldon's books are about romance and espionage and they're a little more intriguing than Danielle Steele's. There's usually one central theme that runs through each of his books that keeps my attention. The characters will get caught in some desperate situation, and of course there's always a couple that has a wonderful affair. In one of his books a woman's face is totally destroyed by her husband; she gets a new face put on, but she's miserable from then on out.

I won't read a book if it has too many characters because I'd have to keep up with them and I don't want to have to think that hard; I read to relax. Some of the books I read are so ridiculous that they take my mind off my problems. Reading them clears my mind so I can go on to something else. I like the quick, to-the-point romance stories because I like to do everything fast. I cook fast—cooking a dinner all day long is a waste of time to me—I finish people's sentences, I ask them, "What is the bottom line here?" People who work with me have to get used to this. So whatever I read has to go very fast. If it's slow, I'll never finish it.

I read government publications every day at work, wading through the garble to interpret them. I've been doing it for about eight years now; I started at the bottom of the company twenty years ago when I was nineteen.

I read the regulations and decide how we'll pay claims based on what they say. What I write then gets interpreted into computer jargon. Since the rules change all the time, I have to read a lot. I can't say I enjoy that kind of reading, but it's part of my job, so I do it, and I am good at it.

I didn't read to my daughter when she was young. Although I was twenty-four when I had her, I was about as mature as a nineteen-year-old, and it didn't occur to me that I should start to prepare her for school at four or five. I guess I expected her to learn to read by osmosis from watching me, or just by going to school. Her school didn't have a standardized program for teaching reading, and she had a difficult time learning to read. I know now that reading to young children is a big key to their reading success, but I didn't know it then. I got her a reading tutor in the fourth grade.

Now she's in the tenth grade. She's a very different person than me, but I respect who she is. I had to come to grips with the fact that we are more different than we are alike. I wanted her to take algebra, trig, and geometry all in the same semester, and get straight A's. When she was about in the sixth grade I had to say to myself, "Eileen, this is not going to happen," and adjust myself to the kind of person she is. A parent can really screw up a kid sometimes; at one point I noticed she was really down on herself, so I decided not to say certain things to her again—I decided to leave her alone. She's perfectly happy now, and that's what I really want. She's a good kid. Reading is just not her favorite pastime.

I often wonder how people are able to function if they don't read. When I listen to a foreign language, like when there was some Russian being spoken on TV, and it means nothing to me, I think about what it would be like not to read. Reading is something I do without thinking about it; it's like breathing. Everything in my life has something to do with reading.

◇ CHAPTER 4 ◇

Voracious Readers

Books are intense, mini-human beings, and bookstores are the souls of humanity.

Kosta Bagakis

Voracious readers seem to inhale reading material, often reading quite fast, sometimes reading every word, other times merely skimming articles to catch just a glimpse of their content. They typically read both fiction and nonfiction—whatever crosses their path. They read anytime, anywhere. Voracious readers read magazines and newspapers (sometimes two or three a day), literature, novels, mysteries, science fiction, history, politics, sociology, science, technology, popular psychology, repair manuals, how-to books, and cereal box tops.

If you're looking for voracious readers, a good place to find them is at the library or in a bookstore, somewhere between the cookbooks and the science fiction section. Many voracious readers prefer an evening browsing the bookshelves in their favorite bookstore to an evening socializing with friends. Reading is their form of play; it's their favorite leisure-time activity. When you visit the homes of voracious readers, you'll most likely find bookshelves crammed with their favorite books, sometimes neatly arranged alphabetically, sometimes just shoved and stacked on the shelves randomly, wherever they could find space to put them.

When they were children, voracious readers tended to read more books and books of greater length than their peers. They were also the ones who were most likely to pronounce the words correctly when they read aloud in their fourth-grade classrooms, and had a larger vocabulary than their friends. These children often finished their assignments before the rest of the class, and regularly read ahead in their textbooks.[9] One voracious reader described how his mother bundled him up and drove him to the library when he was very young. She gave him freedom to choose whichever books he wanted to read. As a result, he began checking out adult books even before he could comprehend the nuances of their plots and characters. Another voracious reader spoke of parents who allowed her uninterrupted time to read, and let her escape chores in favor of reading. Most likely, the parents of both of these children were readers themselves and therefore approved of, and even directed, their children's reading lives.

A voracious reader once told me that she thinks it is a tragedy if someone doesn't read, that nonreaders must live in isolation because they don't have the opportunity to easily and frequently enter the minds of others. On the other hand, a nonreader wondered how people who read all the time don't become totally isolated from their families and friends. Voracious readers and nonreaders may have something to learn from one another.

This chapter includes narratives of people enraptured in their reading and, for the most part, enjoying themselves immensely. If you're a voracious reader, I hope this chapter validates your own reading experiences. If you are not, I hope you glean from these stories an insight into what it's like to have a passion for reading.

MICHAEL KRASNY

Michael Krasny's factory worker father's belief in "a life of the mind" and his own passion for intellectual activity led him to pursue his interests in literature and world affairs, leading him first to become a professor of modern American literature, and currently, host and interviewer of his daily talk show radio program, "Forum." In each of his professions he is able to "cross-pollinate" the stimulation he gets from reading to the world at large.

I wasn't really motivated to read throughout most of my youth; I was involved in athletics and socializing and ran with the wilder crowd. All this changed in high school when I discovered, much to my surprise and delight, that I had an intellect. I hung around my friend's house quite a bit because his parents didn't care if I smoked. His older brother, though a bit crazy, was also a serious would-be intellect. He would be reading Bertrand Russell or Sigmund Freud or C. Wright Mills or Eric Fromm, and I would pick up his books, sit down with an ashtray, and read. I discovered these authors were good food for my mind.

Then I started hanging around libraries, taking out books to feed my desire for more. I was closeted about it at first, especially when I read poetry, because the days of the sensitive male came much later. Then I discovered that girls from the better neighborhoods actually put a certain value on intelligence and knowledge. My attraction to the realm of ideas led me to a course on international relations in high school, which opened my interest to world affairs and so eventually to my current path, my destiny.

After I became interested in thinking, I realized my dad had been a good model for me. He was a factory worker who read a lot, who believed in the life of the mind. He worked in blue-collar jobs his whole life and he was very frustrated at having never attained greater stature in the world. But he did have this rich inner life, which he had built through reading. As I get older and approach a little wisdom myself, I get a sense of how my father had tried to inculcate in me a love of books. He thought of books as mind-expanders, as ways of ferreting out greater knowledge, as ways of feeding intellectual curiosity.

My father had a brother-in-law who was very competitive with him, who was a show-off about what he knew. This brother-in-law would find some minute point in the Bible and challenge my father with it. My father became more and more adept at arming himself for these assaults. He read to prepare himself so he could defend his point of view against his brother-in-law. This might sound like a Philip Roth novel, and in a way it was. My family argued a lot about ideas and politics my whole life. I learned a lot through these encounters.

I felt a good deal of sympathy for the civil rights movement at a very young age, and would get fired up because some of my relatives were bigoted. I wanted to take them on; I wanted to bait those whom I felt were less willing to be open about race relations, those who were more inclined to be narrow-minded. I would read to inform myself so I could take a strong position and be able to support it. Even now I often fight against bigots on the radio. Perhaps I got some of that from my father. He liked to display what he knew; he was a bit of an exhibitionist. He also had a desire to inform people, to communicate with them in ideas. Like father, like son, I guess.

I read newspapers and magazines every day to prepare for my work on radio and television. I read them omnivorously between five and eight hours a day, sometimes more. Fortunately, I need less sleep than most mortals; five hours a night is enough. I get up early because I have a child to get off to school, and then I walk down to the newsstands and buy as many newspapers as I can: I read *USA Today,* the *New York Times,* the *Los Angeles Times,* and three or four local newspapers each day. I used to feel compulsive about reading everything in each paper; I don't anymore. Now I look at the stories that interest me or that might be useful to know about for discussion, editorializing, or commentary. I have to absorb a lot of information because people who call up on the radio talk about a wide variety of topics.

My other life, as an academic, requires a different kind of reading—fiction, poetry, drama. Sometimes I read these things for the classroom and sometimes just for the love of it because I still feel planted in the world of scholarship. When I read a novel for the classroom I worry about technique, style, metaphor. But if I read it for pleasure, I just let it waft over me. I don't brood about the meaning of the work; I'm there as a reader to enjoy and find pleasure in it.

If I read a novel because the author is going to be on my show, I read it differently than I would either for use in my classroom or for my own enjoyment. When I read for broadcasting, I look for hooks that will get my audience involved. I pay attention to the parts that I'm curious about and ones my audience might find interesting as well. Right now, I'm finishing a couple of novels by authors who will be on my show next week. I usually try to book authors whose work I'm familiar with or who have written about something important that we can talk about. It's hard to interview fiction writers on radio because people are listening for news hooks, for things that are directly tied into current events. They're not interested in taking a literature seminar, so many would tune out and turn off if I did this type of interview. The challenge is to make literature palatable to a broad audience.

I'm certainly not an especially spiritual person and I'm far more secular than religious, yet when I read, I find a kind of illumination, I have epiphanies. Reading encourages me to see things differently. I get knowledge from reading that sometimes I can't even define. I understand the processes and dynamics of so many things to such a greater extent and in such greater depth than people who don't read. I thrive on reading because it stimulates me. The added bonus is that I can stimulate others with what I have read. I enjoy that process—it's like cross-pollination.

KAREEM ABDUL-JABBAR

Kareem Abdul-Jabbar's career as center for the Los Angeles Lakers is legendary. During his twenty-season career with the National Basketball Association he scored 37,639 points while appearing in 1,815 NBA games, and remains the only player in NBA history to have won the Most Valuable Player award six times. Both his revealing autobiography, Giant Steps, *and his chronicle of his final NBA season,* Kareem *(written with Mignon McCarthy), have appeared on best-seller lists. He developed a reputation for being one of the nicest people in basketball and has devoted countless hours motivating youth to stay in school. An avid reader, Kareem's life has been affected deeply by the books he has read, even though "books aren't big on the NBA agenda."*

As a young boy, I already saw reading as a source of entertainment as well as knowledge and information. I was always very curious, and my reading skills developed accordingly. It also had to do with what I learned at home from just watching my dad—he was my hero and my role model. When I was young, Dad and Gary Cooper kind of blended into the same person at times. My dad was a prolific reader. Through him I could see there were tremendous advantages to be had by reading. He started off as a police officer but he ended up being a lieutenant, and he got to that point by taking Civil Service exams, so he was always studying his books. I just watched him read. He used to read a lot on firearms and the history of firearms, and events like the Alamo. He read a lot of science fiction, so I read it too. I got all of my dad's reading habits and then developed some of my own.

I went to Catholic school in New York City and it was a very good system. They strongly emphasized reading. By the time I finished grade school I didn't need any encouragement—I was reading comic books, but I was also reading Alexandre Dumas, Robert Louis Stevenson, and Edgar Allan Poe on my own. Later I read Shakespeare and Dickens in high school, but for fun as well.

I started out as an English major in college because reading had always been a passion for me, but I switched to history in my sophomore year because I didn't have enough time to write all those papers. With history you just had to read and do a term paper instead of having to write something every week as you did in English classes. That's when I began reading history as well as literature. I was particularly interested in black history. At one time I wanted to be a journalism major, an interest I've used recently by writing two books, one an autobiography, and the other an account of my last year of professional basketball.

When I was playing professional basketball, all I had time and energy to do when I was on the road was read. We might have a two-hour practice during the day and then the rest of the time we'd be sitting around the hotel, so I filled those hours with reading. I realized I had to rest a lot and eat well in order to play basketball well, so I wasn't a huge party animal on the road. I would spend a lot of time in the bed with a book or asleep. They seem to go together. Reading helped me pass the time in a productive way that kept my mind expanding, and kept adding something to my life. The other guys on my teams never read that much. It was rare to find someone who read, so I didn't talk about reading to the other guys because they weren't into it. They talked music and maybe a couple of films, but books aren't big on the NBA agenda.

I'm a very eclectic reader. I still read a lot of history, novels, you name it. I like spy novels, especially, because of the whole mystery of who-done-it and why. I also like novels about the Cold War; John Le Carré is a favorite. And historical novels always interest me.

Whenever I travel somewhere, the fact that I've read a lot about wherever I go enables me to understand what I am seeing and where I am. I get a lot more out of traveling. For example, I used to work for Adidas and that work took me to Paris a lot. I read *A Tale of Two Cities* while I was there one summer and I got to know Paris much more from having read that book. And knowing the history of Turkey and then visiting Istanbul changed my experience of being there. Knowing the history of the British Empire and then visiting places like Pakistan and Hong Kong enriched those experiences, too. When I read about a place and then go there, it's different, because what I read enables me to see the place in depth as opposed to just being wheeled through it and not understanding what I'm even looking at.

Reading *The Autobiography of Malcolm X* had a profound effect on me. It started me investigating Islam, and I eventually became a Muslim. The Koran is our religious text, and the Pickthall translation is one that I read early on and still put great value in.

"Knowledge is power," that's what Malcolm X said. You find knowledge in books, all types of books.

DEBBI FIELDS

Debbi Fields grew up in a blue-collar family in which "priority was not given to reading." After her marriage at age twenty to an economist, she often found herself in the company of highly educated, financially successful people. At social events, she felt unable to contribute to the conversations because of her lack of exposure to current trends and events. At one such party, the host asked her, "Debbi, what are you going to do with your life?" When she replied that she was trying to "get orientated," the man dropped a dictionary in her lap and told her to "learn to use the English language." Her humiliation drove her to find something she could do incredibly well. She opened her first cookie store in 1977 at twenty, and is now chairperson of Mrs. Fields Inc., which runs over six hundred cookie stores worldwide.

Reading was not important in my house when I was a kid. I read what was required by my teachers, but I was never intrigued or excited about any particular subject. My view was pretty much limited to the city I grew up in—I didn't really know there was a world outside. How can a kid learn to be aware of the world without reading? I wasn't even aware of books; I had never had the curiosity to pick one up and see for myself what was inside. I guess it's shameful that I didn't have that curiosity, but I'm glad it finally came.

I learned the richness of reading from my husband Randy. Whenever I saw him, he would have books with him. He had every periodical (Did I say that right?) and magazine imaginable. He had a thirst for knowledge and insight and information which both intimidated me and drew me in. He would encourage me to pick up a book and read, or look at the contents of a magazine. At first, I had to force myself, but then I slowly found articles that I actually enjoyed.

Once I had made the decision of pursuing my dream to bake and sell cookies, books became my teachers. I had the inspiration, the desire, and the guts to start the business, but I knew I didn't have the knowledge or the experience, so I went to the library to learn what others had done, to hear their suggestions and insights. Through books I met the people who had traveled the road before and were now there to guide me.

That was the beginning of my quest, and it has led me to becoming the really avid reader I am today. I would read self-help books to find out how to set up an inventory system or a marketing plan. It was so exciting at the time because these books were telling me how to make my dreams happen. Once I had a passion, I developed a passion for reading.

Now I'm very committed to reading. I have five types of required reading for myself. First, I have books that I challenge myself to read to develop my mind. Then, I have information books about things I should know for the business. Another set of readings is about things that are happening in the world today. And the fourth group is what I call my development work—books that make me a better business person, a better manager, like *The Seven Habits of Highly Effective People* and *Principle-Centered Leadership* by Stephen Covey. The last group is what I call my fun stuff, like Danielle Steel and Mary Higgins Clark.

But reading has done more for me than just entertaining me or enriching me with information and knowledge. Reading has also improved my vocabulary immensely. Did you notice how I practiced the word *periodical* on you? I force myself to use new words that I see when I read. I put them in sentences. Reading has also improved my grammar and writing skills, and it's even helped me to speak better. It's a gift.

I don't read a whole book in one sitting. I'll read a chapter of one, then I'll go to another one. That way I get a blend of a lot of information and having more information helps me improve my decision making. It enables me to think and be challenged to agree or disagree. Reading also helps with my communication, and you know, you don't have to communicate only with other human beings—you can do it internally. I love to cry and laugh with a book.

There is one book that I always come back to, a book by Kahlil Gibran, who was a poet and a philosopher. It was probably one of the first books I read, called *The Prophet*. I remember one particular line in one poem that says something like, "You can never experience joy without experiencing sorrow." I think about this day-in and day-out, when I'm feeling sorry for myself or feeling depressed. I know I feel that way because I also know how great it feels when I'm joyful and jubilant and excited. It's a balance, a process.

Looking back on my childhood, I wish I were more interested in reading. I wish someone had said, "I recommend that you pick up a very tiny, thin book about something that gives you joy, or intrigues you." There is one book that I love, and it's a kid's book, *The Little Engine that Could*. The engine says, "I think I can, I think I can, I think I can. I know I can, I know I can, I know I can." I got the book for my kids but I read it for myself. I found it right after we opened the business. I needed help and people kept turning me away, and then I found somebody who said yes, but who didn't really believe that I could do it. I just said to myself, "I think I can," and then later I moved to "I know I can." That lesson is the key to my life—believing I can do it. I take one step, one chapter at a time.

JACK PRELUTSKY

Although his parents were not readers, Jack Prelutsky loved books as a child, a pleasure he kept secret from the other kids in his tough Bronx neighborhood. While trying to "find himself" in his early twenties, he fell naturally into writing children's poetry and has published more than three dozen books during his twenty-year writing career, including New Kid on the Block, *a book of his own poetry; and two anthologies,* The Random House Book of Poetry for Children *and* Read Aloud Rhymes for the Very Young.

The only books in the house where I grew up were the complete works of Mark Twain and Charles Dickens, which my father got from cigar coupons. He never read them, but I did. My mother used to shop at the A&P, where she bought *Women's Day,* and every issue had a poem from *A Child's Garden of Verses* by Robert Louis Stevenson, which I would clip and save. I enjoyed poetry when I was a small child; I was musical so the rhythm and meter appealed to me. Most kids like riding their bicycles and chewing gum, but they don't like spinach or poetry. I guess I was just different.

I spent a lot of time reading in my room by myself. I read books like *Robin Hood* and *Alice in Wonderland.* I read all the *Hardy Boys, The Lone Ranger,* and *King Arthur and the Knights of the Round Table.* I used to think Sir Lancelot was the greatest guy on earth—I'm sure that book taught me something about honor and purpose.

We lived in a tough, blue-collar neighborhood, so we kids spent most of our time fighting, running like lunatics through the street, playing stickball, or setting stink bombs behind the movie theater. I was small and introverted so I spent much of my time defending myself, and I kept my enjoyment of poetry private.

I became really discouraged in school but I did enjoy playing with words—doing puzzles and making up word games as a distraction from my teachers. They would give an assignment, I would pick out one word and make a word game out of it rather than write whatever I was supposed to. My parents didn't particularly encourage me to play with words because they expected me to get a job in the trades at some point. My father was an electrician, and all his friends were plumbers and bricklayers and shoe salesmen. It was just a fluke that I loved to read.

I had one particular teacher who obviously did not like poetry herself and she was determined to perpetuate her loathing of poetry in her captives. She would find the most boring book on the shelf because the curriculum told her that once a week she had to recite a poem to us. She would open the book to a boring page, and in a boring voice would recite a boring poem, looking bored while she did. Since nobody else was encouraging me, I became turned off to poetry, but luckily I didn't get turned off to reading.

My junior high school had a librarian whom I hated and feared. She was short and dumpy and wore only black dresses. She had wire-rimmed glasses and fixed her steel-grey hair in a bun. She wore support hose and sensible shoes. And, she loved books but hated children. I hated going to her library. The first week I was there I pulled a book off the shelf, which happened to be *Wild Animals I Have Known* by Ernest Thompson Seton. I hid it and every week I'd go back, pull it off the shelf, and read it right there so I wouldn't have to check it out. That way, I never had to deal with her.

As an adult, I don't use the library much because I collect books. Right now we're in the process of moving and the movers said we have almost twice as much weight in books alone as most people have in all their possessions. They estimated we have fifteen thousand pounds of books.

I have five thousand reference books alone, which I buy whenever I want to know about something. The books aren't in any particular order on my shelves because I believe in serendipity. I like them strewn all over the place because I get some of my best ideas when I come upon books by accident. Let's see, I'll pick out a few books at random and tell you why I bought them: I have this book, called *Name Your Baby,* because when I write poems, I look for the right name. Names have meaning in themselves so if I use one in a poem, it will add subtly to its overall meaning.

I'm working on a set of poems from outer space so I bought *The Science Fiction Encyclopedia, The Visual Encyclopedia of Science Fiction, The Transgalactic Guide to the Solar System,* and *Barlowe's Guide to Extra-terrestrials* to get some ideas.

I also have this one, *Dictionary of Foreign Terms,* so that when I see a foreign word in a crossword puzzle, I can look it up and find out what it means. I have a lot of books on word play, like *Almanac of Words at Play* and *The Game of Words.* I've gone through all of them because I'm writing my own word play books.

I bought *Joys of Yiddish* when I got married because I often used Yiddish expressions that my wife, who is Asian, didn't understand. I wanted to get a book that would help her out so I got her that one, along with a bunch of books by Isaac Bashevis Singer, to give her a cultural background on me.

I buy coffee-table books on ceramics, woodworking, folk art, Japanese art. I want to build a Japanese garden in my new house. Do I know how to build one? No. So I bought some books. I'm reading books on how to tie bamboo together, how to make stone basins, how to orientate the garden, and how to make a waterfall. Books can be very practical.

I also own over three thousand books of children's poetry and I've read them all cover to cover. When I collected the poems for my anthologies, most of the research came from my own collection. I didn't discover most of the children's poems I know until I was an adult and I like them more than I like adult poetry because they have form and meter and rhyme. I'm old-fashioned; I like poetry that rhymes and so that's what I write. My poems have clear messages and are easily understood, accessible.

I got drawn to poetry in my twenties through the words of folk music. I was a coffee house folk singer in the late '50s and early '60s and I liked the English/Irish/Scottish ballads, bluegrass music, and the blues, all of which are about basic feelings expressed by ordinary people, sometimes very poetically and poignantly.

I get my own poetry ideas from many different places. Once I was sitting in the bathtub reading *National Geographic* (because it didn't matter if it got wet). I was reading a pictorial essay about wolves and thought, "Why not write a poem about a wolf taking a bath?" Later, as I was writing the poem, I thought of a terrible pun and I realized it would be the last line of the poem, but in order to get there I had to change the poem's focus, so it became a poem about a wolf washing his clothing in a laundromat. It's in *The New Kid on the Block*, and here's how it goes:

A wolf is at the laundromat,
it's not a wary stare-wolf,
it's short and fat, it tips its hat,
unlike a scary glare-wolf.

It combs its hair, it clips its toes,
it is a fairly rare wolf,
that's only there to clean its clothes—
it is a wash-and-wear-wolf.

JULIE CONGER

Following an early career teaching college mathematics, Julie Conger entered law school in pursuit of more humanitarian work. She practiced law for eight years before being elected Judge of the Municipal Court. Reading for her is a way of life, both on the bench, where she reviews hundreds of cases each week, and at home, where she finds relaxation in reading fiction, mysteries, courtroom dramas, and biographies.

I probably read two hundred pages a day in the course of my work as a judge. At this moment I'm reading case law. I have to read some administrative information on a proposition that just came through. I also have penal codes, briefs, cases. I try to do reading on cases that are applicable to the cases I see every day.

I have to keep abreast of current law, and I read advance sheets on all the cases that the Supreme Court and the Appellate Court decide. I've fallen behind two advance sheets, so I will read them during my lunch hour. First I read the head notes to determine if they have any relation to my cases, and if they do, I read the whole case. I usually read all the criminal law cases.

It's fortunate that I read very fast because I have so much to read to keep up with my work. I just did my afternoon arraignment calendar. I had a hundred and twenty cases on it starting at two. Let me pick out a case at random as an example of what I do with each one. Let's say I'm handed this particular file. I immediately read the charges, the complaint on the defendant, and the police report. I note that he was cited to appear before and he didn't show. I read the OR report, which tells me his ties to the community. Then I look at his rap sheet, which tells me his history of criminal cases. This man had a rape case, a drunk-in-public case, a burglary, and he failed to appear fourteen times. So in the space of thirty seconds I get an overview of this person who is on his way out of the holding cell: what the nature of his offense is, if he is a serious alcoholic, and what the likelihood is of his coming back to court (which in this case is not very good because he didn't show up before). I have to make a very quick decision as to whether I will release him on his own recognizance or if I will keep him in custody. All this in thirty seconds.

I do over a hundred of these cases in an afternoon. With each one, I do the reading as he or she is being brought out of the holding cell. I have to tell him his charges when he appears, so I have to memorize what he's being charged with and the date of the offense so I can make eye contact when I talk to him. While this is happening, I'm also making the decision. In this particular case I decided I wasn't going to let him out and I wanted him to be represented by an attorney, so I had to tell him he was going to stay in custody, and also that the public defender's office was going to talk to him. And while I was doing this, I was writing on his file, "Refer PD." That's the kind of reading I do at work. Needless to say, I get kind of tired by the end of the day.

In the last three or four years, my clerk, another judge, several of the marshals, and I have been trading books. We even have a little lending library which I started. We read a lot of mysteries, courtroom dramas, and novels having to do with criminal law. I do this type of reading at home, where I read primarily for diversion. I can read a book every other night or so, and maybe three on a weekend. I can usually read a three-hundred-page book in a night if I'm not too tired. Last Sunday afternoon I took five kids to the beach. We got there at two, and by the time we left at five I had finished a book.

I'm very high energy and I can do things very fast, but I also tend to have a certain impatience. One of my faults is that I don't spend time savoring things but instead focus more on doing things as quickly as I can. Maybe that's why I read so fast. I want to know right away what's happening, what's going on. One of the books I read last week was about a courtroom trial. It was about a very circumstantial case, and it became bogged down because the author hadn't edited the trial transcript. It could have been edited into, say, thirty pages, but it took up two hundred. I didn't enjoy reading that so much. Another book I read last week was *A Gathering of Saints,* about the Mormon Church. By page three hundred we still had this guy forging documents and nobody had ever been arrested. I thought, "Couldn't you collapse that into less than three hundred pages?"

I do hundreds of crossword puzzles, hundreds. I do at least two before six in the morning. I even wait up on Saturday night for the *New York Times* to be delivered so I can take a look at the crossword puzzle. The legal newspaper always has one, too. Crosswords are almost a mania for me. I have a whole stack of them. I really enjoy words, their meanings, their preciseness. I'm interested in their etymologies and their derivations.

My marshals and I are trying to do vocabulary improvement together. We select a word every day and try to use it as much as we can. I have a bunch of kids at home and we select five words every night out of a Barron's vocabulary book, post them in the house, and try to use them. One of the puzzles I did last week had the most wonderful word, *canoodling,* which means petting. Isn't that a great word?

I have a degree in mathematics and I'm reading about that now, mainly because my nephew is living with me and I'm tutoring him. We're going step-by-step through algebra, geometry, trigonometry, calculus. It's pleasurable for me. I still do reading in recursive function theory as well, which is the field of math I specialized in. I don't keep up with the cutting edge, but I read maybe two or three pages a night; it's really intensive reading, but I enjoy it as a diversion.

One reason I got into reading so much is that I grew up in New York City, where I lived on the twentieth floor of an apartment building and couldn't play outside. My parents didn't get a television set until I was about fourteen or fifteen, so the only thing I could do, other than play with dolls, was read. I don't think I'd be so much of a reader if I'd had the opportunity to play outside until dark the way my kids do. It's definitely a function of environment, location.

I hate reading aloud, so I hardly ever read to my kids when they were younger. I always felt guilty about it, but I just cannot stand reading out loud, probably because it takes so long. It's absolute torture for me. It's not the content that I mind so much, but the fact that it just doesn't go as quickly as I would like.

My daughter reads for amusement in spite of my not reading to her. She's now decided she's in love with anthropology, so she's reading that voraciously. My oldest son just got a degree in engineering; he's not much of a reader, although he'll read Stephen King or science fiction on vacation. My nine-year-old son doesn't read as much as I'd like.

Since I make decisions all day long, I do two things for relaxation at home: knitting and reading. When I knit, I do my own thinking at my own pace. Other people aren't pulling on me. And when I read, I can shut out everything and just concentrate on the story, on its interesting aspects. I don't have to *do something* about what I have just read, which is a great relief.

HOWARD FAST

As a child Howard Fast read his way through the books in his branch library, beginning with the A's and ending with the Z's. An author of more than thirty novels of his own, he uses historical contexts for the settings of his books. Freedom Road, *for example, is set in the South during post-Civil War Reconstruction, and* The Immigrants *begins with the 1906 San Francisco earthquake.*

I don't have any real memory of how I began to read. It probably happened in the first grade, but from that point on reading was the center of my life. Fortunately, when I was a child, there was no radio or television, only books and movies. My book collection came from the New York Public Library. I owe everything, my pleasure, my education, my vocation, to that library.

I grew up in Manhattan and I played in its streets. All the kids I knew went to the library. The times were different from today. It was not a case of us finding the library, but of the library being the focus of the neighborhood.

In 1926, when I was twelve years old, teenagers' knowledge of history was shaped by the books of Joseph A. Altsheler, who wrote about the American frontier. We read Altsheler, and we also read Mark Twain. We were poor kids, very poor kids, who grew up in the streets and had no loving parents to guide our reading. We had no one to say, "Read this," or "Read that."

If you're twelve years old and are shown a copy of *Tarzan and the Apes*, you'll find it to be the most wonderful book in the world, but then a point comes when it turns into utter nonsense. This process happens with so many books. Occasionally, a man like Robert Louis Stevenson can write a book that you love at age twelve, love more at age twenty, and more yet at age thirty when you discover the brilliance of the structure and language he uses in his tales and stories.

No kid I knew ever had a book in his house—books were something that were in the public library. Nobody owned books. Our reading was chaotic, which was the best thing in the world because it meant we read everything. From the library I would read all the "A" writers, then the "B" writers, then the "C" writers. The critic Alexander Wollcott once asked me how I knew the writings of Eden Phillpotts. I said I was reading in the "P" section of the public library at the time.

It was a great moment in my life when I bought my first book at the age of sixteen or seventeen. Later, when I began to make money as a writer, I said to myself, "From here on I will buy any book I want and I will never ask the price." I've kept that pledge.

I used to read a great deal of fiction; now I read it less and less. I find that today's fiction writers leave me bored and disinterested—except a very few. There are a few writers whom I love, whom I do read, but very few. I think that Tom Wolfe's *The Bonfire of the Vanities* is a wonderful book in terms of our times. I enjoy Kurt Vonnegut and I read Gore Vidal, who is probably the wittiest and most literate of writers today. I still reread Faulkner and Mark Twain a great deal. I've tried rereading Sinclair Lewis, whom I admired at one time but I now find a clumsy writer. There is a spectrum of writers whom I still read and enjoy, but it's not too broad.

Now I read history, I read religion, and I read physics—these are my passions. I became interested in these areas many years ago. I've been on an endless journey through the world of physics, especially nuclear mechanics. I read physics for pleasure. However, sometimes I read a book that is sheer nonsense, and enjoy picking it apart for its nonsense. Other times when I read a book, I'm filled with delight at how the writer is doing his job.

I do a tremendous amount of research for my books. Yesterday I researched certain events written in the *New York Daily News* of April, 1949. I went to the New York Public Library's newspaper building and I pulled out the microfilm reel, put it through the machine, and read every day of the *Daily News* of the period that interested me. I always take notes. I usually look for exactly what I want. Some researchers will read five books to get one fact, which wastes a considerable amount of time. I simply look for the facts I want. I've been reading history all my life, so I have a background of historical information already. I fill my shelves with books that can provide me with whatever information I want, and I read all the time.

Good readers don't read letter by letter as young children do; they read symbols, they read the way the Chinese read. The Chinese see a whole symbol, which is a word. Western man also reads symbols; he no longer reacts to letters. At first, each word is a symbol, then as you add to your reading knowledge, a group of words may become a symbol, so the reading process can become rather extraordinary, totally different as you age, providing that your reading grows.

Referencing is an important part of my reading and reasoning process: I translate symbols into images and then back them by references, and the reading becomes even more understandable. For instance, as I read the word *Egypt,* I recall a series of images and references to that country—for instance, that it is the land of the Nile, the place where papyrus grows. I have in my mind a whole picture book of references for a single word. An intelligent reader reads steadily through his life and builds clouds of images to surround each word.

It is a tragedy when someone doesn't read. Such a person cannot enter into the world of the mind; he lives in isolation. Perhaps he can watch television and gain a certain sense of the world, but man's inner world is barred from him. This inner world is found only in literature.

WALTER STACK

Eighty-two-year-old Walter Stack has been running, swimming, and cycling daily for the last twenty-five years. He has participated in the "Iron Man" competition, and even today runs marathons in six hours. He complains that his memory is beginning to fade, but after speaking with him, this is difficult to believe. Mr. Stack is a retired seaman who reads a great deal.

I've been an avid reader, and *avid* is the word all right, ever since I left the orphan home when I was about fourteen. I remember going up to the library and getting what I could on religion because I was mistreated by some of the grown-ups, the nuns and so on. And so I became an atheist at the same time.

Now I don't try to tell people what they should think—if they want to be religious, that's OK with me. I don't hold it against them and we can be friends. I've been a member of the Civic Club for the last twenty-five years and I've gotten the top votes by the board of governors. Most of our members are policemen or soldiers, officers, and so on.

I've always found what goes on both internationally and locally to be important. I subscribe to the *New York Times* and the local newspapers, and I pick up the *Wall Street Journal* and the *Christian Science Monitor* when I get the chance. I read the *Times* religiously, especially for the international news. When I get a chance on a sunny day, I go out to the garage, which has no roof over it, and read for a few hours. I do my swimming and running in the morning, pick up some papers on the way home, and read most of the afternoon.

I aborted my academic learning halfway through high school and went to work. I went to sea for twenty-six years, and then I was in the slaughterhouse for a few years. I worked for a long time as a hod carrier, too. Then I was a business agent for the Marine Fireman's Union for about ten years. You might say I'm self-educated, because I read a lot during those years.

I don't remember ever having somebody I enjoyed reading or talking about books with—I just took it for granted that reading was a lot of fun, but it was a person's thing to do by himself. It didn't occur to me to find someone to read with, someone to help me understand what I was reading. It just came natural for me to read alone.

I read about the records of outstanding athletes—I have many books about them here at the house. I get *Runner's World* and I read everything on the subject of running that's come out. I think reading has helped me become a better athlete. When I got into running, I read everything I could to improve myself. I did the same thing with swimming and cycling. I'm sure reading has had a great effect on my progress—I'm very interested in paying attention to how I do, what's bad for me and what's good for me.

I've also read the health food books, but I'm not exactly what you would call a vegetarian, or a meat company wouldn't have invited me to Chicago to run one of their races advertising the meat-eaters.

We have a library full of books here at home, so I've got a whole lot to read through between the newspapers. My wife's got a lot of books in the library, so I've been reading two or three of 'em that I find very interesting. One is *The Feminine Mystique*—you've heard of it, haven't you? I'm also reading this five-hundred-page book called *Sexual Politics*. It's like a study of books, you know; they quote innumerable books throughout this thing—they quote philosophers and artists and what not. It's a very interesting book, and I've found out very interesting things about women that I didn't know. One is the question of orgasm, that it is possible for women to have orgasms indefinitely until they just can't stand anymore and poop out. That's just one of the things in the book that comes to my mind; I've learned any number of things about women from that book.

Reading gives me ideas to think about, it gives me a greater understanding of the world. Without reading, I'd be lost, completely lost. It would be like not having the sun shine after a cold swim when your teeth are chattering. Somebody once asked me, "How do you keep your teeth from chattering after swimming in that cold water?" I said, "Well, I leave 'em in the locker."

MO YANAGI

As a Japanese-American, Mo Yanagi and his family were sent to an internment camp during World War II. Ironically, he was later drafted to do intelligence work for the Army, where he was valued for his knowledge of the Japanese language. He did not become an avid reader until he had back surgery at fifty-five. Since then, he has read nearly every spy novel ever written.

When I was young, I went to live with my grandmother back in Korea. That was right after the Russo-Japanese War when the Japanese occupied Korea. Although my family lived in the United States, they thought it would be cheaper to raise my brother and me there. The schools were segregated: Korean schools and Japanese schools. A Japanese publisher there used to publish magazines for boys and for girls of different age groups and my grandmother would buy me the magazine only if I kept up my grades. Books were very expensive, so the only books my family would buy for me were textbooks. If a rich kid had money and was able to buy a book, I'd try to borrow it. I'd get a few pages at a time as he finished reading them. That's how books got traded and read among the Japanese kids in Korea at that time. There were fifty-five kids in my class and only four or five were able to buy books.

My father's oldest brother was a school teacher. I spent winter vacations at his house in Fukuoka, Japan. He had a bookcase, just solid books, all in Japanese, and all bound in red. When I first saw his library, I was stunned. How could a person have so many books? One day he found me reading one of his books and he got really upset. He said, "These books are not for you to read." They were for decorations! I complained to my grandmother and she said, "No, no. He's the head of the household. Whatever he says, goes." I still wonder where he got all of those books.

When I came back to the United States in 1936, I was twelve years old. One day a strange man came to our house and said, "I'm your father's cousin from New York." It turned out he was the head butler in the Doubleday household. He said, "Do you like books?" and I said, "Yes." After that, I began receiving books from the Doubleday office. They came regularly for two years until we were interned.

All of the people of Japanese ancestry were interned during World War II. Within two weeks of Roosevelt's decree, all persons of Japanese ancestry were restricted to five miles from where they lived. We had to get rid of all of our furniture and sign up at the courthouse to leave for the assembly center. It was chaos. Even though my family had been in the United States for three generations, we were sent to a camp in Utah. I was sixteen. Strangely, all the books from my high school on the West Coast ended up in that camp. And my dad had kept books on the game of *Go* and a Japanese game similar to chess called *Shoji*. I still have those books today.

My real reading started about ten years ago when I had back surgery. I read Tom Clancy's *Hunt for Red October* through my recuperation. The nurse wondered why my light was on all the time. She asked, "Why are you still up?" I was laying on my back for weeks with nothing to do and I could only sleep so much. That was the first novel I read through just like that. I couldn't put it down. Since then, my reading has mushroomed into reading just about every spy novel ever written.

It intrigued me that Tom Clancy knows more about the submarine than the people in the Navy Department. He is fascinating. He researches any topic he writes about and I like to read his books because I like fast-moving plots. Other authors like to develop the whole story and then get you at the end, but Clancy tends to move fast from the start. I used to read spy novels about espionage and intelligence all the time, but lately they've become scarce because the Cold War is over.

I wasn't that much of a reader before I started reading spy novels. Now I feel I'm wasting time if I'm not reading. I'll take a book to a restaurant to read while I'm waiting to be served. My wife doesn't like it but I do it if the book is engrossing. I have to read one more page to find out what's going to happen next.

I'm a very slow reader. I listen all the time and pay attention to the details. I read everything. I can recall many of the details even five years later. When I was drafted into the Army, I was attached to the Intelligence Unit and was trained as a translator. I was assigned duty in the Japanese police department, where I had to listen carefully and remember everything. It may be due to that training that I attend to details and remember everything when I read. My wife reads differently; she reads so fast and isn't that interested in the details. She doesn't remember them later on.

I would be lost without books to read. I always have one in my pocket and I carry one or two spares just in case I mislay one. There are always books someplace—in my car, on shelves in my office, in my bag. Reading is a big part of my life now.

RONNIE GILBERT

During the 1950s, Ronnie Gilbert sang with The Weavers, an internationally acclaimed music group that popularized hundreds of traditional folk songs. She has survived political blacklisting and media blackout to remain active in the entertainment business for well over forty years. Here she recalls with fondness the libraries she frequented as a child and describes her own personal library today.

I remember entering the library on a rainy day, coming into the room full of polished wood and the smell of wet wool, umbrellas, and rain gear lying around, a woman reading to a group of children sitting in small chairs. The library was a wonderful sanctuary to me where I could imagine, discover, and escape, all because the adults thought I was learning. And I was learning, but not for school; I was in storyland, adventureland.

My mother valued reading quite highly, but she worried about me because I was a true bookworm—I far preferred to read than go out and play. She would yell at me, "Why do you always have your nose in a book? Why don't you go out and play?" Well, outside was a jungle, and the library was the only other place I was allowed to go.

The library that really did it for me was the one on Fifth Avenue in New York. It was so full of smells and textures. I loved the quiet and the mustiness, and the feel of those long wooden tables with the big, heavy library chairs. To this day I love to read by laying the book flat on a table, my elbows propped, my head in my fists.

By the time I was seven someone had given me *Minute Stories of the Opera* and *Tales from Shakespeare*. I loved these books and kept them for years until the bindings fell apart. I also read the Nancy Drew mysteries, which drove my mother wild because she didn't think they were cultural enough. I finally gave them up on my own when I realized that each book was just advertising the next one in the series. I was disappointed and bored with them after that. Then I read all of the Agatha Christie mysteries. At that time in my life, I read to escape from scenes in my immediate life, as well as to probe my imagination. It was wonderful to be able to escape into the pleasurable, exciting, beautiful images in books.

My mother used to read stories to me when I was very young. She read with a kind of drama; I can still remember her voice and the texture of the story as it was filtered through her. I can feel the excitement from the way she read those stories. As a result of her reading to me in this way, I already knew how to read when I went to school, so I was often chosen to be the one to read aloud in class. I read with intonations that gave the sense of the story, not with that flat monotone I hear kids today read with.

Even now I love to read aloud, and have read poetry and stories on the radio. Radio is a very intimate medium because it goes directly from the voice to the imagination. I often read a poem or two in my concerts. When I read poetry, I feel like I'm on the inside of something. I'm seldom interested in a song unless the lyrics move me the way poetry does.

I used to be a person who moved a lot; I lived in New York, then I moved west, then north to Canada. When I moved to Canada I took very little with me—a chair to sit on, personal clothing, kitchen things, and books. They weren't all necessarily books that I longed to read, some of them had been important in my life at various times. I left those books in Canada, but do you think I've forgotten about them? No, I want them back, even though it's been years.

The other day I visited an old friend, who said, "You know, I have some books of yours that you may want back. You gave them to me years ago." They were books of folklore that I had given to her when I went to Canada. Giving away those books had been a symbolic action at the time, but once she showed them to me, I had to have them back. Fortunately, she was glad to return them.

I have other books in my library that have more to do with their history than with what's in them. I looked on my shelves the other day and found a pair of books that belonged to Lee Hays, one of The Weavers. When I pick up one of his books and open it, I think of him. Just seeing his books on my shelf keeps his memory bright. I also have a book of "complete" Shakespeare that belonged to my mother. It, too, has a physical presence that connects me with her life when she was young.

CHAPTER 5

Habitual Readers

When I walk into a bookstore I feel a physical change, an adrenaline rush, just like other people get when they walk into a gambling casino. I take out my charge card and spend too much money.

Maggie McBride

Many chronic, compulsive readers would consider joining a readers-anonymous support group if there was one. They are self-described read-a-holics, who are sometimes unable to stop reading. One habitual reader told me she thought of her reading as a disease that makes her spend inordinate amounts of time engrossed in the pages of books rather than joining in life's activities. She confessed that, although she had been reading all week, she once declined an invitation to take a bicycle ride with her husband on Sunday because she was involved in a new book. Another said that her extensive reading allows her to keep from becoming too involved in difficult situations. For her, "Reading was an escape as a child, sometimes a pathological escape, and it has continued to be so into the present day."

Habitual readers are bibliophiles, but they can become obsessed by their love of books, often to the exclusion of other activities. Some habitual readers laugh at themselves; others are embarrassed by their compulsive reading behavior, especially when it infringes on their lives to an uncomfortable degree. For example, the woman who refused a Sunday bicycle ride with her husband fears that she reads even to the detriment of her marriage, but avows that she can't help herself.

When a habitual reader leaves the house, she will typically check to see that she has both her keys and a book because she fears being stuck in an elevator, a subway train, or a traffic jam without something to read. Habitual readers read at every opportunity: while vacuuming the living room, at a stoplight, in the bathroom, and of course in bed before sleeping.

I once described three of the habitual readers I know to a frustrated reader. The first races through one book, sometimes without enjoying it, simply to begin another. The second will read several books at the same time, even though he confuses their plots. And the third uses books as a reward for completing difficult tasks or as an antidote for frustrating situations, much as others use shopping for clothes or eating a favorite candy bar. Upon hearing these practices, the frustrated reader shook his head in disbelief. He was particularly baffled by the concept of reading as a reward because he viewed reading as a difficult task that must be endured.

For some habitual readers, reading provides an escape from un-pleasant realities. One particularly compulsive reader recalled that dur-ing childhood, reading provided him with the perfect escape from his difficult family since no one questioned the time he spent reading. At ten he kept alphabetical lists of books he wanted to read. At twelve he planned to read all the books in his small branch library, and he was well into the T's when he graduated from high school. He noted that as much as he enjoyed reading, he sometimes wished he weren't so shy.

Such exceptionally well-read people amass a tremendous reservoir of knowledge on a wide range of subjects. Like other avid readers, habit-ual readers are quite familiar with the world from the experiences they've gained through reading, even if they've rarely traveled beyond the pages of their books. One habitual reader insists that he actually prefers to travel through novels than explore on his own. He finds the landscapes in books more appealing than the ones he can visit as a tourist. "What's more exciting," he asked, "sitting in an English pub watching old men get drunk, or reading about the goings-on in a pub in a well-crafted nineteenth-century novel? There's simply no comparison."

ADAIR LARA

One of the worst punishments Adair Lara could imagine as a child was be-ing sent to a desert island without books. Her passion for words has led her to a career in publishing, first as a magazine editor, and currently as a regular columnist for a large metropolitan newspaper. She lives with her two children and is working on her first novel.

When I was little, I'd be walking down the street and my ears would be cold, but I didn't believe they were as cold as the cold described in books. I thought the descriptions in books were more real than my own experiences, and that my own experiences would be more real if some-body wrote them down so I could read them. I thought of books as real life, and of everything else as wan imitation. I was totally wrapped up in words—I was wordstruck.

Scenes from books constantly played through my head. Once I was riding in the back of a pickup truck and I suddenly picked up a pillow and hit it, yelling, "Take that, woman," because I was playing out a scene from a book I was completely involved in. I totally startled the other two people sitting beside me.

Both my parents were compulsive readers, although out of the seven kids from my Irish-American working-class family, I'm the only one who reads a lot. My mother loved reading about the lives of other people. Her attitude was that she'd had her life and her disappointments and now she was going to read and find out what other lives were about. My mother and I used to tear books right down the middle so we could both read them at the same time. My dad used to get drunk on books. I never saw him without a paperback of some kind in his pocket, and he always had one in his lunch box when he went off to work.

About ten years ago I realized I, too, had been reading compulsively—I just raced through books. I would read them, toss them aside, and go on to the next one. As a teenager, I even read books at stoplights. If the light turned red, I'd pick up a book. I would read books during lulls in conversations—I didn't think of it as rude, I would just look down at the book that I always had open in my lap. If I was out somewhere, I would be thinking about whatever book I was reading. It was wonderful.

If you had asked me then what punishments I couldn't have endured, I would have said: having books taken away from me, being blinded, or being sent to a desert island without books. I constantly thought about which books I would take to the desert island if I could only take a few. I decided I would take books that were very dense that I could keep rereading, like Shakespeare.

Nobody asked me, "Why are you reading so much? What are you looking for?" But being a compulsive reader for me was a way of hiding from what was going on in my life. The real question is how much I read books for the pleasure of reading, and how much was escape.

Then about ten years ago, I stopped reading so much and started writing, which I did just as compulsively—I just switched gears. I would read a good passage and think, "I want to do that," and I'd go to the typewriter. Or I'd read a bad passage and think, "I could do better than that," and go to the typewriter. It's the same kind of energy—all words.

When I was younger I could read certain kinds of books, like blockbusters, that I can't read now because the writing bothers me. I'm a more sophisticated reader now and I feel this as a major loss because those blockbusters gave me many wonderful hours. Now I will only spend a lot of time with a book if it's finely written. The last blockbuster I read was *Lonesome Dove* by Larry McMurtry. It's a wonderful book that's nearly a thousand pages long. I love books that go on and on because I can trust them not to stop right when I get into them.

I don't read escape literature and never could. Mystery writers withhold something they know, as opposed to allowing the characters to unfold. After reading a mystery, I don't feel I've had anything resembling an important experience. It's like eating junk food; I feel I have wasted four hours of my life.

When I read *The Eye of the Needle*, a spy novel by Ken Follett, I just loved it and I thought, "This is great! Now I can read this genre. There are ten billion books that I can now read and enjoy." So I went out and got a couple more of his books, and found out that they were all the same. They had different settings, but the plots were essentially the same and I couldn't read them. I also tried reading a Stephen King book on a trip to Mexico and was tremendously diverted by it so I thought, "Now I can read more of him," but when I picked up another of his books, I just couldn't read it. I don't like books with contrived plots that descend from above and order the characters around instead of arising from the characters themselves.

When I was younger most of the books I read, that anybody read, were written by men. I didn't grow up with much of a female viewpoint; I identified with whatever book I was reading and its portrayal of women, men, horses, dogs, whatever. Now I find myself more and more drawn to novels by women, contemporary novels. These novels are often about people who face the same kind of problems, fears, questions, passions that I do. The same sort of personal connection sometimes happens through my newspaper column. People write to me and say, "We're alike. I feel we could be friends." It's like we're talking over a back fence.

I was in my twenties before I met any really bright people who didn't read at all. One man I knew had all this archival information in his brain that he got just by soaking it up from conversations with people. I didn't quite know what to do with the idea that a person could be bright and have lots of information, but not read. I've known this same man now for a long time, and I'm finally getting impatient with him. He keeps rediscovering the wheel because he doesn't read. He'll have an idea and I'll say, "Well, that's been done. Read a book." There is a vast experience to be picked up in books that he doesn't have. Yet he is so bright, he keeps working his way around it like a blind man. This makes conversations with him tedious sometimes. He relies so much on his own insights, which are staggeringly good, but his ideas aren't tempered by what other people have thought and said throughout the ages.

A friend of mine told me about three types of information-gatherers: hunters, browsers, and grazers. I think the theory applies to readers as well. Hunters turn to the index or look up the chapter that has what they want, read it, and get out. Browsers may be looking for something in particular in a book, but just like shoppers in a store going from aisle to aisle, they'll let something else catch their eye. Grazers read like cows eat: they read whatever is in front of them and discover all kinds of unexpected things as a result.

Grazers are people who really love books and love giving themselves over to the experience of reading them. Like most ardent readers, I'm a grazer. I've heard the argument that grazers are going to drown because we aren't very efficient since we read every book or newspaper that comes our way. But many scientific discoveries were made when the scientists weren't looking for them, when their attention was diverted or they were just curious about something. Reading everything does take a colossal amount of time, though.

Hunters miss all those things you find accidently, but they're very efficient. People who are hunters are not what I consider book lovers—they're trying to get something from the book, usually in the most efficient way. Hunters almost always read nonfiction. At one time I was seeing this guy who was clearly a hunter, and whenever I gave him a book he didn't want to read, which I was continually doing, he'd get mad. I would say, "This is a wonderful book, you'll just die when you read it." He'd get mad and say, "I don't want to read that!" If it didn't have information he needed for something he was already doing then reading a book was an intrusion, a chore. Hunters feel that in this speeded up world books are going to go by the wayside because people simply won't have time to read them. I think to some extent, they're right. My own life has speeded up quite a bit, and sometimes when I come home tired, even I don't want to read.

I still don't ever leave the house without something to read in my purse in case I get caught somewhere. It may border on the neurotic, but I carry books in my car. Once I got a flat tire. It was a very hot day but I was completely happy and absolutely calm because I could read. I had a little lawn chair in the back, which I set up beside the road, and I was very sorry to see the repair truck when it came to rescue me.

TARA THIRTYACRE

One of Tara Thirtyacre's favorite Sunday activities is to sit all day and never move, just read. She previously worked for a number of years in marketing and public relations, but currently she is following in her mother's footsteps and working toward a degree in English literature.

My very favorite "Twilight Zone" episode is about the bank teller who loves to read. He has a nagging wife so he locks himself in a bank vault and reads during his lunches. There's a nuclear explosion one day while he's in the vault reading and everything outside is destroyed. He leaves the bank vault and is totally alone, so he finds enough food and goes to the library and reads. But then he falls asleep and accidentally breaks his Coke-bottle glasses so he can't see to read anymore. He has been robbed of reading, which is my own ultimate nightmare.

Perhaps because my family life was full of tumult, reading was the security, the comfort, the place of refuge, the one consistent activity throughout my youth. The least chaotic time in my home was when my mother was reading to my sister and me late at night. We would curl up in her lap or at her feet while she read. My mother had a wonderful voice and a great delivery. She would take on big novels like those by Charles Dickens that would take six months to read a few pages at a time. She had very eclectic tastes, but she always read fiction. Before I was in third or fourth grade she had read us *Catcher in the Rye, A Tale of Two Cities,* even books by Truman Capote. She read to us whatever she was interested in reading herself. We'd talk about the plot, especially with stories like Truman Capote's and J.D. Salinger's, because I was very young and became confused. But with books like *Pinocchio* and *The Wizard of Oz,* I would create a whole visual fantasy in my mind. I remember those books as being very colorful.

I remember my mother reading to us even when I was in the tenth grade, around the time of the spelling bees in our house: At the end of dinner each night we would learn a new word. Usually my parents would come up with a word, and my sister and I would look it up to find out what it meant. We'd talk about it and then we'd use it in a sentence. My father would usually try to make a joke using the word. A few days later we'd bring the word back up and spell it out loud. Then we'd have spelling bees every month or so with all the words we learned and if we spelled them all correctly, we'd get fifty cents. I always thought every family did that!

Even now, I often get my husband to read to me because I still love to hear the sound of well-written prose. As with poetry, it's the sound of the words that is appealing—the snippets of words that produce a fragrance, a feeling, a transport into another world. Reading is the place I go where time does not exist, which to me is the most enjoyable place to be. Once I get hooked on whatever I'm reading, I disappear, I escape; I lose sense of whether I've been reading for half an hour or two hours; things can happen around me but I'll be so far away, I won't know what's going on.

I read every night before I go to sleep. I feel there is a reason for each word to be on the page so, in order to have the full experience, I want to read each one. I start at the beginning and read through until the end. Maybe I do that because of my mother reading so much to me and oral reading, by nature, is reading every word.

I love novels when I can envision myself in the position of the hero or when something in them touches what I relate to. I will also get hooked on a book if it is written eloquently and has a marvelously woven plot that's plausible, even though it may be far-fetched. For several years I read a lot of twentieth-century novels and plays but right now I'm on a kick of reading Victorian novels. I've picked up Dickens again, *Great Expectations*. I'm totally absorbed in it and I don't know why I didn't pick up classics before. This year I've also read *Crime and Punishment*, a lot of Kafka, and Hardy, also.

Sometimes I think I should be incredibly wise because I read so much but I wonder how much of it I really retain. I wonder if I just suck it up and then let it go out of my body. I have this enormous appetite so I gobble up novels, but after a few years have passed, I look through the bookshelf and I can't remember what particular books are about even though I know I've read them. I feel I should remember every book that I ever read, but then what I love about reading is the time-warp experience, so perhaps the most important part of reading the book is the moment at which I'm actually reading.

I grew up with a certain set of circumstances in my home and at the time I had no idea that anyone outside my home had experienced anything similar until, through reading so much, I saw characters in books play out various parts of my own life. I've always been very sensitive and hyper-aware, mostly because of how emotionally crazy things were for me as a child, and reading has become a way of reliving some of my own experiences, of explaining my own life and validating it from the psychological side. Reading is a way to hold up my life before me so I can examine it. Sometimes it's hard to read books that uncover things in myself, but can do it because the book is at the end of my arm—it's not happening in my real life.

I have a certain amount of pride that I read more than anyone I know. I just can't understand why people don't read more. What do they do when they ride the subway if they don't read? I always bring a book with me wherever I go, just in case I have to sit and wait for the doctor for half an hour.

My absolute favorite thing to do is to sit all day Sunday and never move, just read. It's hard to pry me out even to do things I enjoy, like bike riding or hiking. It could be a beautiful day, and I've been reading all week anyway, so why do I have to sit inside all day Sunday and read? I could go for a bike ride and come back in an hour. I know it's a little indulgent, but I just can't imagine my life without reading as much as I do.

ANDREA BEHR

Andrea Behr's lifelong voracity for reading has provided her with both a deep understanding of the world and a "sometimes pathological" escape from her own troubles. She works as a newspaper copy editor for a major newspaper.

As an adolescent I would check out six or seven books at a time from the library and go home and read them. My parents let me read whatever I wanted to so if I found books in the adult section, I read them. As a result, I read a lot of things that I didn't understand at all. I would go through entire books and not understand what I was reading except the meanings of individual words. I read *Treasure Island* even though it is written in an old-fashioned English prose and I had no idea what it was about; I also read *The Brothers Karamazov* before I could understand it—I actually read the whole thing!

Reading was an escape for me, sometimes pathological, and it has continued to be so into the present day. As a child, if I wasn't feeling happy, I could forget what troubled me, just block it out, by going into my room and reading. I had this little daybed with a bunch of pillows on it, and I'd curl up and read for hours at a time. I'd read until all my muscles were stiff and I didn't know where I was. I'd kind of stagger to my feet afterwards, shake my head, and stumble out the door to dinner.

Later, when I was twenty-five or so, I isolated myself again with reading during a difficult year in my life. At the time I had a job at a public library and one of my duties was to sort books that came back from the branches. As I sorted them, every fourth or fifth book would look interesting to me so I would throw it into my pack. I'd bring home an eighteen-inch stack of books every night. I'd get what I wanted from each book; I'd either skim it for five or ten minutes or, if I got hooked on it, read it all the way through. Then I'd return them all the next day. I would read from the time I got home until bedtime. I'd read fiction, books about medicine, picture books, interior design books, you name it. It was nice because the books were ones that other people had found interesting; the library patrons did the selection for me. Those books were interesting in all kinds of far-flung ways and many of them I never would have picked out on my own.

Although that year was a great reading time, I used to feel vaguely embarrassed or ashamed of myself after reading so much. I was doing it to escape pain, to escape my life. It was like being a drug addict or not being able to stop eating from a box of cookies. My reading is still a compulsive behavior sometimes. I just can't control it. I'll say, "I can stop anytime, just one more chapter," but I can't stop. It's really bad when there's something I know I should do, but I don't get to it because I just want to read.

I'm an auditory reader, so I used to skip over visual descriptions. I didn't understand the pleasure of reading descriptions, and sometimes I still have to force myself to read every word of one—I just want to get to the part where the people talk because I tend to hear what I read rather than see it. But for a while I worked nights and drove the freeway to work, and I started listening to taped books while I drove and this got me into paying attention to descriptions.

You see, the person on the tape reads at a constant speed, and by listening to so many books, I realized I don't do this; rather I speed up and slow down. But as I listened, I couldn't speed up through the description, which forced me to get more into it. But neither could I slow down. I was always reaching over and punching the button to stop it because a character would say something important or interesting, or something would happen that I wanted to think about. I began to realize that when I read to myself I often stop and stare into space and think about what I read for a minute. If I do this while listening to a book, the tape just keeps rolling. When I read to myself, I'm more in control of the flow of my reading.

There are other things I find interesting about listening to books. One is that any little error or glitch in the flow of the writing is really much more glaring to me when I listen than if I read it on my own. It could be a grammatical error or a piece of dialogue that just doesn't sound true. Another is that I can't listen to taped books while I'm driving through beautiful scenery during a vacation because I can't focus on the scenery when I listen to a book. I see what I'm hearing on the tape rather than the scenery. I've learned to just turn the machine off through beautiful country.

I think the average American would probably define us compulsive readers as lazy because we really love just lying on a couch and reading a book. We're not accomplishing anything, we're not changing the material world in any way, and 'doing' is valued more than 'being' in this country. People are judged worse for being well-read and poor, than for being nonreaders yet successful in the material world. I don't necessarily buy into that American ideology, but it's what the general culture says, so I end up judging myself by those standards—it's hard not to accept that sort of judgment.

Although reading is sometimes like a drug for me, I also think it helps me understand the meaning of civilization. If I didn't have the understandings I get from reading, I'd be stuck in my own life, in my own body, and I'd be an extremely limited person. Whatever I read I take into myself even if I don't remember everything. I think the cumulative effect of reading helps me formulate my ideas; it influences and changes me. Reading lets me go places I wouldn't go otherwise. It helps me gather information of every possible sort: facts, emotional information, philosophical information. Reading can be communication with another person, too, since when I read a book I communicate with its author. Reading is all these things, and it's also a friend who keeps me company when I'm down.

MAGGIE MCBRIDE

Maggie McBride, professor of mathematics and education, is a self-described book-addict. In addition to consuming large numbers of books herself, she also loves to give them away to her friends. One such friend is Michele Oldman, who describes elsewhere in this collection how Maggie's gift of a book helped to open the world of reading to her.

Some people are addicted to gambling, and others are addicted to alcohol and drugs. Well, I'm addicted to bookstores. It's a very physical thing. When I walk into a bookstore, I feel a physical change, an adrenaline rush, just like other people get when they walk into a gambling casino. I take out my charge card and spend too much money. If I have a stash of books at home to read, all is right with the world. But if I see my stash getting low, it's time to go to another bookstore. I have to have at least five to ten unread books—that's the safety limit for me. I'm convinced that, although reading is socially acceptable, it is an addiction.

Fortunately, nobody has started a book-readers anonymous club—or have they?

There are times when I read too much and I use it to hide out. I go through periods when I'd rather not be with people or be outside. I'd rather not deal with the traffic and the noise, so I stay home and read. Sometimes I think I read too much and I should be going out more, but in the end, I don't go anywhere.

Reading is a vicarious experience: I can read about Alaska instead of going there; I don't have to live on the edge, because I can read about people who do. Maybe reading is voyeuristic, but it enables me to anticipate and articulate ideas. Can people read too much? I really don't think so.

Reading other people's stories also gives me a better perspective on my own life. Reading about how other people work out problems gives me a way of thinking about issues in my own life. For instance, my mother died recently. It was a very, very difficult time for me. I couldn't finish my work or even keep up with it, so I just came home and read. I read Simone deBeauvoir's *A Very Easy Death*, which is about the horror of her mother's death. That was the first time I had read that sort of description of one's mother dying. Reading it was really helpful to me because she wasn't talking about the beauty and the passage from life, but of the realities of the deterioration of the body and how she came to deal with it. I've given that book to my friends to read so they can understand some of what I was going through.

When I'm with my friends who read, I enjoy their company so much because we talk about ideas, we talk about awareness, philosophies. There's no right or wrong, there's no debate—we just have wonderful, rich conversation.

I exchange books with other readers all the time. I'm always losing books because I lend them to people and they don't come back. I have a couple of friends in particular who I'm always exchanging books with or getting lists of titles they've read, but mostly I give people books. I'm always buying books at the large bookstores where they're discounted and then I give them away to my friends.

I once gave a friend of mine named Michele a Wallace Stegner book, *Crossing to Safety,* to read. I wasn't aware at the time that she didn't read, and I am still surprised when I think about it. I make the assumption that people read more than they often do. I just happened to have the book lying around—I think I got it real cheaply in a discount bookstore. When I gave it to her I think she was stunned. I don't think anybody had ever given her a book to read before. She fell in love with Wallace Stegner and really enjoyed the plot and the style of writing. When she found out that he would be speaking, she even invited me to go to his talk. Later that summer she decided we should meet every week or two and talk about a book we'd read.

I can't empathize with people who don't read. In my own upper-middle-class intellectual-snobbish way, I feel their lives aren't as full as mine. But I have to watch this attitude because I do have some dear, dear friends in Montana who don't read, but have a lot of good, common sense and are very kind people. But when I sit with these friends, whose experiences are more narrow, we talk about events of the day: what the cat did, what the dog did, what they did. I find myself getting bored very quickly with that sort of conversation. I will feign interest, though, and chat with them. I can talk about events of the day as easily as anybody else, but I would rather be talking about the implications of those events or the awarenesses that people have about them. I feel that reading, regardless of what one reads, brings about the ability to reflect on one's relationship to one's family and friends, to one's world. I guess I'm being judgmental, but I can't imagine why somebody would go work on a car or paint something instead of reading.

My family's houses back in Montana don't have books anywhere. I grew up like that and now I find it a bit appalling. I was about twenty-one when I started college full-time and began to hang out with people who read a lot. Bit by bit, I got into reading. My one brother earned his BA in English, but he stayed in Montana as a carpenter. He has more books in his house than I do in mine. He has introduced me to a lot of fiction about the Northwest, the cowboys and Indians, and the development of the area. Having the respect I do for him, I've read those books. In fact, he introduced me to Wallace Stegner.

Reading Wallace Stegner's work gives me a very healthy appreciation of Montana and people we might describe as primitive or backward or lacking in culture. He writes about that country so beautifully and so simplistically that it makes me feel real good about the area that I came from. His books show me things about my childhood that I didn't even experience in my childhood. They make me understand some of the frustrations and happinesses of people living there. They show me the peacefulness of the open spaces, the beauty of the simplicity of people's lives. In fact, they affected me so much, I'm moving back to Montana myself.

DENNIS MILLWARD

An eclectic reader, Dennis Millward will read anything at any time, for a cumulative average of three hours each day. He supports himself as a bartender while attending chiropractic college, and takes a highly active role in raising his three-year-old son.

As a boy, I worked in a fish market. I would wrap the fish up in old newspapers until my bosses finally took them away from me because I'd flatten them out to read some article and wouldn't be able to tear myself away.

My grandparents in Las Vegas where the temperature is usually 105–115 degrees during the day. They were quite overprotective; they didn't like the neighborhood kids and discouraged me from playing with them, so I would end up reading inside all day long. I started reading a lot of grocery store authors like Arthur Hailey and Frederick Forsyth, mostly out of boredom. I liked all the details I learned in those books. From the Frederick Forsyth novels, I learned how to muffle the motor of an outboard boat when landing on a beach, and how a certain car bomb can be made using hacksaw blades, pencil erasers, and condoms. I enjoyed these kinds of details since I like using my hands and building little things.

My grandfather used to buy me kits, like kits to build your own doorbell. I would read the instructions before I started to build, and I remember my grandfather telling me that it was great that I did this. I still love to build things and I always read the instructions on equipment I buy. I like to know everything about something before I start playing with it. I want to know all its capabilities and what to do in the event of difficulties. This goes for power planers and belt sanders, digital watches, and VCR's. I know so many people who buy a VCR, plug it in, push the "play" button, and never do anything else with it.

I read motorcycle repair manuals since I do the work on my own motorcycle. I'll read about a procedure before I begin working on my motorcycle, then I take the book with me and refer to it while I'm doing the repairs. I don't think I would have had the confidence to learn how to do the repairs just from reading, though; I've also watched other people do it. After I watched Norm Peterson on "This Old House" on PBS, I had the desire to build my own bookshelves. I got the idea and some general knowledge from Norm, then I bought a Sears Craftsman book on how to use tools, which gave me more exact ideas on how to join ends for a good bookshelf. I even made dado cuts on the sides to give the shelves better support.

Sometimes when I have a spare evening, I'll go out and buy a couple of motorcycle magazines. I read them cover to cover because I like motorcycles and I like the absurdity of the magazines. The bike I have is twelve years old; today's motorcycle technology is phenomenally ahead of that, but by reading the magazines, I can know what's out there anyway.

I subscribe to the *Smithsonian* magazine because I like its eclecticism. There'll be an article on the history of some general back in the 1860s, and then, on the next page, an article about Barbie dolls. The quality of the writing in this magazine is very high, and I read it cover to cover. The "letters" column is pretty interesting because the people who write letters to the *Smithsonian* are at a fairly high level in society and they write about some amazing things. Like somebody wrote in about some momentos she has from her own uncle, who was a general back in the 1860s. The letters in the motorcycle magazines are mostly just complaints about the magazine's style of coverage, and the fact that the magazines cause the motorcycle companies to create motorcycles that only motorcycle journalists like. I never write letters myself, but I'm getting closer to doing it. Oh, yes, I also read *National Geographic* pretty much cover to cover, mostly in the bathroom.

I try to take in a broad variety of reading materials. I'll think of authors I want to know more about, whose name I always hear, and go find their books in the library. I want to get a base knowledge of the books I hear referred to in other books. *Tortilla Flat* by John Steinbeck is my favorite book I've come across that way. After I read it, I read three or four of his other books until I had a real feeling for what his books were like. Someone mentioned Kafka to me the other day, and I realized I've never read anything by him, so when I get a few weeks off pretty soon, I'm going to go to the library and pick up a Kafka book.

Reading a book gives me the experiences that are recorded in it, and in that way expands my own experiences. Even though I might not have the time to do something, there are people who have done it and recorded it in their books. I know about the bullfights in Spain through reading Hemingway, for example. When I read Hemingway, I enjoy the story, his telling of it; if I read an article in the *Smithsonian* with a color spread on Spanish bullfights, it would be an entirely different experience. The experience of reading a novel is very different than that of reading nonfiction.

I was once with a woman who tried to stop me from reading because I became so absorbed in it. Luckily, my wife enjoys that I read. I have a young son, and it's hard to read when he's around, but I still probably read two or three hours a day. Sometimes a book or magazine or the Sunday newspaper will catch my eye, and I'll just sit down right then to read it. If I have something to get done, I try to stop reading soon enough to get it done. Or I try to cover my commitments before I sit down to read, or at least know that I'm not too far behind in my various household duties, because once I sit down to read, it's hard to stop.

I barely got to my bartending job on time last night because I was caught up reading the Sunday paper. All the while I was reading it I was thinking, "OK, I can wear these pants, but what am I going to do for a shirt? If I wear that shirt I'll have to stop reading early to iron it. If I keep reading I'm going to have to take my motorcycle instead of my car because the parking is easier." I was enjoying reading too much to stop.

Lately I've been reading books like *The Pathologic Basis for Disease* for my chiropractic courses. I find them fascinating, but it takes a conscious effort for me to absorb what they're saying. I've never had to work this hard before. I have a lot of confidence as a reader, and I think that's helping me get through these courses. Plus, I've always loved to read about how to do things. In some of my textbooks, for instance, there are chapters about where to put your hands and move the person's body to feel the certain movement in a certain vertebral segment. My favorite thing about chiropractic is the way it deals with the body as an integrated whole; it takes into account the connection between the mind, the hands, everything. I will certainly get to practice with my hands doing this work.

It would be pretty hard for me to accept it if I couldn't read for some reason; I just crave my reading time. Taking time out to read helps me get control over myself; it relieves tension and helps me avoid frustration. It can take me away from my life, or put my life in a larger perspective. I'm more self-reliant because I can read, and hopefully, reading has made me a more well-rounded person. Perhaps because I read so much, I realize that my own point of view isn't the only one, and my way of living isn't the only way of living; my immediate surroundings are only a very small part of the world. I'm very thankful that I can read.

RICHARD VOSSLER

Richard Vossler's inner world is filled with characters and places from both his wide reading and extensive traveling. He speaks five languages, holds season tickets to the opera, and enjoys scuba diving and white water rafting.

I couldn't wait until reading hour when I was in the first grade. I remember when Mrs. Coolidge read us *The Wizard of Oz,* how different the story was from seeing it on television—the descriptions in the book were more vivid than in the movie. She held up the pictures and I would sit on the edge of my seat and listen, feeling the warmth of the afternoon light. I was very calm while she read. I loved listening with the group, while being totally alone with my thoughts at the same time.

I enjoyed books even at a young age. When I was in third grade, I belonged to a summer reading club called "Rocket to the Moon." I would ride my bike three miles to the public library, even on days it was closed, to see through the window where my name was on the chart. I went to bed with books rather than bunnies that summer. I have always liked being inside libraries. I get an immense feeling of security with all those books around me. I know I will never run out of something to do, there will always be a new experience in a book.

My interest in languages began on the school bus in fifth grade. There were these girls who talked in sign language, and I thought they were talking about me, so I went home and studied from this book I happened to have on Helen Keller. After practicing for a week or so, I was able to sign somewhat, and sat down in a seat facing the girls. They were talking about me! I surprised them when I signed back that they weren't being fair. That incident encouraged me to take an interest in languages.

I have always liked foreign things, and reading made me realize that there was much I wanted to see in the world. I went to college for a year and a half directly out of high school, but then I decided I wanted to travel to Europe, so I dropped out of college. I still don't have a de-gree to this day. I guess I don't want to grow up; I have the Peter Pan syndrome. I like to take classes just because I am really into the subject, a new language, for instance, and I have a hard time fitting myself into a pattern. I'd rather go to college part time and take only the classes I want.

I am constantly reading. One day a number of years ago when I was working in Germany, I started reading a really good book on my way to work. I just couldn't put it down when I got there, so I stuck it in the bib of my overalls and kept going to the bathroom to read it. One time I was gone for forty minutes. Soon it was lunchtime, and I went off to the bathroom again. When I returned late, my supervisor came up to me and grabbed the book from my bib and yelled at me for reading in the bathroom. I told her the book was too interesting to put down, and she asked me how many pages I had left. I said twenty, and she told me to go back to the bathroom and finish it and never let it happen again.

Even today I read everywhere. When I ride the subway, I read on the platform while I listen for the train, and then I always sit in the same seat so I can see the station names without having to look around too much. I get off the train and put myself on automatic pilot while I walk to the building where I work, reading the whole time. I feel naked without a book in my hands. If I forget to bring a book on the subway, it will bother me all day long.

I'm often reading more than one thing at a time, often in languages other than English. Right now, I'm reading an Italian musical score. I will have to repeat a couple of parts because my concentration goes. I am trying to read the words without putting the melody to them. When I read French, I read in a different way, and the same with Spanish. In English, I skim a lot, especially if I'm reading a magazine. If I'm reading a novel, however, I comprehend totally because I start living the story as I read it. It usually takes the first one hundred pages of a novel before it's set in my mind, but after that, I can jump in and out and still keep the continuity. I often read an entire novel in one sitting, though. I'm in heaven when I read a good novel.

These days, I'm reading books about England; I've read about the royal matriarchs and patriarchs: Charles and Diana; Edward VII; Queen Victoria and her daughter, Princess Beatrice. I often go through "topic" or "author" periods. Last summer I read Mark Twain. Once it was George Orwell. Another time it was Jane Austin. I love reading her—her English is so good, proper, pure. I love the sound of the English language as she uses it.

I also read a lot of religious material. I have a Bible dictionary so I can cross-reference passages I read in the Bible. During Lent this year, I read discussions on the Psalms after Mass every day. I always bring the missal to church so I can read along. I read religious materials because I am concerned about my own spiritual growth. I know many of the Bible stories already, but I look for messages in them about what I can do inside, for something I can apply to myself, or reflect on.

I have always loved looking at books I've read. I look at the books sitting silently on the bookcase in my kitchen and know each one is like a symphony, waiting for its music to be released.

PEGGY SULLIVAN

The city in New Mexico where Peggy Sullivan grew up had very few other black families, no black educators, and few black professionals. As a result, it took her until adulthood to realize fully her identity as a black woman— a process that was greatly helped by reading African-American women writers. Following a career as a human service professional, she has now chosen to do temporary work in order to spend more time on her own writing.

In the 1930s my grandmother worked as a housekeeper for a man who collected first editions. He let her read them after he and his wife were through with them, and my grandmother let my mother read them after her. My mother read to us kids quite a bit when we were young, and even though my father was not a reader—he was a third-grade push-out—he was very indulgent about buying us comics and books.

I read my way through the children's reading room at the library before I was eleven so my mother made a deal with the librarians: I could pick out the books I wanted from the adult section, but if the librarian said no, I couldn't have the book. I picked out a lot of biographies and of course, I fell in love with Florence Nightingale and Helen Keller. I didn't realize it then, but I wasn't reading any books about black people. Except for the obligatory books about George Washington Carver and Booker T. Washington, they just weren't there.

Reading certainly gave me a wider window on the world than I could have had at that time and place without it. It gave me all kinds of wonderful thoughts and ideas. My mother's *Ebony* magazine articles were the only black literature that was available to me, but I still grew up knowing I could be somebody from reading about so many other people who had succeeded. Nobody could stop me because I knew about people who had been successful.

As an adult, I can be an obsessive reader, but I don't think I'm a compulsive reader. Compulsive readers have to have a book in their hands, not just in their briefcase or backpack as I do. It is really easy to cut myself off from life by reading too much, though. As a child, reading was a retreat from the world when my parents started having trouble—it was a way to hide, to block out all the unpleasantness. And I can still build a world that is bounded by my books and not by real people. I delve into a book, or a series of books, and I can shut out the real world. When I don't like what's going on around me, I find a book about something I do like, or I read about somebody else's miserable, dismal life and feel better because it's not mine. Instead of continually thinking about whatever is making me anxious or unhappy, I read. I don't think it's always good for me to use books this way because then I don't deal with what's going on in my life. But I don't know how *not* to read at times like these. And sometimes reading does give me space to discover a way to cope.

I cannot conceive of living in a house without books. I wouldn't want to live in my house if it didn't have any books in it. I have probably fifteen hundred science fiction books on my bookshelves—most written by women. I have books by women such as Andre Norton and C. L. Moore, who wrote science fiction in the thirties, and Octavia Butler and Virginia Hamilton, who are black women. I have books by Marion Zimmer Bradley, Ursula Le Guin, Kate Wilhelm, and Ann McCaffrey, who are all outstanding writers. I also have some by newer writers like Joan Vinge, C. J. Cherryh, and Jennifer Roberson. When I walk into a science fiction bookstore, I probably already own nearly 50 percent of the books by women writers, and I have read many more than that. I collect science fiction written by women, but I also have a few hundred science fiction books written by men.

I hated science fiction until the late sixties because until then it was all "hard" sci-fi about the science rather than the people. It was usually written by male writers, who wrote for and about men and boys. The women in these books were merely props. Then somebody introduced me to Robert Heinlein, who wrote about people, and to E. E. "Doc" Smith, who wrote about super people—psi giants. Sometimes his women even rescued his men. And then I was introduced to the women who were writing science fiction in the sixties. Even though a lot of their stories had male heroes, at least the women in their books had dimension; they had an active part in the story and weren't just something draped in gauze to be rescued by the male hero. And now, women are often the heroes of the stories. I have always been really fascinated with the differences between books written by men and women authors, but lately I'm noticing less difference because men are starting to write more character-based science fiction.

Regular fiction often bores me. Sometimes it takes me into somebody else's world, which is fine, but often I find myself saying, "I already know these people," and their lives on paper aren't as interesting as they are in the flesh. Sometimes I get that feeling about the characters in science fiction, but I get caught up anyway because they are in such unusual situations.

I also have a collection of black women writers, but it is sadly incomplete. I read them because they know the black experience in a way that I don't. There weren't many blacks in New Mexico, and the people of color that I knew were mostly Native American or Chicano. I was almost forty when I began to form my identity as a black woman, and black women writers have helped me take a look at who I am and who I want to be. I read Ann Petry and Rosa Guy, Alice Walker and Alice Childress, and Toni Cade. I read both fiction and nonfiction. Toni Morrison makes me itch everywhere inside because of the way she makes me think about being black in this country. So does Audre Lorde, especially in her essays.

When I admitted the possibility that I am a lesbian, I read everything I could find about homosexuality. I worked in a university library in the fifties and I'd go up to the locked book room to look at Havelock Ellis, and I'd say, "Oh shit, I'm sick." Then I thought, "Well, maybe I'm not sick; these people are all white." Finally, in the sixties, more positive books on lesbians and gays came out and I thought, "Maybe I'm just weird." It was an important step in my life to read these books, even though the characters were white. Even today there aren't a lot of black lesbians saying, "Look, this is who I am," and writing about it. And the black characters in the books written by white women are not black—they may have brown skin, but they're white inside. I keep thinking I'll have to write the great American black-lesbian novel.

Milo Randolph

Milo Randolph learned his love of reading from his father, a farmer who read Zane Grey in the early morning before he went out to work. Before retiring, he taught farm mechanics, shop, biology, and math in a rural junior high school, but regardless of the subject, he always tried to get his students interested in reading.

I can demolish printed material just about as fast as anybody you can imagine, and I can remember most of what I read. I developed my own speed reading style when I was in the Army, and even now it doesn't take me long to go through printed material. I started with the *Liberty* magazine. They had timed articles and a little test afterward. It would say, "Reading time: three minutes and fifty seconds." I'd try to see if I could read it in that amount of time and then I'd answer the questions. At first, I could just barely make it. But then pretty soon, I could zip right through those articles. Later, I took a reading test when I started college. It was a timed test with a booklet and a pencil. I read through the thing and answered the questions and when it was all done, I folded it up and sat there. The instructor came over to me and asked, "What's the matter? You having problems?" "No, Sir." He looked through my booklet and said, "You know, I've been doing this for years and you're the first person who has ever completed the test in the time allowed." Now, I don't claim to be a speed reader, but I do read quickly and I'm able to comprehend what I read.

My dad, he was a farmer. He didn't have very much education, but he just loved to read. He'd get up really early in the morning on the farm back in Iowa, where it's colder than blazes in the winter time. He'd get all the fires going and then he'd sit and read for a little while before going out and starting his day's work. He loved Zane Grey. He read all the westerns. He just ate them up. When I was eight years old, he gave me one of the very best Christmas presents I got in my life. It was a package of six books: *Black Beauty, Robinson Crusoe,* and so forth. I began reading everything I could get my hands on, and that's the way I've been ever since. I just love to read.

I'm busier than sin right now in my cabinet shop, working day and night, seven days a week. But I take a book to the bathroom with me, and I read while my wife's fixing supper. I don't watch very much TV. In fact, lots of times, my wife will be watching and say something like, "Oh, I didn't know about that." Then I'll come up out of my book, startled, and look around for a minute. You see, I get very tied up with whatever the people are doing that I'm reading about. I do like the "Jeopardy" program, though, because most of the time I can come up with an answer before the contestants do, except in the categories like opera and such. Lots of times, I have it right when the contestants don't even get it.

I like to read about things that actually happen. I think I've read most of the biographies at the library. (Of course, the library here is really limited.) I find the biographies to be really interesting, especially ones about people I've heard about, but never knew much about. I also read *National Geographic* cover to cover, and *Reader's Digest,* the *Smithsonian,* and other magazines, and of course, I read the papers. I'm just inundated with catalogues of woodworking equipment.

I also like murder mysteries and westerns. I've read lots of books by the western writer Louis L'Amour, and I've read a lot about him, too. He based his characters' actions on things he knew how to do himself. He had experiences just like his characters—the fast guns, the prize fighters, the barkeeps. It was his own knowledge of the intricacies of western life that helped him to put it all down on paper the way he did. He always said that when he wrote, he didn't have to have a quiet room; he could write with his portable typewriter on his knees right out in the middle of the intersection of the busiest street in America. And I believe that he could.

I go to the library every week. We have a Carnegie library here, the only one that isn't in a big city. It's ten miles out in the middle of the farming community. The building is quite old and it needed some refurbishing. The librarian knows I have a shop and she said they were going to have a work day when people could donate their time to work on the building. A bunch of ladies came and they cleaned and dusted and washed windows. And I patched holes in the walls and the floor and replaced some of the wood that was rotted away on the outside and so forth.

When I retired from teaching at the junior high, the art teacher made me a poster—she always makes posters, caricatures of whoever is retiring. I got one about as tall as I am. It had books all over the place, and something written about how now I'll have plenty of time to read all the books in that library.

I tried real hard to get some of my students into reading. Of course, I mostly had boys when I was teaching shop, and if I saw they were interested in something, I would try to get them acquainted with the library. One of the darn'est things happened one day when I took my biology class to the library. One of the boys didn't finish his assignment by the time we had to leave. I said, "Well, why don't you check the book out and take it home and do it tonight?" He said, "You mean you can take 'em home?" He was a ninth grader and he hadn't found out how to use the library yet.

I tell my kids and my grandkids, "If you can read, you've got it made." My little granddaughter, she's a bookworm. She'll come over and get one of my books and sit down and I won't even know she's there. She gets so engrossed in the story, I can call her three times and she'll never answer. Maybe she's like me.

I always have things I plan to do, but when I sit down to read, I just forget everything I'm doing. I just shut off for a little while. Some people drink, some people smoke, some people like to go dancing or play cards, but I'd rather read. Reading is my habit. There was a quotation in a book I read the other day. It said something like: "People think they only have one life to live, but if you read, you can live as many lives that you have time to read about." You can be a sailor, or an astronaut, or whatever.

◊ CHAPTER 6 ◊

Those Learning to Read as Adults

One time, I even went to the extent of slapping the teacher in the head to keep the other kids from knowing I couldn't read. They sent me away for a year for that one.

Fred Hayes

Throughout the many years I taught adult reading classes, I observed my students as they walked tentatively over the threshold into my classroom for the first time. One student expressed his discomfort clearly: "As I was walking into your class that first day I thought about my thirdgrade teacher, who embarrassed me in front of my friends by having me read out loud when she knew full well I couldn't read to save my life. That was when I decided I'd never read again. Unfortunately I didn't." He came to my class because he was tired of guarding his reading secret. But, as he embarked on his reading studies, he had little idea of the new difficulties he would encounter.

Learning to read as an adult is generally more difficult than learning to read as a child. When adults return to their education after a long hiatus, they seldom learn as quickly as they could have when they were children. When adults who read at the third-grade level begin adult reading classes, they may find it takes several years of night classes to bring their reading up to even the fourth-grade level. The differences between an adult learning to read and a child learning to read are significant. Eight-year-old third graders spend perhaps five hours a day on reading-related activities at the time in their lives when their minds are primed for learning, and when learning is their main occupation. In addition, they don't have the self-concept as a failure that comes from the years of covering up the fact that they can't read. By contrast, adults learning to read generally attend classes and tutoring sessions only two to six hours a week, yet also raise children, work in jobs that are often strenuous, pay bills, shop for food and clothing, and cope with a myriad of family issues.

Adults who can't read develop complex coping mechanisms to save face in countless situations. My students described how they ask

121

directions without letting on they are unable to read street signs, or call up manufacturers to "double-check" instructions; they are forever "forgetting" their glasses, and claim they don't use a checkbook because it "might get stolen." They seldom carry paper or pen to write messages on.

Many nonreaders cope by carefully controlling their interactions with others. One of my students admitted she was naturally an outgoing person, but that as an adult she learned to be cautious around other people. She avoided church activities because she dreaded having to read something in a meeting, and she didn't join her friends at restaurants because she would be confronted with reading a menu. Another had the "gotta go" syndrome—retreating quickly to save embarrassment in front of peers. "Every time I enter a political discussion at work," he confessed, "I risk others noticing my knowledge on the subject is thin. They accuse me of making broad generalizations, but that's all I know."

Many nonreaders control their interactions at work so successfully they become model workers. They work without complaint to cover up their reading disabilities. They have learned to think ahead to avoid potential disasters, and use this skill for both themselves and their company's welfare. Some decline promotions to supervisory positions because of potential paperwork, while others work hard in fear of losing their jobs. They know they may have to fill in employment papers for a future job without having the opportunity to get their spouses' help.

One evening I took a spontaneous poll in my evening adult reading class that revealed fourteen students had been in their present jobs for seven to twelve years, while only two students had been in their present jobs for less than two years. As I thought about this group's endurance, I understood why many of their employers had praised their work. My students were conscientious individuals who disciplined themselves to succeed to the best of their potential. Now they were studying hard in my reading class to push their limits even further.

Four men who were regularly attending another of my reading classes, were encountering emotionally complicated situations with their loved ones at home. They all refused to invite their literate wives to our Christmas party. It seemed that not one of their wives supported them in their reading endeavors. According to these men, their wives were jealous of the time spent at school and weren't seeing enough progress for the long hours spent away from home.

Without having access to information from reading, nonreaders often find it difficult to develop and trust their own opinions on such matters as current events and voting, so the opinions of their well-read relatives and friends hold great weight. Such advisors can hold tremendous power over a nonreader because their store of knowledge tends to be so much greater. The buffer they provide can sometimes be so convenient and familiar that the nonreader doesn't even see the need to return to school.

Although friends and relatives can inadvertently get in the way of a person's literacy efforts, I want to emphasize that most people do support their friends and family members when they return to adult school.

The individuals presented in this chapter have made the choice to return to school and are succeeding in their adult reading classes or their adult literacy tutorial programs. They are the success stories, the ones who are moving out of the narrow domain of nonreading into the wider world of reading, the ones with the desire and motivation necessary to pursue their reading goals.

Literacy Defined

Before you proceed with reading the narratives of adults who are learning to read, I would like to give you a brief overview of the state of literacy in the United States so that you can put these interviews in the broader context of the society at large.

National literacy statistics depict a dire educational situation. A functionally literate person is defined as having the reading and writing skills necessary for everyday living. It is estimated that there are 27 million American adults (15 percent of the total population) who are functionally illiterate—whose reading skills are too low to read medicine bottle labels, consumer product directions and warnings, TV schedules, bus schedules, traffic signs, or job advertisements. An additional 45 million (25 percent of the total population) are barely able to meet the more demanding reading requirements of the workplace, bringing the total to 72 million American adults (40 percent of the total population) with marginal or nonfunctional reading skills.[10] A truly literate populace, one capable of analyzing complex material, forming critical opinions, or making informed decisions necessary for full participation in democracy, requires far more than these marginal skills.

Literacy Programs

Although nearly 3 million American adults are enrolled in some 14,000 federally-funded adult-education literacy courses, this is a small number when you consider that it represents only about 11 percent of the adults with reading difficulties.[11] In addition to the federally-funded programs, thousands of adult literacy volunteer tutoring programs arrange for individual tutoring of adult literacy learners. These programs encompass private nonprofit literacy organizations, federally-funded and state-funded programs, and community, church, library, and workplace programs as well. If you'd like to find out more about these programs, either because you want to volunteer or because you want to enroll, call your local library or adult school for information.

Costs of Illiteracy

Management is finding that many of its workers' skills are not up to the demands of even non-technical or semi-technical jobs. One of my adult literacy students confessed that he incorrectly rebuilt a car engine because he was unable to read an updated section in the manual. His error caused the rebuilt engine to malfunction, which resulted in a serious accident. This accident was the crisis that brought him to my class. Poor workmanship and lowered production attributable to illiteracy results in losses of hundreds of billions of dollars each year. A few more enlightened companies are now developing their own literacy programs in response to their need for a more skilled work force.

What happens to people when they lose their jobs and are unable to find or maintain new jobs because of their poor literacy skills? They remain chronically unemployed or underemployed. Seventy-five percent require additional reading and writing skills to enable them to successfully compete for entry-level job openings.[12] The government has put into place a number of programs to address this need. Yet, as I discussed earlier, learning to read as an adult can be an enormous undertaking. Rather than endure the years it takes to make up for their educational deficit, nonreaders can become disillusioned and opt for a short-cut. A small percentage turn to crime to make up the deficit in their pocketbook.

Prison operations cost the United States about $7 billion annually and are directly linked to illiteracy rates. If we include the cost of court appearances, lost income of prisoners, welfare expenditures to prisoners' families, and law enforcement, the amount jumps to $10 billion and is increasing annually. Functionally illiterate prisoners account for 50 percent of the prison population, while 60 percent of prisoners have not completed high school.[13] In addition, an incredible 85 percent of all juvenile delinquents are considered functionally illiterate.[14]

For every $1 spent on preschool education, perhaps $4 are saved in future welfare and prison costs.[15] If you consider the fact that preschool is where the children with parents who don't or can't read to them first encounter the prereading skills that will prepare them to learn to read later, and that without such preschool experiences children enter kindergarten already behind, this statistic makes the importance of funding education, especially early childhood education, profoundly clear. If society cannot give a child a solid foundation in literacy, the child may easily grow into an adult who finds it more difficult than literate people to positively function in society whether creatively, socially, politically, or economically.

In addition to experiencing economic barriers, many of my adult literacy students found it difficult to take their full place in other parts of society. I once spent three weeks with one of my classes reviewing ballot initiatives before an election, only to find later that none of them actually voted because they were just too intimidated by the process or feared humiliation at the polling booths.

There are no measurements for the effects on individual people of the sense of narrow career options, or the poor self-esteem, or the feelings of failure and inadequacy that undereducated people cope with on a daily basis.[16] This chapter brings you into the lives of nine individuals who cope with the myriad difficulties related to poor reading skills.

HELEN GARRETT

Helen Garrett hid her reading problem from her husband for five years even though they worked side by side in his home siding business. She has attended adult school classes and tutoring sessions for the past three years, and has managed, with considerable effort, to raise her reading level from first to third grade.

When you can't read, you're always a little bit on guard. I'm a very private person, almost standoffish. Even if I could read better, I think I would still be a private person, but because I have this reading disability, maybe that made me the way I am, too. Which came first, I don't know, but I think my reading played a big part in it all. I have people who I'm close to, but I don't get so close to anyone that I have to tell them about my reading. I don't trust what they'll do when they find out.

I dated men who never knew I couldn't read. I was afraid that if I told them they might have kept on dating me, but maybe would start joking about me with their friends later on. That would have hurt me. I once dated a man who wanted me to put my voice on his answering machine, and he wrote out what he wanted me to say. I said, "Fine, but let's do it later, I don't want to do it now." He got upset with me and did it himself. Maybe he would have continued dating me if I told him, but I'm sure he would have thrown things up in my face later on. I married the right man; my husband would never do such a thing, never.

I have always been curious about why I have a reading problem— why me? When I was younger I'd lay in bed and cry, "Why did this happen to me?" I'd go to Sunday school and the other kids could read, but I couldn't. Sometimes I would break down and cry, but no one knew why I was crying. I didn't think anybody would understand. I was desperate. I didn't want to get up to read with everybody looking at me. I was afraid everybody would say, "Wow, can't she read?" At that time I thought I was the only one who couldn't read, but now I know that's not true.

My brothers and sisters can read fine—I was picked out of the bunch. Recently, I asked my mother, "Did you read to me? What happened?" She said, "I don't know what happened. I read books to you." I said, "Well maybe you didn't spend enough time with me. What went wrong?" She said she just didn't know. She said she took me to a specialist who couldn't find anything wrong with me. He said that a lot of kids are slow in reading and some just pick it up faster than others.

My mother said that I was always kind of stubborn. Well, maybe I was. She said, "Helen, when I tried to help you, you didn't want the help. You wanted to do things on your own." I said to her, "But you were the mother and I was the kid. Why didn't you whoop me or discipline me?" She said, "You know you wouldn't let me do that." Maybe I did have too much pride to let her help me, I don't know, but it's hard not to blame her. I'm still trying to put together the bits and pieces of the puzzle; I'm still trying to understand. I'm pretty strong willed now, so I suppose I was strong willed as a kid. I knew I couldn't read, but I didn't know it would stagnate me as I got older, that it would stop me from being able to do things. I had no idea.

I've been married for seven years, but my husband only found out about my reading two years ago. We have a business, and even before we got married he wanted me to help him with it. I would make excuses, but finally I started helping him. When I would have to spell something, like a person's name or the name of a company, I would call my mother to spell it out for me over the telephone. Finally, one day I told him about my reading. He said, "Helen, I did notice your spelling, sometimes you would spell something wrong, but I really didn't know you couldn't read." He was really sympathetic, and thank God for him because a lot of men wouldn't even want to date me if they knew I couldn't read. He helps me a lot now.

Sometimes I ask him if people know I can't read. He says, "No, nobody would ever guess it." He says that God lets things happen to people for certain reasons. Once he said to me, "Maybe if you could read you would be uppity. As you are, you're really down to earth." Maybe he's right that not being able to read humbles me. I know God is not going to put so much on me that I can't bear it, but it's rough.

I have to worm myself out of so many things. One time a friend mailed me something and then asked me, "Helen, did you read it?" I had to make up an excuse. I said, "I haven't had time to read it." Another time I was at a friend's baby shower and she wanted me to read the cards. I said I didn't have my glasses. In church, I would go to classes and I get so nervous because the pastor might call on me to read something. My husband told me to be truthful with him, so I pulled him aside one day and told him I had a reading problem. He said he understood, and that there were other people there who couldn't read also.

About four years ago, I went on an interview where these people wanted to hear my voice, so they asked me to read something off a card. I asked them, "Can I do it later?" They said, "Can we ask you a question? Can you read?" I said, "I can read but not very well." You can imagine how I felt when I got out of there. I felt backed against a wall. I cried all the way home. Later they told me they still wanted me, but I never went back. I never told anyone about it, either. I only told my husband a couple of months ago. Every time I think about that incident, I almost cry.

I've been back in school a few years now. I've learned my vowels that I wasn't sure about as a child: a-e-i-o-u and sometimes y. I've learned about using periods, commas, and question marks. I've learned to not skip something I don't know, but to go back and sound it out. Now I'll use my dictionary, and I'll write a letter. At one time I couldn't even look up a word, and I wouldn't dare write a letter to no one.

I expected that in six months to a year it would all come together for me, but it doesn't happen like that. Learning to read is a long process. Sometimes, sure, I might get frustrated, but that's not going to help. I used to break down and ask my teacher, "How am I doing? It seems like I'm not doing very well." But she said I was doing fine. I've come up maybe two or three levels in a few years, and that's pretty good.

I have to go through the mail at work and figure out if something is important so I can give it to my husband. It really made me feel good one day when a letter came in that was important. I was able to read that letter and then I was able to give it to him and tell him it was important. It made me feel good, it really did.

When I first started at adult school, I told my mother, "I don't know about going there because I might run into someone I know." She said, "They wouldn't see you there if they didn't need to be there theirselves." Then one particular evening these two women I know did come in the class, and none of us said anything to anyone.

I don't want what happened to me to happen to my daughter. She's eighteen months. I've wondered if I should tell her about my reading problem, but she's my child and I think I should be truthful to her. I buy little children's books for her and I read them over and over until I know the words thoroughly, and then I read them to her.

I'll keep on fighting until I can read. I'm never going to give up. I've made God a part of my life, so He'll help me. God has already helped me a lot. If it wasn't for Him, I don't know what I would do.

JAMES RICH

Marathon runner and rower James Rich raised ten children while working at multiple jobs, often having to keep his reading difficulties hidden. He had the remarkable perseverance to reach his impressive goal—increasing his reading skills from elementary to college level by his forty-fifth birthday.

I've always had a problem with reading. I lived with my grandparents in South Carolina and went up to third grade there, then I went to New York to live with my mother. I was terrified going to school in New York because it was a big school with kids of all ethnic groups. I was shy and quiet so my teacher, who had thirty-five kids in the classroom, was happy to have a kid who didn't give her any trouble. Unfortunately, she never helped me with my reading. We moved a lot and I changed from one school to another, so I never got to feel comfortable. I just didn't open up in school.

My mother only had a fourth-grade education, but she could read. She worked long hours doing domestic work, so I didn't see her much. Actually, no one I knew read much, no teachers ever encouraged me, and no one ever picked me out to talk to about reading.

In 1955, when I was in the sixth grade, I moved back to South Carolina and began school there once again. The kids were pretty sharp and I couldn't keep up. It was an all-black school with all-black teachers who were strict and very traditional. They made the kids go up to the board and do their math, for example, and there weren't too many kids in the classroom. I was so far behind I quit school to go to work. At that point I probably read at second- or third-grade level.

Soon I moved back to New York to live with my father. He had a third grade education, but he was a hard-working man, very determined, very ambitious. He read the Bible and taught Bible school. I stayed away from the school because they made us read out loud to each other, and I didn't want to be embarrassed.

By the time I was eighteen, I got a girl pregnant, got married, and went to work. Eventually we had ten children together. During that time I would try to read occasionally by getting the newspaper and trying to pick out as many words as I could and guess the rest. I became good at picking up the drift of an article. My wife had finished high school and read very well. When she read a book or newspaper article to me, I'd listen carefully and remember what I heard because I have a very good memory.

I worked two jobs most of the time I was married, and I memorized as many words as I could on my jobs. For a while I worked as a chemical operator in a plant mixing chemicals and sending samples to the lab. They would send back written instructions detailing how much acid, let's say, to put into the chemical and at what temperature. It could explode if the temperature was too high. No one knew I couldn't read. I got a helper to read things to me sometimes, and other times I would call the lab up and say, "The instructions got wet, what do they say?" It took a tremendous amount of my energy just to maintain.

Finally, at age forty, I went back to school, to adult education. The most difficult thing for me was sitting and reading one word at a time like I was a kid. It just didn't feel good, especially since I moved pretty well in the world; it was hard on my ego, on my self-esteem. But I struggled long and hard with my reading for a number of years and finally got good enough to work towards my high school equivalency diploma, my G.E.D.

I work better when I set a goal, so six months before my forty-fifth birthday I decided I wanted to get my G.E.D by that date. I got up really early every morning and studied, and had three tutors who each studied with me one night a week. Fortunately, I was able to connect up with the local adult literacy program so the tutors were free. With the tutors helping me figure out how to read the paragraphs and answer the questions, I slowly moved through the G.E.D study books. I put in an incredible amount of work and actually got my G.E.D a month ahead of time!

Now I'm attending a community college and I'm beginning to understand how a person learns and knows how to read. My first class was a public speaking class because speaking is one of my strong interests—I had already been through the Toastmasters program. Next, I learned how to read articles and write papers on them. I had decided to be honest with the teachers about my background, so I went up and told my first writing teacher what a bad speller I was. She really tried hard with me. She thought my content was pretty good, and just corrected my spelling. Now my spelling is getting better, and I've gone from writing three, four, five words at a time to writing whole essays. I use a dictionary, but spelling is still the most difficult thing. Now I can ask someone how to spell a word and I don't feel bad because I know I've already given it my best.

The most important thing I've learned is that if I want to learn how to read, I have to read a lot. I have to face where I'm at to start moving from here. I have a lot of endurance because I'm a long-distance runner; running helps me focus and clear my head. In turn, reading has helped my running—I now have more information available to me about running. If you can read, you can do almost anything.

Reading has made me a lot more aware of the world around me. For instance, with issues and events, I don't have to just listen to the news and only hear what others say, I can also read and form my own opinions. I started voting in '84 after I went back to school by educating myself on the issues with my tutors. For the last few years I've been an inspector at the polls.

The overall result of reading is that it has enriched my life and changed my relationships with people. I can be a lot more open and comfortable with people because I'm not trying to hide anything. I have new and different kinds of friends now who I've met at school or through my various activities. People used to wonder what was wrong with me because I was so closed. Reading has a hell of a lot to do with your personality.

Fred Hayes

Fred Hayes is a construction worker who has recently returned to school in order to get his high school diploma after years of living "out of the mainstream," avoiding any situation that would expose him as a nonreader.

While volunteering in a preschool, he discovered that he has a way with small children, and he is now determined to become a day care teacher.

It all came from not being able to read. When I was thirteen years old, and in junior high, I still couldn't read, so when the teacher asked me to read in front of the class, I got scared, nervous, panicked. But I had taught myself by then what to do: I got smart, sassy; I'd say, "Ah hell, where's the book? What page you guys on?" Anything to throw them off. One time, I even went to the extent of slapping the teacher in the head to keep the other kids from knowing I couldn't read. They sent me away a year for that one.

When I was about sixteen, a doorman told me, "You're a leader, man. You don't know that? When you come out of that shell, you're going to be a decent human being." "What shell?" I wondered. I had a car, I had money. What shell was he talking about? Around the same time, another guy, a policeman with red hair, walked up to me and said, "I've been watching you for about an hour. Either you're going to become a policeman or you're going to end up in the penitentiary. You're a leader; all these kids are following you and you don't even know it." I knew they were trying to tell me that if I ever grabbed a hold of something good, I'd be something. But what they didn't know was that my not being able to read was holding me back. I knew it, but I just couldn't let it sink in.

I was in a high school street gang around the time the Vietnam War was beginning and we were all told to join the Army. I wanted to do it because of the war, the fighting—I was in a street gang, after all; my business was fighting. But I knew I'd have to take the Army reading test. Sure enough, when I went to enlist, I was put into a room full of young men like myself. I opened the book, and I couldn't read it. Everyone else passed the reading test, but I didn't. They told me they would call me only if we declared war on Vietnam. All my friends went to either Vietnam or Germany; they all went except me.

By the time I was in my twenties, I was getting through life, but I wasn't in the mainstream at all. Not being able to read kept me out of it. I wouldn't associate with people who were educated. I knew, deep down inside, they would find me out. But what I said was that they bored me, that they weren't my kind of people. I said, "I'm over here, and they're over there, and that's the way it is." I stayed in places where education or reading didn't matter, where all that was important was how I looked and how I talked and how I fought. I lived in that world for a long time; it was my world. I kept busy making money and driving cars and fighting and dancing and partying, but if I had learned how to read, with my mind and some help, things could have been very different.

When I was thirty-seven, I jumped off a bridge and lived. TV wanted my story, people wanted me to make speeches to crowds, to audiences, to businessmen. No one knew I couldn't read, they just knew about my history and wanted to make money off of me. None of it came to light, and certainly none of it changed my life because education still hadn't come in.

Then I went to a drug rehabilitation program where they took everything that was inside of me and ripped it out and put it right in front where I could see it and where everybody else could see it, too. They moved around every feeling in my head and heart so I could finally open up and see who I was and why. I realized then that I had the choice to change my life or to die. I had nothing left to hide, my reading problems included, so I tried to change. They said I had to go to school and get a diploma, but every time I went back to adult school, I would get a job offer the same day. I'd sign up for school, then walk out and go to work. I never let school come first. Jobs and money were always more important.

But while I was still in the rehab program, I volunteered in a preschool. I would ask the kids questions, and they would immediately get close to me and tell me what was wrong at home. I gained their confidence, and they felt safe with me because they were safe. I felt for those little kids because I knew where they were coming from, I knew what was happening to them, and that they couldn't do anything about it. They needed somebody big to be there for them, and I'm pretty big.

Once a week these rich, white teenagers came to the preschool to volunteer. One of them slipped up to me and said, "Boy, you sure know what to do with these kids. Damn, you're a dynamite teacher." I said, "I'm not a teacher. I'm a volunteer." He said, "Go to college. You're too valuable to waste. You bring tears to my eyes, what you do with these kids." He just dove right into me. He saw me from behind and sideways and everyways and he was only eighteen. It went right into my head—"college," but I couldn't hardly even read.

I had to leave the preschool to make enough money to get an apartment. My counselor at the rehabilitation program told me I'd been there too long. He said, "We love you, we need you, but you've got to go make a life for yourself. Cut this preschool loose and get a real job so you can move out and begin your life."

Recently, three things happened that brought me back to school for good. The first was, my mother passed away. I really felt the loss. I finally saw what she had gone through being Cherokee and Creole and married to a black man. I finally opened my eyes to what her life had been. I realized I had been asleep, and I woke up and began wondering what my own life was worth. When my mother died, she gave me something that went from her body to mine. It was her voice saying, "Do something. Keep changing your life, Fred. I'm gone man, but you still got yourself and your kids and your future. All I can give you is what you already got, so put it to use."

The second thing had to do with smoking weed. Marijuana had been a good thing for me for awhile, but it also became my enemy—it also kept me out of the mainstream. One Friday, my dealer said, "No, I ain't got any for you, man." I knew he was lying, but he had the power to say whatever he wanted and hang up the phone. I said to myself, "This is going to ruin my weekend." Then I thought, "I'm going to let this man ruin my weekend? No, no, no, I'm going to stop smoking this shit instead. I have to be in control of what I do on the weekend, not the guy who's got the marijuana." So I stopped smoking weed right then and there.

The third thing happened around the same time—I saw the Jane Fonda and Robert De Niro movie, *Stanley and Iris*, about literacy. I really took in what he said to her at the bus stop: "Teach me how to read," and then the bus door closes. I said to myself, "Who's going to teach me how to read?" I knew I had to go to school and get that piece of paper. Now I'm back in school for good.

JOSEPHINE ROSE-ANTEBI

Joesphine Rose-Antebi wrote poems even before she learned how to read, which for her happened after age thirty. She began writing poetry to resolve her traumatic childhood, but now just wants to take whatever beauty she sees in the world and leave it for other people.

My family members were very superstitious people who came from Sicily where my mother's oldest sister was a witch. They all thought I was a bad seed from the minute I was born. You see, I was born on April 30th at midnight, May Day. Hundreds of years ago, the witches would go to a mountain in Germany and have their orgies on that night. The devils would go around and find any new babies that were born, and they would steal their souls and then enter them. The babies became the bad seed; they were the devil's children. My mother was convinced that I was not human, that the devil took my soul, and that I was the devil's child. By the time I was seven years old, I really believed that I was a witch and a devil myself.

I also had the bad fortune to be born with the veil over my head, which meant that I had special powers. The veil is the afterbirth. At one time, sailors would spend any kind of money to buy the afterbirth because it was good luck for them on the high seas—they wouldn't drown. I also had a natural ability with words, which was another proof that I was possessed. One day I accidentally said that somebody was going to die and the stupid guy had to die the next day. That did it. That was proof that I was possessed.

I don't want to say anything against the Catholic religion, but when I was still little they were afraid of my powers. They did all kinds of weird things to me to try to chase the devil out. And then my father got drunk and raped me. That was the finishing touch. I didn't know about books when I was eight years old, and I probably hadn't even thought about reading, but I was already an alcoholic, drinking my father's booze. I declared war against my family. I thought I *did* have special powers and I started using them against people. I was diagnosed as paranoid, schizophrenic, and homicidal—a very, very sick and dangerous person.

Fortunately, I never wanted to go against the Ten Commandments, especially "Thou shalt not kill," so when I got out of control I would beat myself against the wall in order not to commit murder. Oh, the anger, the violence that was put into little Josephine. Finally, today they're beginning to acknowledge that a lot of men who commit heinous crimes have come out of abusive situations themselves. They could have asked me, I'd tell them. I had always wanted just to be a good little girl.

My father died before I was eleven years old in 1943, but from him I thought that Jews had two heads and a tail. I said to myself, "Well, if they're devils and they're bad people, and I'm a devil and a bad person, then I belong with the Jewish people." Then my mom had cancer and committed suicide before I was seventeen. My parents dying when I was young gave me the opportunity to get away from my family, and that is what saved me. I grew into adulthood and moved towards the Jewish people. That's where my salvation came in. I am now a converted Jew.

I married and had children, and when they were grown, I went to adult school, at the age of thirty because I still couldn't read. I did very good in math because the teacher was excellent. He taught me how to balance my checks and I managed very nicely. But I had another teacher for English. I studied and studied. I worked so hard, but I couldn't learn. It was humiliating. I went up to that teacher and tried talking to him. I told him I just had a nervous breakdown and had been committed and that I was in therapy, but that I was trying hard. He turned around and said in the classroom that he didn't care what people's problems were, if they had nervous breakdowns or what, that he was there to teach. If we couldn't learn, that was too bad. When he did that, I flipped. I called my husband on the phone and all I remember is that he came, the police came, and they took me out and that was the last time I tried to enter school for a long time.

Although I didn't have much education, I'd write to Washington, D.C., about anything having to do with abuse of women and children. I've got to say my letters were very crude since I could hardly write. You can imagine—handwritten with no concept of grammar or past tense or anything. I'm surprised I even got a response. I even got a beautiful letter from Mrs. Bush that said, "It's never too late for a new beginning." I've got that one framed.

I picked up reading only within the last several years when I saw a literacy program advertised in the newspaper. Before then, I couldn't read at all. Not at all. I got the nerves to apply and I got a wonderful tutor who was patient and taught me so much. I had the most difficult time trying to break the barrier of *not* learning.

I wanted to be able to read so bad. Everywhere I went, my school books went with me. Every opportunity I had, I worked in my book, twenty-four hours a day, seven days a week. I lived, breathed, and slept with my school books. I jumped one obstacle after another. It was so painful to learn to read. I got stomachaches. I got nauseous. I got headaches. I went temporarily blind. I would sit there in a pool of fear. I had all these physical effects but I was determined to learn. There are still times when I have a blank brain. I don't get upset or give in to the aggravation anymore. I just say, "Oh well, my brain went somewhere for lunch and it didn't have the good graces to let me know where it is, but it'll come back. I'll just go ahead and do something else until it comes back."

I want to give credit to both of my tutors and the others at the literacy program for staying with me and supporting me in jumping the hurdles I had to jump. They took their time to volunteer with me. They took the time to share their brains, their intelligence with me. As long as I have a good, caring person to work with me, I flourish.

I started writing poetry in 1983. The words just came to me even though I didn't know how to spell them. As I said, I've always been good with words. I would use a tape recorder and have a friend take the words off the tape for me. Now, since being in the literacy program, I write my own poetry and have a Franklin spelling computer with me at all times. I'm a textbook dyslexic who reverses letters, so I need the dictionary to put words in their proper places. I've had several poems published, including this very short one:

> *Heart*
> If I give you a red rose
> that is my heart
> and when you hold it
> be gentle and kind
> because it bleeds
> so very easily
> fragile
> like life and love.

I want to be able to tell the world wonderful things, nice things. I want to leave nothing but pretty words and happy thoughts behind. I've moved away from all the tragic poetry that I was writing to resolve what I came out of, and now I want to take whatever beauty I see in the world and leave it for other people.

My mind is hungry for knowledge, for learning, and for passing what I know onto whoever wants to learn it. I am good with children. I have absolutely phenomenal insight with them. Working with children is like working with a bud that's blooming into a flower. You are aware of the fact that whatever you expose them to, whatever you teach them, puts a print on their brains. The greatest gift that anyone can give another human is time.

It has taken me thirty-two years to undo the first thirty years of my life. There are still obstacles. At times, things come back, but I just handle them one day at a time. I was recently accepted into a community college. I don't need anything else in life but that acceptance letter. There is so much I want to learn. Reading and learning to me is more pleasurable than an orgasm. It is! I just open up my whole mind like two big arms and grab the world. I have a little quote, and it's my own: "My dreams moved from my pillow to becoming alive."

JORGE PEREZ

While working as a diesel truck mechanic for the past twenty-five years, Jorge Perez has spent his off-hours investing in real estate. He buys older homes that need rehabilitation, does the needed work, then sells them at a profit. He has become so knowledgeable about this process that he now coaches other investors who want to do the same. Although his drive and ambition have enabled him to succeed in real estate, he identifies his greatest and most difficult accomplishment as learning how to read.

I managed to graduate from high school, but I never did learn how to read, even though I always tried to make sense of what was on the page. I don't feel sorry for myself for not learning how to read as a kid, I just don't. Maybe it's society, or the school system, but I don't blame anyone but myself. When I was in high school I didn't put enough emphasis on reading, I just wanted to horse around. I had one friend who was always in class or in the library studying while I was out cutting class and partying. He's a lawyer now. We get together and have a big laugh about it. He tells me, "Remember when you guys used to come and tease me? Well, now I have my own office. Come on up." He knows my problem, but he doesn't ridicule me. I envy him, but he envies me sometimes, too.

After I had been a truck mechanic for ten years, I began working in a national shop, making a good salary. A real estate friend did my taxes, and he noticed I was making money, so he helped me invest in real estate. With three thousand dollars I started buying homes, fixing them up, and selling them, all in my off-hours. As I bought more and more homes, I received a lot of legal documents, but since I couldn't read them, I had no idea what they were about. I just had no idea, so my wife helped me. I would give her whatever I needed to read and say, "Read this to me," or "I need a letter, make this here for me." Or sometimes my broker would actually sit down and read the documents to me himself.

Then, a few years ago, I went through a divorce and realized that I had to begin to depend on myself. That's when I stopped and looked at my life and thought, "It's time to learn how to read and write. You don't have a wife any longer to do it for you. You can't go along in life depending on other people." That's when I first went back to adult education classes. No, I don't usually feel I'm stupid, but when I do, it's for not going back to school earlier.

Learning to read has become the biggest goal in my life. I still feel I need a lot of help, that it's a long, long road, but I have improved in the three years since I started. In only three years I've learned how to pick up a newspaper and understand maybe 75 percent of it, and I'm still working to get the other 25 percent. I read the front headlines and part of the rest of the paper. I'm now able to read a full article within thirty minutes; it would have taken me two days before. So yes, there's an improvement, but not enough. I want to be able to read a newspaper in a reasonable amount of time so if somebody asks me about something, I can at least tell them about a small portion of it. I'd like to be able to know what was in the editorial, the news section, and so on.

All my life it's been hard not being able to read. I've always depended on someone else to tell me what this word or that sentence meant. It has been very embarrassing at some points, like when some friends of mine came over to visit with their children and the kids wanted me to read to them. Well, even *The Cat in the Hat* was too hard for me. Or at work, where the oldest truck I ever work on now is three years old, so I'm always having to learn new methods. I've been with the same company for fifteen years, and I've had to rely on somebody else for a lot of my information. The company's constantly sending us to school to learn the new technologies, or having people come in to talk to us about brake systems, power steering systems, refrigeration, what have you. They tell us what we're supposed to look out for, how we're supposed to handle these things, and a lot of my co-workers take notes, but I can't write them. I have no idea how to change another person's thoughts into print because I don't know how to spell. So when I listen, I really have to concentrate on the person speaking. I can't be bothered with the other people in the room. I have to block everyone else's comments completely out of my mind and pay attention to the speaker so I'll be able to grasp everything. I've been working with most of those other mechanics for all these years and and they still don't know I can't read. Sometimes I feel ashamed of it, and a lot of times it hurts.

Once my company fired a person who hit another person. I had to go to a hearing where there were five bosses plus the arbitration group, probably ten people in all. I had no idea before I went in that they were going to make me read a statement I'd made earlier that they had written down. I had to bluff my way through it by just remembering what I had told them. It was very embarrassing; I wanted to crawl under a rock and die.

Now that I can read some, I find I can have longer, more interesting conversations when I talk to other people. I'm starting to mingle with pretty intelligent people who read a lot. They're moving up on the ladder and they have conversations, debates, and I'm starting to sit there and talk with them. Before, when they would say something, it would go right over me and I'd say, "I gotta go," because I had no idea what they were talking about. Now I'm getting more background knowledge, I'm filling in some of the holes, although there are still a lot more to fill. I don't think I'll ever fill them all; I don't think even the best readers do that. There's always more to read. There's no end to it. Whatever I learn today gives me more to learn tomorrow.

Ray Christensen

As a journeyman electrician, Ray Christensen has had a difficult time keeping a job—not because of poor workmanship, but because he couldn't read. Ray finally entered an adult literacy program, where he has raised his reading to twelfth-grade level. He believes that self-confidence and close friends are the most important factors in reading.

In grade school my teacher told me that they had to have some A students and some D students, and that I was just one of the D students. With us who have dyslexia, at fifth grade we're maxed out. By then we either learn how to bluff or cheat real well.

They graduated me from high school anyway. If I had it to do over, I'd take the toughest English teacher there was in high school and get him to flunk me. Not that I'd want him to necessarily flunk me, but the teachers with the toughest reputations are usually trying to teach the most. And if you're willing to go the extra mile, they're willing to do the mile with you. That's much more helpful in the long run.

My children are grown now, but when my kids were young they would tell me that when I read stories I was putting in words that wasn't even there. I'd just go along and read and when I come to a word I didn't know, well, I'd make up a word. I'd get the idea of what the story was, and I'd put in something that would kind of make sense, and go on and read it. Finally they said, "Hey, that's not right." And so then I got discouraged and quit reading to them altogether.

I went to trade school to become an electrician. I would go to school and listen to what was read there, and I'd bring the textbooks home, and my wife would read them to me. That's how I graduated from a technical college. When I got out on the job I would fake it when I was supposed to read something. If I could get a copy, I'd bring it home and my wife would read it to me. But if I had to read something right on the job, I couldn't do it. I would procrastinate. Sometimes I could get somebody else to read it to me by telling them that I was having a headache or that I couldn't understand it. Quite often they would. But one time I got recommended for being a lead with a crew and I had to fill out the paperwork, but I couldn't do it, so I got let go. They knew

I could do the job but that didn't matter because I couldn't do the paperwork.

I lost a couple more jobs because of low self-confidence and low reading. I was working for the power and light company and when they found out I couldn't read, they told me I wasn't capable of doing the job. They reduced me from a journeyman electrician and gave me a laborer's job, and cut my salary in half. They also sent me to see a psychologist. They ended up sending me to trade school and then I went to the university, but they said I'd have to hire a private tutor plus take a full load. This was ridiculously out of my price range, so I didn't do it. I had chosen an occupation where I needed to keep on learning and my bluff finally caught up with me.

Then I happened to get hired on with an airline as an electrician. My self-confidence was so bad that I couldn't even go up and talk to my foreman. I told him that he was on a pedestal in my mind. He said, "Well, what can we do to change that?" I told him that he would have to come and see me for at least two weeks for five or ten minutes a day and talk about something, anything. He did it—he came back every day for two weeks. After that time, he came off his pedestal and then I told him I wanted to get into a literacy program. He said, "Well, go do it." It's easy to lose your self-confidence because you live a lie with yourself and other people, and the failures just keep multiplying until somebody says, "Hey, you can do it. Go get into a literacy program."

So I went down and joined the literacy program. I told them I had dyslexia and that I had lost my self-confidence. I tested out at the seventh-grade level, but they started me on a fifth-grade level so I would have some success with reading. I'd been taught to sight read so I had to learn phonics. When I started out, I could read maybe a five-letter word, but I didn't understand what a prefix was or what a suffix was— you take a word and you stuff these things on the front or back and make a big bunch of letters. Most words are made by adding or subtracting them.

I was successful and I started to build up my confidence slowly. My foreman still come down and see me every day, and I could tell him that I have a problem or that I think we ought to do this or that or something else. Now I can talk to him and it don't bother me. When you have dyslexia, you get discouraged because you know there's something out there that you're missing. And then you start to learn how to read and it's like opening up a new world.

My son, who was in the Army, got hit by a truck and had a brain injury, so I dropped out of the literacy program for a year because I was emotionally upset. I dropped out for a year to recuperate. I've gone back now and I've gotten so I can read to the twelfth-grade level. Within the past three months, I've gotten so I can read technical stuff, but I still have trouble with it because, with your technical stuff, if you lose a word you can lose the whole meaning. Most of the words in technical stuff are pretty good-sized, at least ones in the electrical field. I can't read as fast as other people can, but I manage to do it.

One of the side effects of reading more is that you build up your self-confidence and then you're less reliant on close friends and family. One or two of these people might try to talk you out of going to tutoring because they're losing your dependence on them. On the other hand, there are people who come up to a plateau in their reading and get discouraged and quit the program because they didn't have a close friend or family member to encourage them.

My wife was used to me depending on her because she was good with reading. She read a lot of books to me. When I started getting better at reading, she said, "If you're going to read, go ahead and do it. You can read for yourself now." It hurt me a lot. There's a lot of things you can learn by reading along with somebody. And it helps you be a little more secure in how to pronounce the words you're not familiar with. That was a difficult time for my wife and me, but we worked it out.

SAM JEFFERS

Sam Jeffers has come a long way from his younger days of being a burglar and later, a prison inmate. Now he is a successful carpenter and acoustical ceiling layer. He is determined to learn how to read, even if it takes him a lifetime.

As a kid, I'd do anything I could to keep from reading because I was literally scared to death of it. The other kids made fun of me and the teachers didn't take time out to help me read; instead they worked with the kids who already knew how. I would sit at the back of the room and pretend I was busy doing something else, like math, and they never bothered me. I felt stupid and embarrassed, so I wouldn't say anything. I got my friends to do my homework for me, but I wouldn't know what I was turning in because I couldn't read it. I was pretty good in math until it got to the time you had to read the problems.

I was put into the slow learning classes where, if I did the work, fine; if I didn't, fine. They would pass me because I was an amenable kid,

I wouldn't cause any shit in the classroom; if I was supposed to be quiet, I'd be quiet.

I had nine brothers and sisters and they can all read except me; they tried to help me, but I guess they couldn't. I don't know why, but I would always run from it. I remember one day we were in Sunday school and the teacher asked each of the students to get up and read a chapter in the Bible. When he got to me, I got up and ran to the restroom.

My father tried to help me but he couldn't read that good himself. He didn't preach education, he preached hard work and making a living for your family. I think because he didn't know how to read himself, his value system was more on working hard. He had two jobs to support all of us kids. We were never on welfare, but there wasn't any money for tutors either. He taught me how to work, and I do work hard now.

As time went on, I pushed reading further and further away. In school I took classes that didn't entail a lot of reading—wood shop, metal shop, automotives. I was always good at hands-on activities. Maybe I can't read so well, but if I see someone fix something, I can fix it myself, or if I see someone build something, I can build it too. Whatever I see other people do, I can do. As I got older, I knew I wasn't stupid, I just had a problem with reading.

I went to a continuation high school after I dropped out of regular school, but since I wasn't feeling good about myself from doing school work, I started stealing. Eventually, I quit going to school altogether and went off into selling and using drugs and making burglaries. I felt good about the burglaries because they were something I could do better than some of the other kids—remember, I was good with my hands. I didn't steal because I needed to since I had a job and was making money; I just wanted to be good at something, to be better than anybody else. I don't know if the other kids could read or not—we didn't exactly sit around talking about the books we just read. To be honest with you, they couldn't give a damn if I could read or not.

They had me up for attempted murder and burglary, but it really wasn't attempted murder because I just took a gun away from a police officer who had pulled it and tried to hit me in the head. I was just trying to stop him from hurting me. I was born strong and I have always been a pretty nice-sized guy. Later they dropped the murder charges.

When I was in prison I went to the prison school. I knew I wouldn't learn anything, but I went to try to get a good mark on my record so when I went up before the board they would let me go because I was trying to better myself. It was all bullshit. No one took the classes seriously. In prison, power doesn't come from being able to read, it comes from whoever has the dope. Anyway, you can buy your diploma in jail: give someone a couple cartons of cigarettes, they give you a high school diploma.

I was lucky to get into a really good rehabilitation facility. In some of the group encounter sessions there they said I should go back to school, that I should put my false pride aside and go do something with my life, so I finally did.

I really started learning to read when I started reading classes at the adult school. Some of the teachers took pride in their work, and helped me overcome being ashamed and embarrassed. And the other people in the classes were there for the same reason as I was, so they'd be kind of crazy to laugh at me since they couldn't read no better. Occasionally, I still do get embarrassed or nervous depending on who's in the class, especially when I have to read aloud.

Getting to those classes was a hurdle, but the process of learning to read is also difficult. Sounding out the words, breaking them down, getting a headache—going hour after hour like that is hard. I'm miserable until I feel like I've learned something, and then it all becomes rewarding. Bettering myself, learning how to read, to me that's a priority. Just to be able to sit down and read a book to my kids is a priority. I don't care about the G.E.D (high school equivalency exam), I can buy that. It's more important to me to just learn how to read.

Everybody I know reads. They read novels and the newspaper. Even my kids are reading. I keep myself from feeling sorry for myself by remembering there are some people who can't talk. I look at myself and see I've got no shoes, then I see somebody without any feet. It may take me a lifetime to learn how to read, but every day I do a little bit better than the day before. I don't want to be a doctor or a lawyer, I just want to be a better person walking in the world. And how could I tell my kids to go to school if I don't go myself?

Not being able to read makes me kind of humble. I wish there was a pill that I could take so I could wake up in the morning and be able to read. It's something I really want to learn.

MADISON BLAND

Madison Bland loved people for their inner selves, and refused to judge them harshly for the lives they might have led. A deacon of his church, he became a role model for young people, inspiring them to create their own futures, and was a natural teacher who guided them in their progress along the way. Mr. Bland died three months after this interview took place.

My family were sharecroppers in Texarkana, Texas, during the Great Depression. I tried to go through school, but I only went to the eighth grade because we were constantly taken out to do farm work in order to help the family. My mother was married three times and my father twice, so there were twelve to fourteen people in my family until I was fourteen. I had half, whole, and stepbrothers and sisters. No one was a reader per se, in the home, but we were all doing a lot of thinking and preparing in those Depression days. It was pretty hard getting by. By the time the Depression was over, my father's eyes had grown dim, and he lost interest in reading. My mom would read Sunday school literature, and we read the Bible as a family. Life was different in those days, without TV and all. On the farm, we kids had to be in the house when darkness came, and we all gathered around the table and listened to my mother read for entertainment. There wasn't too much discussion; we just listened.

Even though I never made it to high school, I've always wanted to gain as much knowledge as possible. Coming from an environment where I was deprived of certain rights made me conscious of the fact that I wanted to learn. As a child I read mostly religious materials, but around fourteen or fifteen I began expanding my reading to magazines. I read magazines like *Ebony,* and others put out by the black press, or anything I could to find out what was going on in the world. After I entered into World War II back in '43, my hunger for knowledge got even greater. I started to see how little I really knew, and began to read everything I could get my hands on.

I came out of the war with a thirst for religious material. A young lady invited me to church one Sunday, and after I went, I began reading more of the Bible. Since then, I have read it from beginning to end, from Genesis to Revelation, and I've tried to retain everything. When I first started teaching Bible classes, some of my pupils knew more about the lesson than I did. They had studied, they had read the commentaries and handbooks. Then I started getting all those materials too. Now when I read the Bible, I put these materials down in front of me, so if there's something I don't understand, I can look it up. If three or four say the same thing, I know I'm on pretty safe ground.

I worked with the church auxiliaries and later became the chairman of the board of deacons. In order to do that, I had to really get into the Book, learn what it's all about, know what I was talking about. I also had to know how to preside and how to present. I've always said that if I have something to say, people will listen. My message was being well received, but I fell short as far as my speech was concerned, as far as grammar, so I knew I had to do a lot of self-education. My verbs, nouns, pronouns, and adjectives were not up to par; so I decided to correct my grammar and make it proper. I needed to know which of my statements were correct and which were wrong, so I decided to go to adult education classes. I feel now that I have overcome much of it, but I still want to get better.

Last year I took a science class and good God Almighty! I found out how much more knowledge there is for me to learn. There are the planets, the earth, the seaboard, and the ocean floor. There's how the plants give out and take in energy and oxygen, and how the human body does the same thing. This is a whole new world of knowledge that I haven't tapped, that I didn't know about until I started to read about it in adult education classes. Neither did I know so much existed as far as humanity is concerned, like how other people live in other countries. It's just beautiful.

Learning to read better has made me more self-confident in the world. It has made me feel able to mix and mingle with people. No man is an island; we all have a desire to talk and discuss different issues and get each other's opinions, and reading has made me want to share what I think, as well as be the recipient of what others have to offer. Before I could read OK, I was hesitant about speaking; not having read about a subject caused me to be silent.

Reading means a new life, it means the whole world. If I'm able to read, I'm able to communicate and to understand. I think people should read, read, and reread. Once you read, you can climb out of the gutter and become something better.

GARY LEE

"The world is set up to where you've got to read and write to be able to function in it. It's really frustrating if you can't, and you beat up on yourself a lot," says Gary Lee, who is now learning how to read, fifteen years after receiving his high school diploma. He and two other students from his adult literacy class have written and produced a play that dramatizes the frustration and limitations of life without literacy.

Schools are big factories. When you're a little kid, you're the raw material, and when you get to the end, they spit you out. Somewhere in between, if you don't keep up, you get chucked off into the reject pile. That's basically what happened to me.

Reading has been a problem with me ever since I was a little kid. I went to three or four elementary schools. Before I even got to junior high, they put me into a special ed. class and that was what I would call the reject pile.

My mom and dad got a divorce when I was what? Seven years old? My mom was a waitress and was trying to raise two kids. She could read pretty good, but she wasn't a very advanced reader or anything. I went through a couple junior high schools and then I went to two different high schools. I guess I just got lost in the changes.

My mom, she never really stressed to me to go to school and learn stuff. She just said, "Go to school." So I went to school. But when I was in high school, the teachers would never make me do anything. I would go to class and they would say, "Well, you showed up, I'll give you a "D." So I would go to school, but it was basically a big joke.

One teacher was real nice to me and helped me out, but then I moved again. I had to meet new friends, a whole new set of teachers. I guess some people don't realize that moving around really hurts a kid. As soon as you settle down and get used to the new set of teachers and friends, your family moves and you don't have any control over it.

One time in the shuffle, they got my papers screwed up and they injected me into a regular high school format. I went up to this one teacher and told her, "I can't read. I can't do this." They put me into the special ed. class, where we played cards. For two years. But they gave me a high school diploma at the end. Yeah, it's not worth the ink it's printed on. I didn't even care when I got it. I could have left school in the sixth grade.

No one in school ever tried to figure out what I was really talented at. The only thing they spent a lot of time figuring out was what I *wasn't* talented at. Nobody cared what I was interested in. Nobody ever tried to figure out what I could do and try to build off of that.

In the fifteen or so years since high school, I haven't done much. I like going to car races and I guess that's why I started learning to read. I read a lot of car magazines, although when I first started reading them, I was lousy at it. I would just sit down and try to read them as best I could. The words are fairly simple. Those were the only kind of magazines I would read because it was something I was interested in—I wanted to learn about the racing cars.

Then a couple of years ago I went to the literacy program because I was mad at myself. I was still running from this reading thing. I wanted to progress in my life and I knew I had to learn to read and write to do it. I looked in the front of the *Yellow Pages* where there's a lot of community services listed. The first time I went to the literacy program, it felt like I was going to the dentist. I didn't know what to expect. They gave me a couple tests and then they gave me a tutor. They don't have a magical wand or anything. They couldn't just crack me in the head and make me able to read and write.

I had one tutor for a couple of years, but then she went on to something different, I guess. Now I've got another one and she's very organized. She even makes me more organized because she makes me put down what time I study and what I study at what time. I like that. She tutors me for three hours and then she gives me six hours of homework. It really doesn't make my social life too great, but I do most of it anyway. The harder that I push, the farther I go. I don't want to be doing this for eight years.

I came up with this idea that I wanted to write a play about what it was like to not read and write. It's funny because I had never, ever been to a play, and I've never attempted to write one, and I've never attempted acting. It just popped into my head one day. I got together with two other students who were willing to go out on a limb with me. So we sat down and worked for about a year discussing our own personal trials on reading and what we could say out of it all. We sat down and wrote it and produced it and did most of the work ourselves.

We acted out parts of our three stories. My story was about when I got pulled from a regular school and got bussed around town to a special ed. class where the teacher was totally mean to me. She would always grab a hold of my ear and yank on it if I wasn't doing stuff right, or if she was frustrated at me or just was having a bad day. The second scene was about when one of the other students was in high school. I played the teacher and he played himself. The teacher tried to make him stand up in class and read, but he couldn't read and we showed the frustration in that. And the third scene is about when the third student is in high school and she goes to a counselor and he tells her that she doesn't have the ability to even learn how to read.

The play goes from grade school to high school and the very last scene is where the other male student goes to get a job and he can't fill out the application or run a computer because he doesn't know how to read so he's turned down for the job. We're putting the play on all around the area. There's a part in the play that goes something like, "I'm bound by invisible chains, but one of these days, I'm going to get rid of these chains that have bound me." People walk away from the play real sad. I guess that's what we wanted them to do, but I was surprised when I saw some people in the audience crying. But we make them laugh, too.

I used to think that I couldn't do anything, but now I think things are open to me pretty much. Believing in myself is a lot of it. In school all they taught me was, "You're not going to amount to anything.

You're lousy at this, and you will always be lousy." Now I know I ain't the greatest, but if I work hard, I will overcome all of this. I want to be the first one in my family to learn to read and write to a high level. Then I want to go back to school and open my own business.

I know it's going to be a long haul. Learning to read takes time. But over time you get more familiar with it and it starts to become easier for you. It's like the first time I went skiing. I was falling all over the place. I was the lousiest skier in the world. But now that I've done it for a few years, I've gotten pretty good at it. The first time I went skiing, there was a tiny hump and I couldn't get up over it. Now a little hump like that would be nothing to me.

◇ CHAPTER 7 ◇

Information Readers

Whenever I [read] something that seems new so far as my memory goes, I ask myself, "Does this fit into my picture of the world that I've developed over ninety-three years?"

Linus Pauling

They are "self-contained information-processing systems."[17] They are focused studiers intent on discovering information about the various topics that interest them. These individuals find entertainment in the pursuit of knowledge. Information readers are voracious and habitual readers who focus on reading nonfiction; they also tend to be aware of their reading process. They have little interest in reading fiction because, as one man commented, "I view fiction as a waste of time when compared to hard subjects where I can learn something useful."

Many information readers are academics who read books and research studies to keep current in their disciplines, or read extensively as part of the process of writing a book, article, or dissertation. They are keenly aware of the knowledge they seek, and are self-directed in the acquisition of that knowledge. As one subject noted, "I'm an information hunter who compulsively searches for cutting-edge information in my narrow field of study."

But not all information readers are disciplined academics. I interviewed many who have never been to college, yet they are driven to learn all they can on a particular subject. One woman wanted to start her own small business, so she read every book she could find on the subject. Five years later, her business was thriving. Another woman worked as a secretary but educated herself to become a computer consultant by reading computer-related books every evening for three years.

Whether they read for scholarly or non-academic purposes, information readers are able to assimilate vast amounts of material in short periods of time. They thrive on the challenge of reading and analyzing material, and enjoy figuring out plausible solutions to difficult problems and making critical judgments on complex issues.[18] Sometimes they read slowly and patiently, keenly focusing their attention on the details they seek; other times their eyes simply scan the page to gather the essence of the article quickly and efficiently. One woman colorfully recounted how she extracts information she requires while leaving the rest untouched. "I liken myself to a cat burglar. While paying careful attention to detail, and with lightning speed, I grab what I want and get out."

Interestingly, researchers have found that up to 70 percent of information readers' time is spent off the page interpreting the author's ideas and figuring out how those ideas fit with their own prior knowledge on the subject.[19] They engage in a constant dialogue with the authors as they read. One says, "I don't believe this. No way." A second wonders, "Does this resonate with my own experience?" A third asks, "How does this compare with the book I read last week?" You might contrast information readers to many literature and frustrated readers, who both spend far less time off the page. Literature readers can become so engrossed in the plot and language that their eyes float across the page. Frustrated readers lack the knowledge-base and self-confidence to read and think at the same time.

As you read through these narratives, compare your own reading style to those included here and determine if you, or part of you, belongs with the readers inhabiting this chapter.

LINUS PAULING

Dr. Linus Pauling is the only person ever to win two unshared Nobel Prizes: the 1954 Nobel Prize in Chemistry for his work on the nature of the chemical bond, and the 1962 Nobel Peace Prize for his public opposition to nuclear weapons. Dr. Pauling published over 650 scientific papers and 200 articles on social and political issues, as well as numerous books on chemistry, world peace, and vitamin C. With all of his diverse and significant accomplishments, he is still most often identified as "the vitamin C guy." Dr. Pauling died at age 93, shortly after he gave this interview.

I was nine when my father wrote our local Oregon newspaper saying that he had a son who seemed to be very much interested in reading and getting knowledge, and that he needed advice as to what books I should be reading. He went on to say that I seemed to be interested in history, especially ancient history. The editor suggested the classical work *Plutarch's Lives*. Well, nothing came of that because I found it rather boring, but sixty years later someone sent me the clipping from that newspaper about my interest in reading.

When I was young I read anything I could get my hands on. My reading at that time was determined by what books were available to me. I remember reading *The Girl of the Limberlost* and other novels that were popular at the time. I was given a copy of *Through the Looking Glass* and still can quote the poems that I learned from that book. We didn't have many books in the house, but we did have a set of Shakespeare which I still have today.

When I was eleven, I read a book on etymology because I had become interested in insects. I collected insects for a while and continued to read about them. When I was twelve, I began reading about minerals, mineralogy and crystallography. I read about the color and the streak of minerals. I didn't live in a good place to collect minerals, so I didn't do any fieldwork to speak of, but I did look at piles of gravel on the street in front of a house that was being built and found some agate. That was about the only mineral I was able to collect.

I became interested in chemistry because in my high school there was a boy who lived halfway between the school and my home. After school, I often walked with him to his home and then continued on to my place about two miles past. One day he said, "Would you like to see some chemical experiments?" I said, "Yes." So we went to the second floor of his parents' house and he turned out a couple of experiments. I was entranced by the idea that substances can undergo chemical reaction and be changed into other substances with different properties. I could see that wood burned in the furnace, and I knew that gasoline was burned in the automobiles which had recently come into existence, but I hadn't really thought about chemical change until that point.

My father had been a druggist, but he hadn't studied pharmacy in school or university. He had been apprenticed to a druggist in the local drug store in his small town after he'd graduated from grammar school. Later he passed his examination and became a registered pharmacist. He had a book on chemistry, which I read, and from that time on I knew I was going to be a chemist, although I didn't know about chemistry as a profession, only chemical engineering.

I went to the university, and very quickly after I completed my graduate work I became a leading investigator in chemistry. I would get excited reading about anything that was new to me. I had begun to develop the attitude of wanting to understand the world, which mainly meant reading about it. By the time I was thirty-one, I had a worldwide reputation resulting from the papers I had published, papers that were changing the nature of the science of chemistry.

I still keep on the lookout for new ideas and whenever I see something that seems to me to be new, or new so far as my memory goes, I ask myself, "Does this fit into my picture of the world that I've developed over ninety-three years?" If it does, that's fine. If it doesn't, then I ask, "Well, why doesn't it? How can it be interpreted to fit into my picture of the world?" For example, in the last two or three years, I've been publishing papers on the structure of atomic nuclei. The nuclear physicists are apt to set up their equations in a big computer and calculate some values from properties about the nucleus. Of course, if they've done the calculation right, they get agreement with the experiment. They know they're going to get the right answer. So I look for a different model from the one the nuclear physicists develop, and am pleased when I find one. I don't disagree with them, but I'm dissatisfied because what they do doesn't give me a definite picture.

My eldest son says that I'm successful because I have an extraordinary memory, I'm curious so that I often begin reading about a new field in science on my own, and I make the effort to connect to the great body of knowledge that I have of science as a whole with what I read about in the new field. The result is that often I make an important discovery in the new field.

Having a clear mind at my age is probably partly due to heredity and partly due to good nutrition. I was interested in vitamins from the time they were first being discovered. Of course, during the last twenty years, it's been one of my major interests. Even earlier I was well nourished; my wife was a good cook and was well trained in college in chemistry and biochemistry. She saw to it that our children and I received good food and were well nourished. Of course in recent years it may well be that the large amounts of vitamin C and other nutrients that I take as supplements are responsible in part for my still having a clear head.

I used to be a fast reader, but my eyes aren't so good now. I have several big five-inch magnifying glasses with electric lights in the tubes around them. Probably 90 percent of my time is spent reading. In addition to reading scientific articles, I have reread most of the books I have in my library. I've been reading old detective stories and mysteries. I also read essentially all the biographies of the members of the National Academy of Sciences and the Royal Society of London who have died recently. I look forward each year to receiving those books. This is a recent activity of mine. I find it interesting to learn how scientists got interested in science and how they succeeded in making science a profession. I'm interested in the details—

those who were born on farms and developed an interest in genetics, perhaps, and then there are those who just developed an interest in basic science on their own.

My eldest son is a retired physician, my second son is a retired professor of chemistry, my third son is a microbiologist and is head of a university department, and my daughter has some interest in science and is married to a leading geologist. I don't think I particularly read to them about my theories, but perhaps I influenced them by being a role model.

I usually tell young people who want to become scientists or nutritionists or biochemists that the important thing is to get a good knowledge of the basic sciences, mathematics, physics and chemistry, which are hard to learn simply by reading. You need an instructor and a formal introduction to the scientific fields. After you've got this basic knowledge, then you can go into a new field just by reading. That's what I've done over and over again throughout my life.

Reading is my life, reading and thinking, and of course, writing. I couldn't separate reading from the rest of my life if I tried to.

DEAN EDELL

Dr. Dean Edell hosts a popular and lively syndicated radio talk show focusing on medical issues. He becomes excited as he combs medical journals to find "simple home-spun solutions to complex medical problems" because he enjoys explaining these solutions to his audience. He discusses timely medical issues in his syndicated television spot and in his newspaper column, "Dr. Dean Edell's Medical Journal."

I never actually decided to do a medical talk show, it was just an opportunity that came my way. I quit medical practice in '72 and tried to get back into art. I had an antique store and a jewelry store, and I did auctioneering and appraising. One of my clients was a nurse looking for a doctor to work in the drunk tank, and even though I hadn't practiced medicine in a long time, I went down there to work. One night I met a drunk who said, "Hey Doc, you explain things so well, you otta be on the radio. I have a friend of a friend of a friend who I want you to meet." And sure enough, a guy knocked on my door a few days later and dragged me off to meet a woman who ran a country music station. Hell if she didn't want to try a doctor show on the air where people could call up and ask medical questions. Now it's ten years later and I've expanded quite a bit, to say the least. But that's how it all began.

Needless to say, I read lots of medical journals. I used to hate reading them when I was in medical school, and even later when I was in practice, but now I get excited about them. Basically my approach is that of a hunter looking for interesting new medical information that people will want to hear. So when I read a medical journal and find a great story, an article that the media has ignored or the public doesn't know about, for example, it excites me. I get as excited as when I find a fabulous antique that no one has noticed in the back of an antique store.

My approach to reading medical articles varies. I do a lot of speed reading and scanning. Then I'll slow down and read carefully if something interests me or requires closer reading. I read huge amounts of material from the wire services, most of which I read skeptically, and from medical journals and medical books, which I give more credence to. I look for topics people will relate to, ones that are practical and broad based in nature. I love self-help and nutrition articles, and simple home spun type solutions to complex problems. There's a broad range of topics that attract me, but they're all very specific in my mind.

It's necessary to have prior knowledge of the subject in order to read medical journals. When I read articles from psychiatry journals, I have to read a lot more closely and skim a lot less because the subject baffles me. Also, the lingo is unfamiliar and the way the authors present their ideas is different from the way heart surgeons present theirs.

I get excited when I read something new, or when I can predict how the article will come out. Sometimes I doubt the content of the article and throw my head back and say out loud, "Oh, my God, I can't believe this." I often perceive a bias ahead of time and say, "Oh, oh, I can see where they're going with this one." I dig into many articles with my own bias, thinking, "Ech, I'm not going to believe anything I read past this point." Occasionally, the credibility of the article will build, and even though I have some doubts, I find myself becoming a believer towards the end. Yet sometimes I want to say, "What a bunch of junk. Who's writing it?" or "This is amazing stuff here. Who's writing this?" In those cases, I look up the authors and their institutions to determine their backgrounds.

In school, English was not my strong subject, nor did reading attract me. I remember having difficulties with grammar and testing, and even had difficulty taking tests like the SAT and English aptitude tests, for which I had to read and understand paragraphs. But now I have an almost photographic memory for medical journal articles. I look at them once and they're in my mind forever. I've noticed my reading has become much better with practice, concentration, and the fact that I love my work.

I don't take any notes while I read. I tear out an article that interests me and write marks in the margin. I have my little coding system of vertical lines along the side of a paragraph to indicate importance. Three vertical lines indicate special importance. An asterisk indicates one step more important yet. I circle and highlight particular parts also, depending upon my mood, but that's the most I will do. From there I go right on the air, and I have to be able to find quickly what's important to me with my eye. I ad-lib on the air directly from the article.

I enjoy fiction too much. I get so wrapped up reading novels that I can't put them down, and they take up so much time. I used to look at novels the way I watch television: I used to think, "It's just fiction so it doesn't have any socially redeeming value," and yet I constantly find myself reading novels. I get sucked into reading them for various reasons. I'll read Clavell because he writes about Asia, and I've been interested in China lately. I'll read Tom Wolfe's *The Bonfire of the Vanities* because it's set in New York, my home town.

I have an eighteenth-century, seven-volume Chinese novel, supposedly the greatest novel ever written in China, called *Dream of the Red Chamber*. Every Chinese person knows it, most hate it because it's really dry. I love the damn thing; I find it absolutely fascinating. I've spent three years on it now, and I'm only in the middle of volume two. I've made a choice to stretch this book out for the rest of my life, so I'm reading it really slowly on purpose. The problem is that there must be two or three hundred characters and I forget who's who. I spend half my time going back and acquainting myself with some character before I'm able to continue.

I always daydream about the artist who created a painting or object. I daydream about what Van Gogh was thinking while he slopped his paint on the canvas and saw little hairs or lines in the globs. I wonder about the origins of an archaeological object, say a tomb figure from China, and think, "God, I'm really touching this thing." I wonder what the artist would think of me touching this object thousands of years later. That kind of thinking led me to read my first artists' biographies. When I read a biography I not only have the fun of reading about someone real, but I also have their tangible work in front of me. After I read the biography of an artist, I look at the paintings very differently than I did previously. It's wonderful.

ROBERT ALEXANDER

A retired architect and city planner, Robert Alexander is more interested in the way buildings serve their dwellers than in their visual aspects. Here he discusses some books that have inspired him over the course of his lifetime, some affecting him so much that he was moved to seek out their authors.

My father's formal schooling ended in fourth grade, but he taught himself to read and write exceptionally well, play the violin, and even paint. My mother was trained as a school teacher and read to me a great deal before I was able to read to myself. During my youth, my grandmother sent me a twenty-dollar gold piece every birthday, and I would go and buy a beautiful, soft leather-bound edition of a book by Dumas (the one who wrote *The Three Musketeers*), until I had a whole string of them, everything he ever wrote. I know a lot of French words just from reading his work as a boy.

When I was seventeen, in 1925, my father sat me down and said, "What are you going to be?" I said, "I'm going to be an archaeologist," because I had been up to my ears in Indian relics in South Jersey. He said, "You can't make a living being an archaeologist, for God's sake— you'll starve to death." So I said, "Well, how about an architect?" He said, "That's the thing." That was in the post-World War I period when there was a lot of activity in the building trades, and he was a tile contractor in Manhattan. So I became an architect, but even at that, I was always interested in the people who used the buildings more than in the buildings themselves.

I had a lot of time to read during the Depression since there wasn't any work, and also later, during World War II, because I wasn't able to practice architecture. During that period I read Ayn Rand's *The Fountainhead,* which inspired me, yet also tore at me, probably because the hero was an architect. I heard that Ayn Rand lived in the same city as I did, so I looked her up. We ended up having many knock-down, dragout discussions that went on until late in the night. I discovered that she had been born in St. Petersburg, and had been a tourist guide there. She eventually became so disgusted with authoritarian rule that she escaped from the Soviet Union through China, and somehow got to Long

Island. She decided to write a book about the horrors of Communism, of collectivism of any kind, and she very carefully selected an architect as the main character to illustrate her theories because a painter or musician or any other artist may do what he wants with his work, even destroy it, as long as it hasn't been sold to someone else. But not so with an architect; he is intrinsically bound to the social and economic problems of his time. He very seldom owns what he builds, and therefore may not destroy his own work. But she has her hero do exactly that because somebody tampers with his design in his absence.

I was in the process of defining my own philosophy. On the one hand, I agreed with the concept that the individual is the fountainhead. On the other hand, I know there are certain social problems that will never be cured by individual effort, problems that nobody in the capitalist system would even think of tackling, and that require a governmental or group action to improve.

Another author I sought out is Lewis Mumford who wrote a book related to architecture called *Sticks and Stones.* His architectural criticism in the *New Yorker* was the best I'd ever read. Like myself, he was interested in the sociological side of architecture, and wrote eloquently on that subject. One day I knocked on his door, and after that meeting, we continued to correspond for many years. He just died recently at the age of ninety-eight.

I have also read several titles that had nothing to do with architecture as such, but that presented a vision which was inspiring to me. I was always interested in large-scale housing rather than expensive private homes, and I once had the opportunity to help design a large-scale rental project. In preparation, I read Sir Ebenezer Howard's *Garden Cities of Tomorrow,* which was a seminal book in England around 1902. Howard was an accountant who had a concept of a total community, where people both worked and lived. Several towns of this type were built in England at the turn of the century following his idea.

If an architect gets thwarted by not having his designs get built, he writes. He writes about what he admires but cannot do. Le Corbusier, one of the gods of architecture, was a Frenchman and the only design he had built during his early years was an apartment building outside of Paris—insignificant—yet he wrote *The Radiant City:* a vision in which everything was precise and clear. I developed my own vision of Le Corbusier from that book after reading it in my early thirties. Later I went to France and visited the building he designed, which was supposed to contain all the necessities of living for middle-income people, including a shopping area. But when I went to see it I became sick to my stomach. The workmanship was foul and nothing functioned the way it was supposed to, and so it destroyed the dream I had of him from his writing.

I love to read any book that I find inspiring, and many of them have had to do with architecture in some loose, conceptual way. But I also have a tremendous interest in American history because the settlers on my mother's side came over in 1683 and my father's family came over in 1785. I just finished Barbara Tuchman's *The First Salute*. In spite of the fact that the sentences in this book went on for pages, I enjoyed it because I was learning so much that I didn't know before. For example, I remember having seen a painting of Cornwallis delivering his sword to George Washington in his final defeat. Well, it turns out that Cornwallis wasn't even there; he sent his second lieutenant! I've never learned to read fast, but whenever I start a book, I doggedly finish the damn thing in almost every case.

FRANCES MOORE LAPPÉ

Frances Moore Lappé's life quest is to find solutions to world hunger. Her highly acclaimed early book, Diet for a Small Planet, *poses critical questions on this issue, the answers to which she addresses in her subsequent publications, including* Rediscovering America's Values. *She co-founded Food First, an organization committed to reframing questions about food, agriculture, and poverty, and The Institute for the Art of Democracy.*

The most critical period of my life began when I dropped out of graduate school—that's when I started learning. Up to that point I read only out of fear that I would expose my basic ignorance. You see, I grew up in the South in the fifties and believed I was just a dumb Southern female. I went to a very poor high school and so, all during college, I was trying to make up for the fact that I had never written a theme paper—I just didn't know how. I take great pleasure in the fact that two years ago I got an honorary degree from my alma mater. That was a real highlight in my life.

I hadn't been seen as graduate school material in my undergraduate major, which was history, so it just wouldn't have ever occurred to me to enter a graduate program in an academic subject, but I thought anybody who had a heart could do social work. As a graduate student in social work I was not happy, however, because school didn't address any of the problems that really interested me. I was in my mid-twenties and I was insecure and terrified, but I finally decided to stop going to school until I understood what I was doing and why I was doing it.

Once I dropped out of graduate school and started listening to my internal questions, I realized I had a quest that I had to pursue. This quest took the form of a series of questions that were very much born out of the culture of the mid 1960s. The concepts of natural food and organic farming were just emerging. The ecology movement was being formed, and I began wondering why there was hunger in a world where there was enough food, where we are rich enough and have the means to feed ourselves. At that time, I had no idea that I would end up writing books or founding an institute; I just wanted to find my direction.

I started doing research in a library that was in the basement of a university building, and had a friendly librarian who helped me follow my nose through the books as one question linked to another. Here I was completely in control; nobody was looking over my shoulder noticing how fast I was reading or how much I was learning, and I quickly became a very active and very critical reader. I developed a burning passion to think things out for myself, something which school simply never afforded me.

I felt that asking the right questions was the most important part of the enterprise, and the more I learned, the more I realized that other people were asking the wrong questions. My intuition told me that if people couldn't feed themselves, than little else seemed important. I read books and tried to organize the information I found to be the most interesting, that raised the most questions, and I paid attention to the patterns that emerged. The only way I could do this was by spending a lot of time with books. Certain ideas began to stick with me, and then the questions began to gel. Soon I realized I wanted to explain my ideas to my friends, and the only way I could do that was to write my ideas down, but I never thought of myself as a writer. I just had all these thoughts I wanted to share with people, and I was compelled to write what would eventually become *Diet for a Small Planet*. It began as a small pamphlet in 1969, and came out as a book in 1971. Today my work is about asking the questions that will lead to the solutions.

Every day involves a lot of reading during the periods when I'm writing. When I'm in that intense process of trying to put together a vision, a picture in my mind of a book, then I search for what I need to put flesh on the image. Reading is always a search, like a treasure hunt.

I hardly ever read books from beginning to end. Instead, I look at a book as if it were the box of treasure; I open it up and start looking for things that I need, things that hit me, things that are useful in the framework I've been working on. I'll often begin at the end of the book; I'll read the conclusion, or I'll look at the index to get a feel for the book and where I might go in it. Or I'll look at the chapter headings to figure out where in the book there might be something meaningful to the questions I'm asking at that moment. Then I'll read that part and later skim through the other parts to see if I've missed something critical.

One simple and efficient system I've used a lot over the years is to mark the interesting pages in books and then photocopy them. I give the pages a code so I know where they came from, so I won't lose the source, and I file them in folders by topic. These topic folders eventually become chapters. When I'm writing I have pages from various books that become my source for information, statistics, examples, quotes, and inspiration.

After I give a talk somewhere, people will often hand me a book or tell me about a book I might be interested in. In this way, I turn up unexpected treasures that I would never find by looking in a card catalogue. It's often by accident that I discover the books that correspond exactly to what I'm thinking about; these books may push me into a new level of questions, or they might give me a fuller level of understanding of something I've intuited. Reading is part of the searching process, and it is so exciting when I find that jewel that expresses something I've been trying to figure out or express myself for some time.

My life is a series of questions that I've tried to answer in large part through reading. Reading is the absolute center of my life's work.

Sharone Abramowitz

Reading is an integral part of Dr. Sharone Abramowitz's intellectual expression. A psychiatrist, she reads many theoretical books and articles, looking for the ways in which their contents compare with her own knowledge, beliefs, and experiences.

I remember reading whole books when I was very young. For many years my mother belonged to a book-of-the-month club, and I knew every single book she bought. Those books were very reassuring to me;

I liked to look at them in the bookcase, and had read most of them by the time I was seventeen and left the house. They were friends to me.

I became a big reader in late grade school. I'd go to the library as an escape from my house. That's when I started reading books like the ones my father read. He's from Poland and survived the Holocaust, so he read books like *The Rise and Fall of the Third Reich,* and huge novels about Jews and World War II. At that time, I read terrifying books about the concentration camps that gave me lots of nightmares.

In college I was a political science and women's studies major, along with being pre-med. My favorite classes were in critical theory, for which I would have to read many theoreticians all writing on one subject, and then I'd have ten days to write a take-home exam pulling together all their different theories. To do this I would go into the university library and hole myself up in the stacks. My world would be totally defined; for ten days I could be completely in my intellect. I'd set up my food thing; I practically slept there. To write the exam, I would find some angle that would act as the sieve through which I could synthesize and develop an argument for my own position. I was very, very focused and disciplined when I did this. I loved it.

My family thought I would become a lawyer, one of my history professors encouraged me to become a professor like her, but instead I went to medical school because I was practical—as a child from a working class family, I wanted to be guaranteed a job, while doing socially useful and humanistic work.

I also holed myself up in the library during medical school, but I didn't enjoy it. The work was harder for me because I lacked the natural enthusiasm for it. I lacked the creative, intuitive feel for the physical sciences that I had for the social sciences. In the physical sciences I understood what the teacher was talking about, I got the basic ideas, but I couldn't be creative or intuitive on my own. In the social sciences I could easily get the big picture. I could make a leap beyond what the teacher was saying. When I make an intuitive leap, I understand the concept beyond what I'm being told.

So it was odd for me to be in medical school since most of the learning there was done by rote memorization and required very few analytic skills. We'd be given these syllabuses and attempt to memorize them from beginning to end, which was very difficult for me because I don't learn by rote very quickly. I understood the broad concepts easily, but not the details. I learned to memorize by drawing things out, by making flash cards. I'd take the syllabus and translate it into graphic representations. Some of the other medical students could just read it and know it, but not me.

I became a very competent doctor, but I wasn't doing the kind of analyzing that I loved. Somehow I always found myself interested in the psycho-social aspects of medicine. I began to realize that psychiatric theory wasn't so dissimilar from other social science theory I had studied in college—a different topic, but also very analytic. Once I began my training as a psychiatrist, I felt I had gone full circle and come back home. I could use all the medical skills I had developed, but also apply my analytic skills. I love being out there working with people. I feel I truly belong in my field of work.

I'm more interactive now with my reading than ever before. All those years I spent reading in the social sciences trained me to read psychotherapy theory. When I read, I am totally focused on what I'm reading. I sit and read every word and really think about the content. At the end of a section I'll pause and think, "What did this just say? What was the author's main point? Is this consistent with what I think? Does this resonate with my own experience?" Or, "This is a new thought and it's really interesting. I'm going to apply it to my work." If I'm not following what I'm reading, I ask myself, "Am I getting sleepy? Is this lousy writing? Or am I just not interested in what's being said?"

Right now I'm reading this book called *Clinical Empathy*. The author will say something about empathy or self-psychology, and I'll write in the margin, "agree" or "disagree," or I'll summarize the main point in the margin. Sometimes I'll write "not sure" or I'll put a question mark if I think something is ridiculous. My reading now applies directly to my work as a psychotherapist, and I want to learn what's being discussed in the books and journals. Partly I'm reading for my work, and partly I just love learning theory. I read it everywhere; when I go on vacation I love to take a good psychotherapy theory book with me. I carefully choose which book I want to take. I often like to read Jungian writers on vacation because of their broad philosophical and spiritual viewpoints.

Sometimes I think I ought to read more novels. I used to read novels more readily, but I'm at the point where I won't read one unless it absolutely engages me; I'd rather go read my psychotherapy theory if it doesn't. A novel has to totally capture my interest, like Marge Piercy's *Gone to Soldiers* did. That book was great; I read it in a few days by staying up until three in the morning. I love to tune out the rest of the world and read.

My life wouldn't be as interesting if I didn't read so much. I suppose I'd be more into athletics or the arts. Maybe I would develop other parts of myself more if I didn't read so much, but why not do what I love? Reading is who I am. Reading for me is an act of intellectual expression—it's the externalization of my intellect.

GERALD EISMAN

A mathematician-turned-computer science professor, Gerald Eisman surrenders to what he describes as his abstract mode when reading technical material. Here he compares reading, which is abstract because it deals with symbolic representations of words, to his profession, which is abstract because it deals with symbolic representations of mechanical processes.

Did you read *Calvin and Hobbes* today? When we were kids, Sunday was an event in my home. We would rush to get the newspaper, spread it out on the floor, and fight over who would get to the funnies first. Now I fight over them with my own kids. Doesn't everyone fight over the funnies? I won't buy a newspaper unless it has *Doonesbury*.

Other than the funnies, I read economics, philosophy, and books in my profession. I especially enjoy playing mental games while reading in the technical, abstract fields. I don't read much fiction. I notice how much time my wife takes to read a novel; that's the time I'll take to play with my children or watch ball on television.

I like to read about the theoretical foundations of computer science, both historical and current. I'm also interested in hardware developments. I'm interested in the way the theory of computer science is being developed using a mathematical approach, using mathematical language, using the way mathematicians think.

Right now I'm reading a book on computers called *Parallel Program Design*. I haven't always liked computers, but I've been around them since their beginnings. I actually used to find them too pedestrian, too down to earth, machinelike. That reaction wasn't uncommon among mathematicians in the '60s and '70s. Now there's a tremendous amount of action in the computer science field. A whole evolution has occurred over the last twelve years that has encouraged a lot of people like myself to switch from math to computers.

After years of reading technical, abstract material, I can put myself into an abstract mode fairly easily. Much of mathematics involves a series of definitions and theorems. The idea is to make the definitions so precise and so clear that the theorems flow naturally from the definitions.

The problem is that if the distinctions become too precise, if they lose their generality, they become meaningless.

When I read something new, I have to adjust my perspective on the material so I know how large a step the author expects me to take. Reading, like any activity, is preceded by certain expectations. Most of the time, one is not even aware of the expectations until there's some sort of breakdown in them. For example, I was reading something yesterday in which the authors were designing a logical system to prove the correctness of programs they were writing. Some common steps in their proofs were occurring over and over again. If a phenomenon is common enough to repeat itself frequently, it is often given a name and then it is referred to by that name. These authors named one of the logical constructs "unless": something was true unless something else was true. As I was reading through the examples, each one had a certain abstract idea of "unlessness." Each proof took a few minutes to read carefully and to understand fully. Then I came upon one that was very simple; it only took a second to figure out. I had already prepared myself for thirty seconds of concentrated thought for each new concept, so I stopped and wondered, "Why did they bother with that? It was so simple." It threw me off completely.

In the course of reading, I develop expectations about what's going to come next. Sometimes, when I read a book by two authors, I can tell when the second author has written a chapter. Suddenly, after having read one author's writing, my expectation of what will be developed next doesn't match the text. I'm thrown off, my strategies are wrong. I'm not even aware I had any expectations up to that point.

I often read a chapter of a computer science book thinking, "Can I make a lecture out of this? Would this take up an hour and fifteen minutes?" I read that way often. I read what interests me, and I also teach what interests me. I'll read about a hundred pages of a book to get the big picture, then go back and read it a second time for details, for examples. My teaching is done by jumping back and forth from theorem to example. I try to be practical for my students, as solid as I can be, rather than too abstract. When I read a textbook for myself only, I usually don't read the examples very carefully. I understand the abstraction, so I'll skim though the examples pretty quickly.

I get very involved reading technical material. It's tiring to read—it's not the type of material I can't put down. An hour session gives me a lot to digest, and it can really inspire me. After that hour, I play with the thoughts I've gained and synthesize them into other ideas I may be working on. I think about how they apply to a curriculum I'm developing, or to the research I'm carrying out in computer science. I'll take the author's abstractions, approach, and manner of thinking, and abstract from them. I mull them over in my mind.

Usually I have two or three technical books going at one time. The books tend to be in different areas within computer science. It's less tiring to read several different authors at a time because they all have different approaches. I like the diversification; it's like stretching between courses. I choose books by browsing through top-rate bookstores which carry current books. I love to look at all the titles—there are always a few that seem exciting. I have one close friend in the field with whom I share titles. We'll exchange books and talk about them together.

Reading is fundamental to what I do. Without reading about new ideas, and attacking new concepts and being replenished by them, my job would be incredibly dull.

SUSAN PETROWICH

Susan Petrowich's daughter, Tara Conyers, relates elsewhere in this book about how she watched her mother read real estate books as part of her effort to rebuild her life after her divorce. Here, Susan remembers reading other books, as well, which provided her with help and guidance during that difficult time.

I was married at twenty-one and had been married for fourteen years when my husband divorced me. I had a seven-year-old daughter and a new baby. Until that time I had lived with feelings of security and certainty and comfort, and when my life changed so abruptly and so dramatically, it was very scary. I had the odd feeling that my feet didn't touch the ground any more, that I was disintegrating, vanishing. It was the first time in my life I felt that strange—my whole body felt strange. I felt like a person who had lived through a disaster and had lost everything.

Finally, after feeling that way for a while, I decided to heal myself. I had to somehow get back the parts of myself I knew were still there, but that I had lost during that time. I needed strength, and reading became my only way out of this situation. All day long I had chattering going on inside my head—my internal thoughts. I was still a prisoner of those thoughts at night as well. When I read, I got to take a break from what I was saying to myself in those endless loops, and I could let new thoughts come into my brain. Reading took me away from where I was and put me in another place. Eventually, I started to feel familiar feelings again; my sense of security slowly came back. If you look at a slow motion picture of something shattering, and then play it backwards in slow motion, that's what reading did for me—it gradually helped put me back together into a whole.

My center was returning. I read spiritual books during that period because I needed to heal my own spirit. I read biographies about strong women—women who had visions and who were out in the world alone. I wanted to find that internal source of power that other women had found for themselves; I wanted to feel connected to them. I had been married for so long, and I had given up a lot of my own life to my husband. I needed to find myself. I needed insight into myself. My therapist said I had been blind, that I had been living each day with blinders on. I had always thought the problem was that I had been deceived, so I began to look seriously at her statement.

I would sit there in the bookstore with the whole psychology section in front of me and go through the titles and the tables of contents of all the books. When something jiggled a part of my brain, I'd go home with the book. I'd read it, put it down, think about it, read some more, and so on. A lot of ideas about how we live in the world started making sense to me during this process. We all go around living life, but if we don't stop and reflect on it, we get into serious problems.

I read Scott Peck's *The Road Less Traveled* for spiritual guidance and his follow-up, *People of the Lie*. I read *The Dance of Anger* by Harriet Lerner to help me cope with the tremendous anger I needed to let go of. I read about verbal self-defense which was fascinating—it helped me pick apart the language we use in interactions to see what we are really saying to each other. If I found a book that I liked, I'd try to get other ones by the same author.

I talked to my daughter about what I was learning from the self-help books. I knew she was hurt from the divorce, so when she was nine and ten I'd sit with her and read her sections from a book I was reading, and then we would talk about it. I would use the book to start the conversation. I wanted to make the discussion sound important and that it wasn't just coming from me. I though she might resent me or resist talking otherwise.

We'd talk about the fact that she can have her own feelings about her dad even though they might be different than mine. It was breaking my heart to see her being split. I knew this was an important time for her, that she had to learn to be her own whole person, too. I found a very good book called *Mom's House, Dad's House*. I told her I was reading it and how it was helping me; I wanted her to know I was not doing so well right then either, but that I was trying to work it out.

Sometimes my daughter would bring the books up later. She'd say, "Remember when you were reading in the book about this? Well, when I was at Dad's house, I had that feeling." She was able to identify it and bring it up because we had read about it in a book together. She caught onto the way this worked, and began using the books I was reading for herself.

Reading for insight is a continuing theme in my life. Developing my mind and spirit and center of personal power allows me to have confidence about my future.

BEN BURTT

Ben Burtt was educated in physics, but became a sound effects fanatic. He has won four Academy Awards for his creation of sound effects in Star Wars, Raiders of the Lost Ark, E.T. The Extraterrestrial, *and* Indiana Jones and the Last Crusade. *In addition to his impressive work on major feature films, he produces his own documentaries, taking the process of making them all the way from the initial idea to the finished product. Here he describes the pleasure and satisfaction he receives from developing ideas for his films through reading and research.*

My mother used to take me to the library frequently. Once, when I was about seven years old, I was at the library reading when somebody from the newspaper took my picture. It got published, and the caption read something like, "Young, studious boy goes to the library each week." Seeing myself in the paper was great reinforcement for going to the library. It was wonderful.

I was always interested in fantasy as a child. I liked imaginary stories of imaginary places—escapism. Many of the ideas I put into films today come from all the time I spent as a kid letting my imagination wander, thinking about imaginary characters and places and things. Besides fantasy, I was also very interested in reading humorous books of all kinds. I read and collected comic books for years, and I think I had every issue of *Mad Magazine* printed from 1952 to 1970.

Although most of my work has been recording sound, I've also worked for twenty years in the visual realm of motion pictures. And now that I've become a writer, director, and editor for documentaries, I have to wear several different hats. Making a film is like taking a course in college. Each film is a new subject and I start out not knowing much about it. First, I try to come up with the idea, then I fine-tune it, put it down

in rough form, edit it to make it better, and by the time the film is released, I feel like I have taken the final exam and graduated. I start out
knowing practically nothing about the subject, so I begin by reading to
add to whatever knowledge I do have. Reading is my main activity when
I start out on a film, and I find that stage is the most relaxed and pleas-
ant time of the film making process. I just leave myself open for ideas; I
clear a space in my mind and say, "OK, book, fill it up." Nobody else is
demanding anything from me, and I'm not trying to make decisions in a
meeting with other people, where I'd have to compromise. The reading
phase is a strictly solo operation in which I'm putting information into
my head and letting it stir up all kinds of other ideas.

I've written several different scripts that deal with historical topics.
Presently I'm working on a nonfiction film about the opening and con-
quering of the American West from the time of Lewis and Clark until the
great land rush at the end of the nineteenth century. It's being produced
for the National Park Service to show at their museum in St. Louis,
which is dedicated to the westward expansion from the Mississippi River
to the Pacific coast.

The film is a redramatization of events which will hopefully stimulate interest so the viewers will go off and find their own books on the
subject. I find, with my kids, that if I tell them a story first about something in history, they'll go to the library and get a book on it because
they've had some vision planted in their minds; they've made some visualization of an event or character which provides a spark of interest for
them.

For this film, I initially started reading the most general history
books on the subject because I was somewhat ignorant of it. I read the
Time-Life books on wagon trains and the American Heritage books on
the frontier. Once I had a general overview, a basic background on the
subject, I started digging into specific topics. I went to a library which
has a tremendous collection of materials on the American West. I found
original, first-hand accounts, letters, and journals. I started reading biographies of the many explorers that went West: the Lewis and Clark
journals, the journals of John Fremont, and the accounts of people who
rode in wagon trains. I had to educate myself by reading enough on the
subject so I could form a valid viewpoint.

So far, I've spent two years of my spare time researching and writing this film and I've spent two months going to the historic sites that
still exist. I followed the Lewis and Clark trail and tramped along the
Oregon trail. I saw what the immigrants saw when they rounded the
corner and viewed the Rockies for the first time. I hadn't realized how
important seeing the actual places would be. It's hard to sort everything
out after reading so many journals and accounts, and I came to a much

better understanding of it all when I went and saw these places for myself. So, in the process of making this film, first there was the general research from books, then the more specific research from reading the original sources in the library, and then there was visualizing the events on location. I'm now rewriting the script based on the new information I learned from going to the sites.

The reading of history has been immensely satisfying to me. I have a strong interest in U.S. historical, political, geographic, and social events as I grope for an identity in this world. Things change so quickly; I study the past to try to get a perspective on the present.

After history, science has always been a subject I've been interested in. I wanted to be a scientist at one time; in fact I trained in school to be a physicist, and also wanted to be be an astronomer. Film making was just a hobby, a form of make-believe that meant I didn't have to grow up. The Peter Pan syndrome. Ironically enough, I've had the chance to do so many films on scientific subjects now that I've fulfilled that destiny, too.

In film school, many students learn to make movies just by watching tons of movies and from making films. Often the only thing they can bring to movies is ideas they've seen in other films, because that is as far as they've looked, whereas those who get away from films, who read and do other forms of study and research for stimulation, for growth and education, can develop viewpoints and story lines that are unique. There's so much information in history that tells you a lot about human nature, that one can easily apply it to making fictional films as well.

Reading to do research for a film is actually a form of entertainment for me. People keep handing me science fiction novels, but I just don't read fiction. Maybe I've had such an outlet in the feature films I do that are all fantasy and make-believe that when I read, I don't want to live in an imaginary universe—I want something substantial. Reading is also a much more effective escape for me than watching movies. I don't go to a movie to relax and forget my cares. Since I make movies, I'm always thinking too much about a movie while I'm watching it. Even though I love movies, I don't find watching them to be as peaceful an experience as reading books.

ATTILA GABOR

As a boy, Attila Gabor traveled with his father, a Hungarian representative, to various Eastern European countries, including Poland and East Germany. He lived in Prague, in the former Czechoslovakia, for four years.

When he was twenty-three, he came to live in the United States. He works as a management assistant, but his passion is international relations. He hopes to earn his Ph.D. in the not-too-distant future.

International relations is living history, and reading about it is more interesting than fiction. A real spy story is much better than James Bond. I am amazed when I see history in front of me. I can stand back and see all the sides of a situation and say, "How could they have not seen that this would be the result?" Of course, I am reading it from hindsight.

Ninety percent of my reading is in the area of international relations and modern history. I think it was in the Kennedy era that someone pointed out that what was on TV is news, but by the time it's in the newspapers, it's history. For me, what's going on right now is international relations. What happened yesterday is the history I need to know to understand today.

I get my information from several sources. For direct access to information, I read e-mail such as *Hungarian Parliament On Line* which is almost like the minutes of what happened that day, and it comes out sooner than the newspapers. For me, it's like living history because I'm seeing it as it happens. I read the newspapers for what happened yesterday, and I read magazines such as *Newsweek* or the *Economist* which usually cover the top stories of the week or month. I also read scholarly journals such as *Foreign Affairs,* which deals with issues going back from a month to several years. And then, of course, there are books. Even the latest book is about two years behind the actual events, but books can provide the in-depth analysis that is useful to understand the whole picture.

With modern technology, there are softwares that simulate historical events with scenario-building capabilities to recreate and rewrite history. What if Hitler would have attacked the Soviet Union a week earlier, or what if the invasion of Britain would have taken place in August of 1940? You change just one little part and let the computer follow the outcome. Of course, this still doesn't prove anything, but it might teach something more to us to look at the theories of what could have happened.

I'm getting to the point, however, that I have to be selective because I think that too much information might actually rob my vision. Take the nationalistic feelings in Bosnia, for example. I don't like to read too many explanations coming out of U.S. scientists or scholars on binationalism in Bosnia because it sometimes gets so theoretical that you actually lose the sense of why the whole thing is happening. When a Serb hates his Muslim neighbor, he is not thinking about the theory that somebody at Harvard created retroactively to explain his feelings. He probably never heard of Harvard in the first place.

I would really miss out on a lot of things if I could not read. I can't even imagine. On the other hand, I would probably try to do more things in real life, rather than passively being involved in them through reading. For example, in the case of travel, you want to do it, but can't afford it, so you just read, read, read about places that you cannot go, like hunting in Africa. It's possible that if you couldn't read about it, but you had this desire, maybe you would actually travel more. Maybe you wouldn't go to such faraway places, but you would go to the near ones.

Of course, when you read, you're trading a fantasy land for reality, and of course the fantasy land is always better. For example, if you read about the jungles of Indonesia, you create a jungle in your own mind and if you go there, you see that the reality does not compare. The one you created is the perfect jungle for you.

This is why I don't go see movies after I've read the book. You create a sinister character when you read a book, but the director, he creates a different character—the perfect sinister character according to him. This short-cuts all the people who read the book. The movie will be very different—it will be a different angle than you imagined, different camera work. Not necessarily better, just different.

As a young boy, I learned Czech by hearing it, by talking to people, whereas German and Russian I learned at a later age primarily from books so I never got them at the native level. In the Czech language, and in English, I primarily communicate through speaking. In these languages I have learned words which I have not ever seen written down, but just learned by watching TV and talking to people. This is contrary to the way I first learned Russian and German. I had to write them and read them, and maybe, on occasion, hear the languages spoken. As a result, the reading is easier for me than the speaking in those languages.

It is true that in both Czech and Hungarian, how you say something is how you write it. The Czech simplified their alphabet in the sixteenth century. It has a Latin origin, just like the English. The only difference is the fonts. In Czech, once you learn a letter, that letter stands for that sound, no matter where you put it in a word, what you put it after, what you pair it with. It's going to be the same. It doesn't become something else like it does in English.

In Hungarian, you have problems in that it is not an Indo-European language. There are sounds that do not occur in the Latin alphabet. Their alphabet has, I think, forty-two letters, contrary to the

English, which has twenty-six. They have letters that would make absolutely no sense in English or in the other European languages.

As far as the grammar, the endings of words, Japanese is the language closest to Hungarian of all the languages I speak. I learned Japanese for only a year, but I have less of an accent in Japanese than in English, which I use every day. Everything is similar in Japanese and Hungarian. In some basic words, there is only one sound difference.

I know I have an accent in English. I came to the United States when I was twenty-three with two of my childhood friends. One of them is a year younger. He has less accent. The other one is two years younger and you have to talk to him for a long time to recognize that he is not native English speaking. If I came a few years earlier, I probably wouldn't have an accent either.

BILL COSTELLO

From among his eclectic reading interests Bill Costello selects baseball as his particular passion. He affectionately labels himself a baseball savant, claiming to have read more books about baseball than any other person on the planet. His secondary reading focus is spiritual enlightenment.

I spent my first three years living with my grandparents because my mother was in the hospital with tuberculosis. My grandmother and my uncle's girlfriend, who was my unofficial aunt, read to me, and my grandfather would tell me great jokes and stories. My grandparents were first-generation, off-the-boat Irish. Their habit was to get the newspaper as soon as they arose in the morning, and go straight to the obituaries. They would sit at the table and say, "Tsk, tsk, tsk. Do you you remember Bridget O'Hara? Oh, she died. Oh, she used to go to church. Oh, she used to play bingo." Irish are very big on death and bingo.

When I was seven I got interested in baseball the way a lot of people get interested in it, from my dad. He wasn't much of a reader since he only had an eighth-grade education, but he did read the sports pages in the *Daily News* and the *Daily Mirror*. I remember him sitting with his coffee and reading the baseball scores to me. Sometimes we would each take a paper and read each other baseball stories back and forth.

I have to credit the game of baseball for my ability to read because the first book I ever read was a rule book—I wanted to know the rules, so I got a rule book and read it, and from then on I read about baseball on my own. I started subscribing to the *Sporting News* when I was nine, so I read that, and eventually, whole books about baseball. My reading had nothing to do with school; baseball was my total focus, my only interest.

Now when I read about baseball, I'm just filling in more little pieces of knowledge to the large mosaic of information I have collected on the subject over the years. I've probably read more books about baseball than anybody on the planet. To me, baseball is more than a game—it's an art form. As someone once said, "Baseball is not a matter of life and death; it's more important than that." Reading a novel is a very different experience from reading about baseball because, with fiction, I don't know what's going to happen next. It's like building a bridge to nowhere; I never know what the next step is going to be.

I read baseball books for entertainment and instruction, but right now I'm reading books about the brain as well. I also read books for spiritual enlightenment, so at any one time I may be reading about baseball, the biology of the brain, and the nature of the soul. Typically, I don't read a single book at a time, but usually have three going at once. I'll read some of one, put it down, and the next night I'll pick up and read some of another. I don't always read the whole book; I frequently get half way through and lose interest and just stop reading. Usually this happens with a fiction piece since I read fiction very slowly. I treat it like good food, chewing it slowly to enjoy the flavor.

I read each type of book with a different attitude, a different approach. If I'm reading a book for enlightenment, I will frequently read for a while, then stop and think about the significance of what I've read, what the lesson is, what it means to me. Sometimes, with books about philosophical and spiritual ideas, I read only a sentence at a time because books that talk about the nature of the soul, the purpose of life, the road to enlightenment are dense, packed with meaning. One sentence can stop me. I'll say, "Well, how 'bout that?" Then I'll have to sit and ponder it for awhile.

I took Tuesday off and went to the bookstore. That's my way of having a good time. Some people like to go to the beach, but I like to go to a bookstore and do a lot of sampling in the sections of philosophical and spiritual books. I spent two hours there and probably read a chapter from about fifteen different books, looking for information on the akashic records. It annoys me that some of these books don't have a key word index in the back, which would have made my search much easier. Instead, I had to scan through a chapter that I thought might have it, looking for those two words. I just stood there and read the chapters, doing a rapid search, and then if I actually found something on the akashic records, I slowed down and read it carefully, maybe even twice. I'd get my information and then put the book back on the shelf.

I found out that the akashic records are basically the book of life. Many religions believe that somewhere out there in the ozone there is a book where all of our past lives are recorded, and if you can tap into the unconscious, you can "read" that record. So when people talk about going into past lives, what they're doing is going back and seeing that record. The theory is that all time is recorded; you can go forward into future lives too, if you have the ability. Time is a myth, according to this idea. There was a famous psychic who claimed he could go into a trance and literally see a book that he would read from. He could see himself turning the pages of the book of life and read about a person. He could also see into the future; he got all his information from the akashic record. Anyway, I became fascinated by the topic and spent my time in the bookstore looking it up.

I can spend equal time reading about baseball, as I've discussed, and also about the biology of the brain. I'm fascinated by all three of these subjects.

CHAPTER 8

Those Aware of Their Reading Process

I hardly ever read books from beginning to end. Instead, I look at a book as if it were a box of treasure; I open it up and start looking for things that I need. . . .

Frances Moore Lappé

When literature readers consider the way they read a novel, they most often say, "I just visualize it, I don't know how." But how do they arrive at their visualizations? What do they do in order to visualize? And when information readers are asked how they read a text, they often reply, "I read it slowly and carefully." But how does slow, careful consideration of the text lead to clear comprehension? How do accomplished readers transform a page of black squiggly lines into vivid pictures and abstract thoughts conjured up from their own creative thinking process?

Although avid readers speak passionately of their intense relationship to reading and the multitude of ways their lives have been profoundly affected by the books they have read, few articulate their innate reading processes. Yet it is this subject that most concerns frustrated readers whose poor concentration and comprehension have a direct negative impact on their reading, while indirectly affecting all parts of their lives.

In this chapter, I bring together an eclectic group of fiction and nonfiction readers, each of whom described the process he or she undergoes while reading. Some speak of their approaches to reading, while others describe their specific reading methods, strategies, and styles. Some are reading professionals, who detail their approaches to teaching reading. One describes a book-reading group, while another contrasts learning to read words with learning to read music. Process-aware readers like those in this chapter describe how they generally approach reading, and also provide great detail about their own unique methods of constructing meaning from print while they move through a book or article.

Whether or not they actually articulate personal strategies, skilled readers do employ a variety of comprehension-monitoring techniques to assist them with their reading. I want to describe some

175

of these well-worn techniques here because I think they are relevant and interesting to know, especially if you are a frustrated reader who finds it difficult to comprehend difficult texts.

Throughout reading sessions, skilled readers pause periodically to summarize what they just read, or to clarify parts that didn't make sense. They ask themselves questions and predict what may come next, or consciously review their prior knowledge on the subject to make new information understandable.[20] (See the sections on metacognition theory and schema theory in the introduction to this book.) Some readers pay attention to the numbering devices and time markers used by authors to keep track of the topic. Others use study techniques that include surveying a book or article before reading in order to create a schema for the selection, or looking at the book's organization in order to think of more ways to remember its content. Another technique for remembering involves paraphrasing the content of each selection immediately after reading. While reading is an 'input' process, paraphrasing is an 'output' process. It is the act of summarizing the text that imbeds it into memory. How do skilled readers learn these techniques? Most of them teach themselves without being aware of doing so. In fact, using these processes seems to come naturally to accomplished readers.

One avid childhood reader recalled, "My fourth-grade teacher had us read stories, then she asked us questions. The good students would wave their hands and answer correctly every single time. I was among the hand-wavers". She wondered, "Why aren't everyone's hands waving? This is so simple." Teachers who ask students to read a section of a book and then ask questions to elicit responses from the better students are not *teaching* comprehension, but only *testing* to see which students already understand. The hand-wavers are those who have already taught themselves how to answer correctly. For those students who have not been able to develop their own reading strategies, this sort of testing does little to help. It is the latter students who grow up to become infrequent and passive readers.

Thanks to the work of reading researchers, teachers now understand how to teach specific comprehension strategies and techniques for giving meaning to print, strategies such as the ones described above.[21] I encourage you to think about your own reading strategies while you read the following narratives. Perhaps they will inspire you to discuss your reading process with others and compare notes. It is my intent that the narratives in this chapter, as well as those in Chapter 7, will motivate avid readers to share their reading strategies with others, especially with frustrated readers. Active readers may develop a new perspective on their own reading and less successful readers may gain access to the processes of more effective reading.

MAXINE HONG-KINGSTON

Maxine Hong-Kingston is a creative and talented author. Her award-winning books, The Woman Warrior *and* China Men, *blend together myths, tales, stories, and her own family's history handed down from her parents and other members of the Chinese American "talk-story" community where she was born and raised. Her latest book,* Tripmaster Monkey: His Fake Book, *is a novel set in the 1960s. During this oral interview, Ms. Hong-Kingston discusses how she works with the ideas in books and actually engages in combat with them during the process of making those ideas meaningful to her.*

My parents told me wonderful tales and stories all through my childhood, stories that were literary and poetic, like the Chinese culture itself. Some were about little girls being slaves, but they also told inspirational stories about women warriors. Both types came from Chinese history.

The Chinese language is so pictorial, has so many images, that it brought lots of pictures to my mind, to my imagination. When I was very young, my parents taught me to read Chinese words, and I found them easy to learn because each word is a picture and makes sense. Then my father tried to teach me English words, but they didn't make sense because the alphabetic shapes of the words and their meanings were so different from each other. I never understood reading in English until later, when I went to school.

When I read, whether in Chinese or English, I mostly visualize—I picture what the text wants me to see. I don't daydream or make up any old picture, I try to envision as closely as I can the picture the author is describing. The process is fun and different with every book. In some books, the scenes are definite and realistic—the setting of the book is important, so I am careful about how I visualize it. For example, if the author says a door is on the left, then I picture it on the left. If I had put it on the right because the author hadn't yet described where it was, I will rearrange the scene in my mind when I come to the part that says it is on the left. If I have to stop and re-imagine a scene, the flow of the story is broken up, but I enjoy the process anyway.

I let a book wash over me in any way it wants to; I let its rhythms carry me away. When I read like this I feel I experience the book totally. I might be more critical and argue with the author later on when I'm finished, but I don't keep hesitating while I read, saying, "but . . . but . . . but." I recently read *Northanger Abby* by Jane Austen; I didn't have to work at the process, I just let her language become my world; reading this book was like eating ice cream.

I don't just record ideas when I read, I contend with the ideas the book presents; I work with them, engage in combat with them, synthesize them into concepts I already know, and then come up with my own ideas. I engage with the world and develop an original vision. This is the process that writers use.

My latest book, *Tripmaster Monkey: His Fake Book,* is about a reader. The main character, Wittman, is a person who has read all the books that were popular in the '60s, all the books that I, too, read at that time. Hermann Hesse, Walt Whitman, Jack Kerouac, he's read them all. He knows the literature of the Western world, as well as Chinese epics. He thinks about taking the humanitarian values that he's learned from reading and applying them out in the real world. I felt that I had that mission too when I graduated from college with an English major. I knew the engineering majors and the MBA's were going to be able to apply their knowledge, but how was I going to apply mine? How could I change the world so it would be more hospitable to the values I'd learned?

There are other characters from literature who are readers, for example, Madam Bovary and Don Quixote, but look what happens to them: Madame Bovary reads trashy romance novels, and wrecks her life trying to carry out what she has read. I think Flaubert is saying a lot about the power of books with this character. And Don Quixote tries to live out what he reads about knights and chivalry. Again, it's tragic; at the end he throws his whole library of books out the window and sets them on fire in a book-burning fury. I was aware of these two books when I was writing mine. Wittman has wonderful humanist values that he sets out to apply in the real world by putting on a show, which I find much more upbeat than *Madame Bovary* or *Don Quixote.*

I like Virginia Woolf because she does such wonderful things with time and space. She can slow time down, and make it expand. I like William Carlos Williams' poetry and prose, especially *In the American Grain.* I read a lot of poetry—I've read most of the contemporary American poets. Poetry gives me beautiful language; I like the way poets experiment with language, the way they simulate a vision, how they create entire states of being with language. I've been reading Emily Dickinson lately. I think she is a very mysterious, powerful writer. I've also been reading Walt Whitman. In between books, I've read all of Yeats. I really like the rhythms of his language.

I'm going to reread Loren Eisley's *The Immense Journey* because I want to see how he takes scientific information and makes it poetic. I don't think scientific knowledge makes its way into the common, human experience when it remains in scientific language. But when it is made into poetry, it can be assimilated into the larger body of world knowledge.

Many people don't know that reading isn't just for getting information, and that it isn't the same thing as turning on the tape deck in your car, even if you've got *War and Peace* playing. Reading takes more participation than just listening. It's a solitary experience with the solitude of the reader meeting the solitude of the writer.

Stephen Krashen

A university linguistics professor, Stephen Krashen has written over 120 books and articles on second language acquisition and the development of literacy. His own personal history of reading comic books as a child supports his idea that "free voluntary reading is the most powerful tool we have in language education."

When I was in the second grade, I was in the low reading group, the "Bluebirds." My father brought home some comics for me to read, and within weeks, I became an "Oriole." It was a definite turning point in my life. From then on, I became an obsessive reader. My reading was entirely self-selected; my parents never prevented me from reading any particular books.

I think the pattern of my reading was typical. I specialized in one genre or author for a long time, and then I gradually moved on to another. First it was comic books. I was such a fanatic comic book reader that when I visited my friends, I would rather read their comics than play. From comics, I moved to sports stories, especially John Tunis' baseball novels. (I reread *The Kid from Tomkinsville* last month—I found it in my ten-year-old cousin's room, and I was amazed that it was still very good reading.) After sports stories, it was science fiction, a phase that lasted about fifteen years. Now my reading is mostly nonfiction, but it is still obsessive. Like many people, I feel uncomfortable leaving the house without a book, even if I know there will probably be no chance to read.

I think my case history is very consistent with what is known about reading. The research says that how much a child reads is related to their access to books. I grew up with easy access to books. My parents readily supported my reading habit. The research also says that the presence of a model influences reading behavior; when parents read, children read. My parents are still avid readers. The research says, too, that comic book reading is not harmful to school success, and that comic book readers read as much, if not more, than non-comic book readers. I did fairly well in school, and my comic book reading certainly led to other reading.

The research also says that free voluntary reading is our major source of competence in reading comprehension, writing style, grammar, vocabulary, and spelling. While I was not a brilliant performer in English classes, or known to be an outstanding writer, my work in these areas was always considered more than adequate, and my verbal SAT's were respectable. Most important, I am sure that all my literacy development came from reading. I cannot remember learning much from language arts or English classes. I do remember reading ahead while the rest of the class was taking turns reading out loud, and so not knowing the place when the teacher called on me. I also remember what I considered to be pointless exercises in grammar, spelling, and punctuation. I think I knew then that these practices were things you did in school, and that they had nothing to do with real literacy development.

My professional interest in reading began in 1979. I had been working on a general theory of language acquisition; the central hypothesis of this theory is the Input Hypothesis, which claims that we acquire language in only one way, by understanding messages. By 1983 I had gathered quite a bit of evidence supporting this hypothesis for second language acquisition. I happened to read Frank Smith's *Reading Without Nonsense* and was amazed to discover that his view of how we learn to read was very similar to the Input Hypothesis. His evidence was different from mine, which gave more strength to the Input Hypothesis. I read all of Smith's work, all of Kenneth Goodman's work, and started exploring the research literature on sustained silent reading, reading out loud to children, and the effect of living in a print-rich environment, all of which confirmed that reading leads to the acquisition of most literacy-related aspects of language. This is strong confirmation of the Input Hypothesis, a point I have tried to make in several papers. I have even written an article on comic books, an attempt to pay back the debt I owe to this genre.

I am now convinced, from the research, from my own case history, and from the experiences of others, that free voluntary reading is the most powerful tool we have in language education. It is the answer to the literacy crisis. It has been established that there are surprisingly few total illiterates; most people can read and write at least at a basic level, and free reading will increase their competence so they can handle the more sophisticated literacy demands of modern society. Free reading is also the single most important ingredient of both first and second language programs in school. When school programs do not provide a print-rich environment, they become merely a test that students who grow up with books pass, and that less fortunate students fail. And foreign language programs need to incorporate free reading, which will provide the linguistic foundation for the study of literature, and give the student a permanent link with the language so he or she can continue to improve after instruction ends.

GLORIA STEINEM

Gloria Steinem cofounded Ms. *magazine in 1972, and is now its consulting editor. She is the critically acclaimed author of several books, including* Outrageous Acts and Everyday Rebellions, Marilyn: Norma Jean, Revolution from Within: A Book of Self-Esteem, *and her most recent,* Moving Beyond Words. *For nine consecutive years, she was chosen as one of the twenty-five Most Influential Women in America by the World Almanac. Here she explains how her strongest feminist thinking comes less from reading than from "just listening to women."*

I grew up in Michigan, where my father had a little summer resort. In the winter time, we would get into a house trailer and my father would sell antiques on the road between Michigan and either California or Florida. He was a vagabond, a gypsy.

As a result, I didn't go to school regularly until I was about eleven or twelve. My mother had a teacher's certificate in college calculus, which was good enough for any truant officers that showed up. I guess they really didn't care. But I did read all the time at home; I read constantly. My father would buy someone's library in order to get a couple of first editions, and he would stack the rest in moldering piles in the garage. I would go out and just pick anything.

I was completely indiscriminate in my reading. I read a couple of volumes of some fifty-volume history of the Civil War. I read *The Whiteoaks of Jalna* when I was seven—which was crazy. I read all of Louisa May Alcott, who was certainly my favorite author—not just her children's books, but also her adult novels, which were quite feminist and also quite dark in a psychological way. I read a novel by Vina Delmar which had all kinds of sex in it that was endlessly fascinating, even though I didn't quite understand it. I would start a book and not stop until I finished it—just sit up all night. I'd walk around dreaming, living more in the book than in reality. I acquired a huge vocabulary—very out of keeping for my age—but I didn't learn other things such as math and geography, which I still don't know. I was a bit lopsided, to put it mildly.

Of course, I wanted to be like other kids, so I regretted not going to school and having a house like they did. But in retrospect, I think I escaped a lot of brainwashing by not going to grade school. If you aren't told you can't do something, you just don't know that you can't. I didn't learn geography, but I also didn't learn what girls "couldn't" do.

I used to read *Little Women* and *Gone with the Wind* every year from the time I was six until my early teens. Those two books were my friends, and reading them each year was like visiting my friends. Aside from one girlfriend whose parents were farmers in a tiny little town nearby, I didn't really see people my own age until I started regular school.

I can now see how *Little Women* was a book about a society of women—excused by the fact that it was wartime, of course—in which women discussed all the subjects of life. That book gave me the idea that women are interesting, and could support each other. But once I was presented with the "feminine" role that comes with being a teenage girl, I shut down in spite of knowing better. I sort of went underground.

The first readings that blew the top of my head off were the feminist essays of the late '60s and early '70s. I had that wonderful feeling of "Ah hah," or "That's why!" very often in those days. I think that the fact so many of us had those kind of insights so late in our reading lives can be attributed to the absence of women's experience from most of what we had read in school. For instance, when it comes to aging, we've been presented with the culturally "masculine" pattern of being rebellious in youth and growing more conservative with age. We've been led to believe that's the *only* pattern. But of course it isn't. The culturally "feminine" pattern has been just the opposite—being conservative in youth, and getting more radical with age.

Even though that feeling of "Ah hah" that sometimes comes from reading is very valuable, my ideas come from the habit of looking at gender politics, not especially from reading. For instance, one day I was talking to a woman who believes in channeling, who maintains that certain people can communicate with those who are dead. As I was talking to her, I realized that women channel men, and men channel men—but I have not yet discovered a single woman who channels another woman. I think women are gaining authority unconsciously by putting their own wisdom in the mouths of men, because then it will be taken more seriously. Once I got into the habit of looking at the politics of gender and race and class and sexuality, these understandings came easily. It's like opening the other eye. If you look at the world as if women matter—or as if everyone matters, instead of just 10 percent of white men as we're educated to believe—then you see a much wider and deeper reality. Looking at the world in this way is what encourages me to write so other girls and women won't have to wait so long to see themselves in what they read.

I also get a lot of ideas from just listening to women. If we tell our stories—what happens to us, our problems, if we just listen to each other—we discover our shared patterns. That helps us to know that we're not crazy, the system is crazy. Our experience is real.

I also think it's possible that some people read too much. Reading can become a drug, because you're not acting; everything is coming in and nothing is going out. Reading isn't completely passive because you're using your imagination, but there is the danger of becoming passive when you're reading too much. There's nothing that can't be overdone, no matter how good it is. Balance is the key.

For instance in the late '60s or early '70s when I was in a television studio doing some kind of show, I met a young man who asked me, "What do you do?" I said, "I'm a writer." He said, "Well, then I wouldn't know your work." At first I thought he was being sort of hostile, but he went on to explain that he was trying to spend five years without reading anything. He didn't want to have the commentary on something before he experienced it himself—he didn't want anything to filter out his own experience.

If reading allows you to expand and enlarge and empower yourself, then it's life-giving. But if reading becomes a way of ignoring and covering up your true self, then it's very negative. If reading is a substitute for acting, being original, thinking your own thoughts—or if you have too much respect for what you read—it's not good. I can't remember where I saw this quote, but it's this: "We read to know we're not alone." Myself, I read to find lights along the path. We all read maps, though each journey is our own.

DEBBIE RUSKAY

After being pressured as a child into intellectual accomplishment by her father, Debbie Ruskay dropped out of college. Fifteen years later she returned when she decided to earn a teaching credential. She currently teaches in a difficult inner-city elementary school where she feels the children are most in need of her talents and energy.

Every summer when I was a kid, my father took us to the free outdoor Shakespeare festival in Central Park. Each night for three weeks before the performance, he would make us go through the play scene by scene, line by line. I understood *Richard III* before I was ten. But it was torture to read the plays this way; I hated doing it because I was forced to. I had been taught to respect my father's and his father's tradition of thinking that one had to know Shakespeare to know anything about reading, so I couldn't contradict him. He also felt I had to be familiar with Beethoven and Vivaldi to know anything about music. Although I eventually gained the love of intellectual accomplishment from him, he didn't give it to me with any softness at all. He constantly corrected my speech, and said that having a New York accent was like being a heathen. All his pressure backfired later when I went to college because I dropped out. I didn't go back until my thirties, when I decided to get a teaching credential.

I see reading as the key to opening the doors of the world. Without being able to read, a person runs into concrete walls. Initially from my courses on teaching reading, and now from my own experiences as a teacher, I have come to understand what teaching reading is all about. Mostly, it's about respect for the students, for the experiences they bring to school which I, as the teacher, have to tap into. Also, as a teacher, I am a role model, and it's very important that I, myself, believe in the value of reading.

When I started teaching, I decided I wanted to surround my kids with books, so I began going to thrift stores to collect them for twenty-five or fifty cents apiece. Now I have hundreds of books in my class-room, and I've learned what my kids will read and what they won't. I may bring in twenty-four copies of *Black Beauty*, but my kids will pick out the adventure stories instead. They like books that are either funny, or have big print, or are not too long, or that other kids have liked. When kids pick out their own books, they don't necessarily choose the best quality literature, but I've learned to respect their own reading choices. If they started out as nonreaders and are now reading some-thing, I don't care what they read. I will still buy books I think they should read because I believe in having them around, but I won't force anything on them.

I have tricks to get them to read. Every time one of them reads a book, they get to add a circle to the "bookworm" that runs around my room. I tell them in the beginning of the year that when the bookworm goes completely around the room, I'll throw a party that will make Christmas look like they were asleep. So they all work together. It's De-cember now and they're about a third of the way around the room al-ready.

I also teach my kids to care about the books. I tell them that I care about my books, and that I don't want them ruining the bindings. I tell them to respect the books themselves, as well as the words inside. I still haven't gotten them to think books are more valuable than a ghetto blaster, but I can continue to show them how I value them. Since I am an important figure in their lives, they pay attention to me and take care of the books without a fight. When they come to love a certain book, I've noticed they do treat it very well.

I've learned from my fourth graders that you can read in many different positions. They sprawl all over the room, get into every nook and cranny. In the beginning, I made them sit at their desks. Then one day a kid pulled out a rug scrap and started to read on it. Now they all do it. They lie on their stomachs and curl up next to somebody and read. They'll read like this for a solid thirty minutes. To me, this is a miracle.

I have some kids whom I'd call readers even though they cannot do the phonics. For example, I have one kid who is at the first-grade level reading group, yet she reads other books, too. Most teachers would call her a nonreader, but I'll swear up and down that she is a reader—she just can't do the tests. I could have listened to all the talk in the teachers' room, or read her folder or her test scores, and I would have had certain expectations of what she could or could not do. But since I didn't, I had only the highest expectations of her. I expect a lot from all my kids. I'm not going to say, "That's OK honey, you just sit there with this first-grade reader." If I had said that to this girl, she would never have become a reader. My kids have taught me not to be ruled by other people's expectations of them, which is a particularly important lesson to learn with inner-city, immigrant, nonwhite kids.

I wish that schools would just let kids read. I wish that reading was taught with literature, and that social studies books weren't so dry. Right now I'm reading a book to my kids called *Indian and the Cover* while we're also studying Native Americans. The book is about a boy who learns things about Native American culture through his friendship with an Indian. He comes to respect tepees and the languages of the different tribes. The book breaks down all sorts of stereotypes, and my kids are learning more about Native Americans from having this novel read out loud to them than they'd learn through twenty lessons on the subject. I know even for myself, I won't read an historical book on World War II, for example, but I will sit down and read a novel about that time. This seems so obvious to us as adults, but as educators we tend to miss this point. Schools are sometimes very backward institutions.

For the last couple of years, I've been primarily reading kids' books myself because I want to be able to suggest books to my students and converse with them about what they're reading. I had just read a book from the Susan Cooper series when one of my kids got it out of the library and read it too. He and I had a three-sentence exchange about it, which made the other kids want to know what we were talking about.

Now one of them might pick it up because of this conversation. I love reading the kids' books. They're very direct, and I always learn a lot. Now I'm reading kids' science fiction. These books have the same battles between dark and light that you find in adult science fiction, but they have a simplicity that makes them very accessible.

The more I read, the more I know how to talk, how to present myself, how to teach. Reading opens up new worlds of ideas, and makes my own world a lot broader. It pushes me to have new thoughts, and enables me to bring others into my own thought process.

TEMPLE GRANDIN

In her book, Emergence: Labeled Autistic, *Temple Grandin describes her experiences as an autistic child—her refusal to be touched or held, her inability to speak, her constant screaming and violent tantrums, and her frustration at trying to communicate her thoughts to others. Fortunately, she had excellent teachers and therapists, and a patient and caring mother, so that by age four her behavior was mostly normal. She is a professor of animal science and is recognized internationally for her outstanding work designing livestock handling facilities for meat packing plants, feedlots, and ranchers.*

Autism is a developmental disorder caused by abnormalities and immaturities of the cerebellum and limbic system. The cerebellum is the part of the brain that involves balance and sensory modulation. When I was a child, I had trouble speaking—I just couldn't get my words out. I could understand what people said to me, but I couldn't say anything back. It was like a big stutter. My worst problems were over by about age three, and the trouble I had with speaking didn't have any effect on my reading. Some autistic kids learn how to read before they can talk. The upper 20 percent of autistics aren't retarded; they have normal intelligence or better, and can function very well if they get the right training. A few nonverbal autistic people who were considered retarded have been taught to read phonetically, and turned out to be really smart. They have even received a high school education; they couldn't talk, so they just used a typewriter.

When it came to my reading, Mother was the most important person. She taught me how to read when I was in the second and third grade. She worked with me, and gradually I learned to sound out my words. If I hadn't learned phonics, I would never have been able to read.

As an autistic, I think totally visually, so memorizing nonvisual symbolic information is very difficult. I could have never memorized a whole bunch of words. Instead, I memorized the fifty phonetic sounds; it was hard, but there's only fifty of them. I remembered my alphabet by singing it since I have perfect pitch and can duplicate any tune (even though I have problems with coordination and rhythm). I had to learn that 'a' has two sounds, and some other rules, like when there's an 'e' on the end, the vowel's long, or if two vowels are together, then you've got 'oo' or 'ee'. Yes, it was hard to learn those rules, but there's not many of them. Then you've got things like 'br' and 'cr' and 'pr'. I assign a visual picture to each sound. For example, for 'd' I make a picture of a dog. I can remember 'dr' as dark and grey. For 'f' I see a picture of a fork, and for 'fr' there's a man named Frank.

We were a reading family so I was read to from an early age, and Mother worked with me on reading every day. She'd read a paragraph out of a book, then she'd have me sound out a sentence. As my reading got better, I'd read more and she'd read less. She'd stop right in the exciting part and get me to read on. We did this every afternoon for about half an hour. Once I learned how to read, I became a very good reader.

Now I read very, very fast, and my comprehension is excellent, but I do have a terrible problem with sequence. I don't like to read romance novels because I can't follow all the interrelationships between the characters: If Jane and Johnny love each other and they split up and somebody else hates one of them, I have trouble remembering the sequence. I have to have a visual image for abstract concepts such as getting along with people. For example, my visual image for relationships is a sliding glass door—if you push too hard it will break.

I would much prefer to read a book with a straightforward plot, and very few subplots—a story describing the pioneers going across the country in covered wagons, for instance. I liked *Clan of the Cave Bear*—that's my idea of good fiction: tons of description and a plot that's not too complicated. I have trouble with history because if I read about a series of wars, I can't remember the sequence. I'd much rather read descriptions of how people lived. I like science fiction because I can make pictures of things I've never seen before, that nobody's ever seen.

I'm not a verbal thinker; I don't think in words, I think in pictures. That's why I'm one of the leading equipment designers in the meat industry, because I can see things in my mind. Somebody asked me yesterday, "How did you make up that idea for the hydraulics on the gates?" Well, I just saw a picture of it in my head. People who are verbal thinkers don't see the equipment all built in their minds, but when I make a drawing for a piece of equipment, the entire thing is already built in my mind. I can just play the pictures in my mind, like putting a tape in a VCR. I put people in the picture, and then put cattle in it, and see how everything works together. And if someone said, "The such-and-such company built a new secret cattle-handling system, but you're not allowed to look at it," I can tell you right now, if I got to look at it for five seconds I'd have it memorized perfectly.

I'm also really good at reading a whole pile of journal articles and making all the information fit into one big picture, at integrating all the papers I read on a subject. If I have to do a review of the literature on a subject I don't know anything about, I read maybe a hundred journal articles and I write what I call "bottom lines" for each one on little scraps of paper. I put the scraps in a basket and mix them up. Then I take them out one by one and stick them on a bulletin board to see how studies that seem unrelated fit together in new patterns. Papers that at first appear to conflict, really don't. I just see a picture of it all, and it becomes super obvious to me. I make a picture of the hundred journal articles on the bulletin board and I remember it totally. Once I understand the field, I can just add a new paper to the board, and modify my picture with the new data.

I'll tell you how I make mental pictures. Let's take the science magazine I have right here. Here's an article called, "The Political Animal: Social Intelligence and the Growth of the Primate Brain." OK, political animal: I saw a bunch of animals sitting in Congress in the Capitol Building. OK, social intelligence: With *social* I saw some people at a cocktail party, and for *intelligence* I saw an IQ test. OK, the growth of the primate brain: I saw a monkey and then I saw a brain. Now it goes on to say, "Almost four million years ago, hairy creatures with long arms and low brows and jutting faces stood on two legs and began to stroll across the African plain." OK, what do I do with a word like *almost*? If I can't make a picture for a word, I just see it in print on a piece of paper in my mind. Basically, I see a picture of everything I'm reading. When I read scientific material, I see pictures of the experiments.

I have a terrible time with algebra because I can't see a picture of it; it's too abstract, I just can't do it. I'll give you an example of how I picture numbers. I've got three different ZIP codes here in town, one for my home, a different one for my mailbox, and another one for the university. OK, the last part of my home ZIP is twenty-six. Twenty-six is half a deck of cards, so I imagine cards scattered on my lawn. OK, the last part of the post office ZIP is twenty-one, which is also the drinking age, so I imagine a bunch of teenagers drinking in the parking lot of the post office. I am a visual thinking expert. I've talked to people who are verbal thinkers who do not believe that I think in pictures. They've got no pictures in their mind at all. They only think in words and sounds, which I find unbelievable.

Since I can't do math, I couldn't get an engineering degree, but I can do designing. I've found that people who can do the math can't do designing because they can't see the finished equipment in their minds. I've seen major design mistakes in meat packing plants that to me were just stupid. I thought, "Couldn't they see it?" Now I realize that they can't. But the price of my gift is that I can't do higher math.

Einstein had a lot of the traits of autism. He probably would be labeled autistic today. Look how weird he acted: He did his theories by visualization, his math was not that great, and he didn't even speak until the age of five.

MARTHA LANE

Martha Lane is nationally recognized as a leader in the field of adult literacy and currently specializes in computer-based learning and training. She rarely visualizes the characters in the many books she reads, but instead experiences them aurally, listening for how their voices reveal their inner workings.

I love to travel. I would love to travel in outer space, or inner space, or any old place. I love to read science fiction because it takes me far away. But when I read, I don't see anything except the print. I do not visualize the spaceship arriving on some planet, but I do imagine sounds—I don't think I've ever heard a voice, but I hear the sound of the spaceship's engine, the slamming of its door. I also get into the characters' emotional states. I feel the expectations of the characters as they leave the spaceship. I feel their anticipation of confrontation, of victory or defeat, of love or hate.

Sometimes truth is more interesting than fiction. I like Studs Terkel very much because I like to read about people I wouldn't necessarily otherwise meet. The oral histories in his books, like *Working,* are fascinating. I meet people through his books whom I could hardly even imagine, people who live and work in places I've never been or would be afraid to go to, people I wouldn't understand or even notice if I were there. I guess you could say that reading Studs Terkel's stories is a way of traveling. But again, I don't see the people in his stories, although I do feel the conflicts they have and try to imagine their lives. Say I read a story told by a waitress. She might describe conversations between some of the people who came into her restaurant. Well, while I'm reading I try to imagine what I would say to those people myself. I don't see them, I just feel their presence.

I like to know what people's underlying values are and how different people handle value conflicts, so I read biographies and autobiographies. I have my favorites: Albert Camus, Albert Schweitzer, and Albert Einstein—my three Albert friends. Albert Camus considered himself to be an atheist, and he said if Christians believed what they say they do, there would be no hungry children in the world. Camus also taught me that the world deserves to know why I do things the way I do, why I act the way I do, that I should be prepared to explain myself. Albert Schweitzer had a love for nature. He said that everything has a purpose so you shouldn't go stomping on things. I still don't have any trouble stepping on ants, but I do see his point of view. He helped me feel a reverence for life. As for Albert Einstein, I'm not a scientist, and I had a lot of trouble with chemistry in school, but I'm impressed with his concept of order in the universe, including the idea that chaos is order. He would go lay on a couch and stare into space, be absolutely oblivious to everything and everybody around him, and visualize the galaxies. He could see things crashing together. I try doing that and I don't see a thing.

Religion is important to me. I like to read about Mother Teresa. Even if I do not get up at 4:00 A.M. the way she does, I consider her to be a role model. She reminds me that one person can do a tremendous amount if she has a vision, that there is always a way around red tape. She's very good at getting right to what people really think, what they really need, what they can really do. I've been greatly affected by reading the Alberts and Mother Teresa. I learned from them that what I believe should be reflected in some way in everything I do.

I read novels the way I watch movies—I read and forget them. I will usually read the whole book though, unless it bogs down in description. I can't stand description since I don't visualize, but I absolutely love the dialogue. I'll buy a book, start reading it, and skip all the description. But when I get to the dialogue, I slow down and read at a luxurious pace, savoring every sentence. When I was in high school my father dictated that I would take a speed reading course, so I glance at everything and pick up two or three key words on a page in the boring parts; at least I will know where the characters are and what their names are. But if I get lost, I do not go back.

I grew up on a farm and I had to make up my own ways of entertaining myself. I lived miles and miles from theaters and stores, so reading was a way for me to escape, to travel, to have adventures. If I had my own way, I would like to see everything that's on the earth and in the galaxies in my lifetime. Everything.

ROSA COUPE

The eldest of seventeen children, Rosa Coupe quit school at nine to be a second mother to her siblings in Guadalajara, Mexico. She met her North American husband when he was visiting her neighbor on a vacation from college. They decided to marry even though they didn't speak each other's language. She has lived the United States for thirty-one years, has two adult sons, and helps run the family business.

My father was a truck driver and only came home in time to make another child. He wasn't around when the children were born. A couple of times, I helped deliver the babies. We didn't even have electricity and I had to hold the candle.

By the time I was in the third grade, we were having a very hard time surviving—by then there were already seven little kids around. There was not enough money in the house, so my mother had to do a lot of sewing. She would sew up to twenty-five dresses a week and I was doing all the hem work. And she knew that she needed me to take care of the kids. She told me with tears in her eyes that she need the help and anyway, education is not all that important in a woman even though she herself had a high school diploma. She said as long as I learn to clean house, to cook and to be a mother, I was going to be OK in life. She said, "You don't need anything more. The boys are the ones who need the education because they are the ones who grow up and look for jobs to support their family. In a girl, this is not necessary." That hurt so bad. I didn't say anything; I just cried.

Even though I didn't have the opportunity to go to school, I always loved to read, but I can't remember how I learned to read so well. I knew my ABC's early on and I put words together by myself. In Spanish, it's a lot different than in English, because the sounds are easier to learn.

Maybe I could read because I always enjoyed cooking and reading cookbooks. My grandmother was a wonderful cook. And I always looked for recipes in magazines. I guess I put one and two words together and figured out the recipes or I asked people, "What this word means?"

I even taught my little brothers to read. I picked up their school books when they came home from school and read to them. I probably got my education from reading their books to them and teaching them. Every time they have problems, I corrected them. When I was a thirteen-year-old-girl, I felt like a twenty-five-year-old mother. Even today, I feel like I'm their mother, they feel so close to me. My opinion is still important to them. They look at me like I'm somebody really special.

When my mother was sewing, she tell me to take the measurements from the people, so I had to measure and write down the waist, the bust, the hips, the shoulder, the length. All that helped me tremendously; I was always great with math, maybe because of the sewing. By the time I met my husband, I was sewing without patterns. My mother never used any patterns.

I did not have a chance to enjoy my teenage life or relax and have a good time. My parents never allowed me to go out much. So on Sundays after I cleaned house and go to the church, I used to come back and read novels about love. That was my afternoon, laying in bed reading. Those novels made me dream a lot. Let me tell you, I never dreamed I would ever be in the United States and talking English.

My husband Bruce and I are like day and night, but we love each other very much. It was very difficult for me to come into his world. I didn't have any formal education and my type of living was different from his type of living.

That first year was very difficult for me because I was only beginning to learn English. I tried to go to adult school, but since the semester was almost ending, most of the people in the class knew more than I did. I got words mixed up like *six* and *sex*. The teacher told my husband to try to explain to me the difference because I was embarrassing the class. He got upset and told the teacher, "If she could do it, there wouldn't be any reason for her to come to school." I never went back after that one night.

I was all alone in the house during the day that whole year. After I finished the housework, I used to watch television and read *Look* magazine. I'd pick up one new word every day to keep in my mind. I'd ask right away, "What this mean?" I remember my first word: I was watching television, the "I Love Lucy" show. I did not understand anything they say, but I figured that sooner or later something is going to stay in my mind. The first word was *sticky fingers*. I asked my mother-in-law what it meant and everybody laughed.

The next day I learned something else. Little by little I learned. Of course everything was backwards because I did it like in Spanish. Instead of "Bruce's mother," I'd say, "the mother of Bruce." When I was reading it was hard for me to understand because everything seemed backwards. But I learned. Now I can read any book that you give me. At first I had a dictionary, but it was too difficult to use, so I quit using it and asked Bruce, "What this mean? What that mean? What is this?" And I just put things together.

Bruce always make me feel strong. He always make me feel special. I was always trying to prove myself because I'm pretty insecure from not having an education. I would read and tell him things and he used to ask me, "Where did you hear that?" "I have read it in the paper." Then he would have a big smile showing to me that he was proud of me.

And now of course, it's very normal that I read. There hasn't been one night that I don't take something to read to bed. I always, always have to bring something to bed. I take anything. I read newspapers, true stories in magazines, books. I have a few prayers I bring from Mexico. And recipes—if I'm going to be doing some cooking, I bring three or four of my cookbooks and I look for recipes.

In our business I deal with bankers and I deal with lawyers. I know I do not have the education that I should, and so it's kind of scary sometimes. But Bruce keeps telling me, "Good job, Honey." I think if I had got an education I would have been something special. People don't take me seriously sometimes, and I feel insecure because of my background. If I continued to go to school, I could have done something more with my life. But I'm not complaining. I have a very good life.

KOSTA BAGAKIS

Kosta Bagakis, the oldest son of peasant Greek immigrants, is a college philosophy instructor and student of life who reads to understand the historical and philosophical connections among his own work, heritage, and worldview. To Dr. Bagakis, "Books are intense, mini-human beings, and bookstores are the souls of humanity."

I love reading. I think it's one of the most wonderful activities that human beings have developed. When I go on a vacation, the first thing I do is get my reading list together. Whenever I leave the house I take enough reading material with me to occupy myself during a five-hour traffic jam. I keep telling myself I should get a little flashlight so I could sit and read if I get stuck in an elevator.

As a Greek immigrant child I felt isolated from the world. Since I was the oldest child in my family, I lost out in terms of attention, so I decided to excel in school instead. The other members of my family were all nonreaders, but luckily I learned to read fairly rapidly since I was shut out from my family. I found my life in books. When my family went to an event, I sat at home and read. I got praise from them for reading, and they often asked me what I read. Eventually, I gained a great amount of power in my family because they would ask me about issues and problems, and I'd tell them what I thought.

I was passive in school; teachers imposed readings on me and I accepted them. My school life was separate from my private life. When I read something that was directly related to my private life, I came alive, and I still do. Right now I'm reading about the Trojan War, and since I'm Greek, that era is part of my heritage. Those heroes are a part of me, and I want to make them clear in my mind so I can understand myself better.

I made sporadic attempts at being an active reader when I was in school, but I had decided that the reading I was supposed to do would not be interesting, so I wouldn't really read it, and there was no one in school to explain how it might be different. I never trusted adults because I felt they were always trying to manipulate me. For example, a high school teacher once tried to force me to read *Silas Marner* without first telling me how the book could possibly connect with my life, so of course I hated reading it. Reading can't be imposed without a context.

By this point in my life I've created my own context for my reading. I have a plan, a specific reason for everything I read: I want to understand my history, my heritage, my job, my worldview. I want to get it all clear and I believe everything is interconnected, so if I'm reading about math, for instance, I try to see how the major mathematical issues fit into my understanding of philosophy and history. All of my reading is focused on my attempt to understand the world.

I maintain that reading is a social act. A book won't stay in my head unless I tell a friend about it, so I like to find other people to read the books I'm reading so we can talk about the ideas together. Sometimes, it's as if we've read different books, our ideas are so different. I have never read a book without sharing it with others—never.

I underline passages in my books that I want to share with others. Depending on my mood, and the book, I underline either a lot or just a little. Sometimes I put a number one in front of important parts; I may mark a reference or a nice phrase, but I only underline something if I expect I will go back and use it.

I used to have a different procedure when I picked up a book: First I would look at the cover and get whatever information I could from it. Then I looked at the table of contents to see if I liked the chapter titles. Next I looked at the references at the back to see what books the author had read before writing it. Then I would read the whole book cover to cover, every word. About seven or eight years ago I was talking to an old teacher about this method of reading and he said, "Just read the part of a book that tells the information you want. You don't have to read everything unless you have the time, or you like the author's style." I was amazed. I rarely read any book from cover to cover any longer.

Every book has its own language, its own vocabulary, its own set of assumptions. I may wonder why an author uses a particular word, but if I keep reading, I'll eventually understand it, and may even begin to use the word myself to express that certain thought. As long as I understand the language in a book, I can understand the material. I take in the information as it is given; I don't restate it in my own words, even though I often think it could have been said in a more direct way.

Reading passively without thinking about what I'm reading is a waste of my life force. If I want to be passive, I'll watch TV. Although it often exhausts me, reading can also make my energy extremely high. Sometimes I have to take a walk after I've read a book that is life-changing. An author can touch me most when he or she explains my connection to the world or expresses my feelings—those feelings I don't usually talk to other people about. A book won't touch me if it's too general.

Each book represents an individual's concentrated attempt at presenting his or her point of view. I can't think of anything else that human beings do that focuses their souls and their understanding of the world more than writing books. Books are intense, mini-human beings, and bookstores are the souls of humanity.

THOMAS (GUS) OWENS

As a professional musician, Gus Owens has traveled around the world playing trumpet with Ray Charles, Max Roach, Art Blakey, and other great jazz musicians. He composes his own lyrics and music and says "reading books and reading music are essentially the same."

My father was a grocery store merchant, so I started as a clerk at the age of seven. He taught me weights and measures, retail and wholesale—all this before I started school. My father learned to read from his father, who started an insurance company. My father would put a book in my hand and have me read it, and then he'd have me tell him the story I'd just read. And my mother was constantly reading to me. This was in Texas in the late 1930s and I was very fortunate to have been born so very well put together for a black child in those times.

I used to write poems all over the walls in my bedroom as a child, just putting words together. I'd take a word and write phrases around it, or I'd take a word and use it as a topic and try to write as much as I could about that word. I just did it on my own.

My father and my mother both played guitar and they would sit and practice when the store was closed, but my father didn't like it when I told him I wanted to become a musician. He wanted me to become a businessman. But I just didn't want to get up at six in the morning and work until eleven at night. So instead I picked a profession where I worked all night and was on the road a lot.

Back in high school I was like most kids who want a little bit of freedom—I didn't do anything in high school except have fun. I stopped reading because I was tired of it and smart enough to read the title and figure the rest out. Or I'd speed read and go through a book and find a sentence in the paragraph that pertained to the title and it worked for me. I got through with a B+ because I had done so much reading up until high school.

Reading books and reading music are essentially the same to me. When I read a book I see the action, I reproduce the action in a book by reading it. And if it's written well, then I also have an image of what the characters look like. When I read a musical sheet, I hear it rather than see it. With music I read one instrument all the way through and listen to the story the instrument is telling me. When I write a musical sheet, I hear it as I write it. When people read my music, they should be able to hear what was in my head when I wrote it, and they should be able to hear the instrument, say the soprano sax, that I wrote it for.

A musical score happens when you put a number of instruments onto the same sheet. You read a score by reading each instrument separately, but you hear it all at the same time, if you're good. That's ear training, which is hard to explain. You know the key immediately, and you know the sound of each note, so you can sing it to yourself if you're trained. A trained musician can also listen to individual instruments playing, say in a symphony, and can hear what each one is doing separately. A layman would just hear the thing as a whole.

Reading music has its differences from reading a book, too. You can read a paragraph in a book and not understand it, but there's no way to read a sheet of music and not understand it. Reading music is reading sounds. To read a song you have to reproduce the sound, and to do that you must read and understand each line. You hear it in your head. The difference is that reading a book is about comprehension and reading music is about hearing.

There are a lot of great musicians who can't read. Did you ever hear of the great Earl Garner? He was a great pianist, but couldn't read. If you can't read words, you can't read music. Reading is reading.

Recently, I had a young student who was having problems with reading because his mother was on drugs. I wanted to help so I went out and looked for a program for the mother. I found a program and she went into it, but when she was there, she didn't like what they were doing. They claimed to be a drug and alcohol rehab facility, but they are not. It seems they're getting these women who are already hooked on drugs and they're using them as prostitutes. When she came back and told me this, I didn't believe her at first, so I went and started asking questions. But when I asked questions, they refused to answer, or they tried to divert away from answering and get belligerent. I thought, "They're concealing something." I went to the proper authorities and they are now investigating it. This is really true.

Now I am trying to write a book about this unfortunate situation because it is exploiting young women. I got the courage to write a book because I have written so many lyrics in the past. Writing the lyrics is what lets me know I can write a book. I looked at the stack of lyrics and songs I've written and knew I could write a book. I know the English language well, although I'm not the greatest speller, but then there's always the dictionary.

I would hate to imagine my life without reading. I can't ever imagine being a street person. I feel so fortunate being able to read. If I hadn't learned to read when I was young I wouldn't have become the jazz and classical musician I am today—maybe I would have gone into rock 'n roll.

NIAMH FITZGERALD

A financial analyst, Niamh Fitzgerald spends her working hours reading financial papers, research reports, and corporate prospectuses. In her off-hours, however, she indulges her taste for literature. Here she describes not only the influences which shaped her interest in literature as she was growing up, but also how she finds people to share her reading interests with today.

I was six when my family came to the United States. My Aunt Peg stayed behind in Ireland, but maintained contact with me by sending books for every occasion—birthdays, Christmas, graduations. I didn't understand the books sometimes, and used to think there was something wrong with me, but in retrospect, I think my Aunt Peg didn't know what books were age appropriate.

Over the years, she sent lots of Irish writers. She promoted Irish writers; she would never send anything English or American. I remember one series of schoolgirl books that took place in an Irish boarding school, for instance. Later, I studied literature in college, and when I finished, I went to Ireland to study Anglo-Irish literature. I still today get an Irish journal.

My Aunt Peg had a profound effect on my life—she gave me my love of reading and literature and words. She gave me a wonderful gift. I'm still in touch with her. She's eighty-six now. I have a goddaughter who I have tried to encourage to read in the same way as Aunt Peg did for me. I have given her books to read. She's only fifteen now, but she writes poetry. I hope the books have helped her a little.

Besides Aunt Peg, I had a literature professor in college who was also a major influence on my reading. I'm still friends with him, in fact. He was teaching Melville, Whitman, and Hawthorne when I took his course. The way he taught was inspirational. He would recite pieces of the literature from each of the authors; a phrase would come to his mind to emphasize a point during a lecture, or he would read a paragraph from a book.

He also would say, "Don't try to understand everything, just read and understand as you can. If you stop and deliberate over it, you lose the context of the whole work. Just be as open as you can to the book." I took this seriously and even now I sometimes read a book I don't like or don't understand. That happened with Rushdie's *Satanic Verses*. I did not get that book. It was frustrating, but I pushed my way through it. My book group read it together and I went to the group even though I had trouble with it because they wanted me to tell them why I didn't like it. Everybody else was talking about it with great understanding and discussing the themes. It's frustrating for me when others understand and I don't, but I just try to get over it. Sometimes, if I return to the book at a later date, the questions I had about it are resolved.

The book group I go to is pretty old, maybe ten or twelve years. I have only been in it about five years. The way I joined the group was serendipitous. My brother-in-law suggested that maybe I would like to meet a friend of his because she lived near me and also liked to read. I arrived at the restaurant with William Kennedy's *Ironweed* in my hand. It turned out that she was currently reading that book for her book group, so she invited me to the next meeting, and the rest is history.

The group meets every six weeks and rotates houses. Whoever's house it is at makes the lunch and chooses the book. People arrive around one o'clock. You're expected to call if you're not coming, which puts a little pressure on you, which is good. We spend three or four hours discussing and eating. There's a core group of six to eight people who come all the time, but there might be ten to twelve people on any one afternoon. I wouldn't say there's any order to what we read. Sometimes we read classics, but more times we read modern novels. These are nice afternoons that I look forward to.

The discussions start pretty informally. No one thinks up questions ahead of time, but some of us mark parts in the books that we want to discuss. There is one woman who I think of as the center of the group because she tries to keep people focused. She's a writer and so she thinks about books a lot. I admire her. She has a fine intellect and is nice to listen to. I don't always agree with what she says, but I really enjoy her input into the group.

Some books are not so conducive to discussion. I remember when we read *Like Water for Chocolate*. It's a great little book with recipes and the magic realism of other Latin American novels. Reading this book is an experience, but the discussion didn't really go very far. The best books for discussion seem to be the ones in which the characterization is developed, not necessarily the ones with great plots. It's more interesting to discuss how the characters interact in relationships. Jane Austen is great for that. Her stories are discourses on the social order of the time, but she also creates a variety of personalities through which the reader can *see* this other time.

We talk a lot about the characters. If we like them, we talk about why we like them, why we relate to them. Sometimes one person will really like a character and another won't like the character at all, and that's always interesting. The Canadian writer Robertson Davies writes stories with great characters. His books make great discussions.

I go through periods when I can't read, when I can't focus on the page and I don't get it. I went through a divorce and from the time when the trouble started until just recently, I had trouble focusing on reading. I could read the newspaper and the *New Yorker* magazine, probably because the articles are short, but I couldn't read books and didn't go to the book group. I would look at the book they were reading and say, "I can't read this." I had no interest.

But even though I have gone through periods like that, I still consider myself to be a good reader, and novels are my passion. Reading novels alters my reality. I enter the books and forget what's going on around me. Sometimes I read out loud so I can really hear the author's voice. Sometimes I go to bed as early as possible so I can read. (I've always liked reading in bed.) Or I might set the alarm forty-five minutes early so I can wake up and read. I feel denied if I can't read for pleasure.

JOHN MORAN

When John Moran began his master's degree in psychology at forty, he had been in a library only a handful of times in his life. In the process of meeting the demands of graduate work, he learned to replace his fears of academic inadequacy with feelings of competence and pleasure. In his work as a coach, he uses basketball as the bait to "reel in" street kids so that he can expose them to the possibilities of success, using his own experience as an example.

On the first night of my master's degree classes, I realized I was in trouble. I was totally unprepared. I did not have the tools to do what they were requesting. I knew it the minute I stepped foot in the classes. It was a real eye-opener for me. The teachers said, "We expect this, this, and this. Read these many chapters. And we need this paperwork. Turn it in next week." I said to myself, "I've never seen this before." It really frightened me. At this point, I realized I had a major stumbling block regarding the process of reading.

Going to the library the next day was an adventure for me. I walked in and saw all these people that were in class the night before, all studying. I said to myself, "I don't think I've been in the library more than five times in my life." I felt the handicap at that point, knowing I didn't have the tools.

In the beginning, the driving, motivating force was more a fear of failure than a desire to enhance my learning. I was so afraid to fail. I even fought a few teachers during the beginning of my master's program. I was constantly nail-biting them and bickering over the smallest of things because I knew I didn't have it. So I said, "Well, why can't I do this?" And they would say, "These are the requirements here. This is the way we do things." One teacher was really outstanding. He'll never realize how much he helped me. It was his openness and his relentlessness in not allowing me a crack to slip through, because I'd have taken it. He said, "No, John, no. Understand, this is psychology which can be applicable to anything. I'm just giving you the process on how to do it." It was the word, *process*, that helped me.

As time went on, I found that I was very capable of understanding what was required, and I also found a joy that had never appeared to me before. It was like flowers blooming in the library, realizing that I was OK being there. My thesis required almost eight months of fourteen, fifteen hours a day in a medical library, and that's where I learned to feel comfortable. I hibernated there, and I came to be able to read for three, four hours at a time, and put off taking a break because I didn't think I had done enough. I was able to deliver, too. I was able to go back to class and sit and participate with all these people and know that I had remembered what I read.

Confirmations come in a variety of ways. Sometimes we don't need to have people pat us on the back and say how great we are. For me the confirmations came when somebody would talk about something in class and I would think, "I read that last night. That's right." And I can remember even raising my hand and saying, "And this is also related to that." It got me feeling real comfortable at being able to talk about what I read, how I remembered it, how I comprehended it.

All of a sudden there was a real gleam in reading. As the discomfort of reading ended, and feeling good about it started, I branched out with it. Prior to graduate school, I was narrow-minded as to reading. I would say, "I don't want to read this. I don't want to read that." But it's not so much that I didn't want to, but that I didn't know how. I was scared. The more I read, the less scared I became, and as a result, what happened? I wasn't as narrow-minded.

Reading was never reinforced in my family. Everybody was a blue-collar worker, and due to the streets and the activities in the neighborhood, reading and education took a back burner. Even though we were put in a Catholic school, there was no reinforcement, so I just hit the streets; that's what everybody in my family did. Nobody went to college. The joy of being in the streets with friends far outweighed going into a classroom. How could you match the two? The street had such an allure. Peer identity and peer acceptance were so important. I mean, if you hang out with people who don't do book work, who don't go into a library, it's not an option. It doesn't exist. You're not going to go to a library in front of your friends. It's not going to happen.

The kids today are a lot like I used to be. They want to go into the streets and hang out. They'd rather be in a doorway than come and sit in a library. They don't realize the safeness and the comfortableness of the place. They could actually drop their guard in the library and not have to look over their shoulders. You can't tell me there's not something in a library that can attract every kid out there. There has to be. It's a matter of getting them there to find it, and showing them the tools for finding the books.

That's what the graduate degree did for me. It gave me the confidence and self-esteem to be able to be comfortable in a library. I'm an incredibly different person now. Reading has allowed me to enter into a new arena and feel comfortable. I find myself going on journeys and picking out books that I never would have years earlier. Reading has given me the freedom to grow from inside out and be wiser. There's things in reading you don't have to go out and shout about, but they're discoveries you make inside.

I'm reading a book now that's a thousand pages on Japan. It's three inches thick. You have to be kidding! And we're talking fourteenth century. It's about the history of the Japanese samurai and how their spiritualness and their emotional development resulted in being a samurai without violence. I go to bed reading it at night. I told my friend who gave me the book that it's so powerful, I'll have to read it again. And he said, "Well, that's right. I read it twice."

I think there are a lot of young people like me out there. Education could open up their world, but how do you bring them over to the other side? That is the fascinating part of this whole experience of education—finding a vehicle to get them to the other end so they can discover they're capable of learning. So many kids are knocking on the door out there, and we have to pay attention to hear them. We have to figure out how to help them discover reading the way I did. If we teach them how to read, then they read for life and everything opens up for them.

I thought I was going to graduate school to get a degree, but I found out that the degree is miscellaneous. The end result was the incredible discovery of what reading is all about, which is the last thing I expected. There are a few times in life when we have special experiences that stay with us forever and warm our insides. I truly believe that learning to read in graduate school was one of them for me. I can read now. I can read a thousand-page book and learn about so many things. It makes me smile.

On Reading Mentorship

Until that point she had just been a grandma who had money, who gave me gifts, and who I had to see as an obligation. Then, during one visit, I realized that this woman was really interesting . . . I just looked at her shelves and . . . I knew that she had read that stuff, and if she could, so could I.

Chris Haight

This book contains the stories of many remarkable people who have revealed their reading history, patterns, and behaviors to you. If you're an avid reader who has seen your own reflection somewhere among these pages, it is now your turn to come to the aid of an infrequent reader. If these stories have alerted you to your own reading difficulties, now is the time to enlist the assistance of a successful reader. Here's how:

Mentoring Adults

Infrequent readers: find someone to mentor you

Are you experiencing difficulty with your reading? Think of a relative, friend, or acquaintance who cares about you, a person with whom you would enjoy spending time. Does this person read a lot and seem to delight in reading? Would you enjoy talking with her so you could acquire some of her pleasure in reading?

Collect your courage and ask her to be your reading mentor. Ask her to tell you how she first became interested in books, how she finds books on the topics she enjoys, and how she actually comprehends the books she finds. Perhaps she would like to read some stories in *Speaking of Reading* with you, especially those similar to your own. If you feel comfortable, make a commitment to each other to meet regularly for a few months to talk about what you are reading; go to the library and bookstores together; read together. Then see how it goes from there.

Avid readers: find someone to mentor

Have books greatly influenced your life? Do you immediately find yourself perusing the bookshelves when you visit a person's home or office? Do you enjoy your self-image as a reader? Then go public as a reader.[22] Let others see you reading, let them know how much you read. Talk about the book you are currently enjoying. If you notice someone listening quietly, notice who that someone is. It may be an infrequent reader who would welcome a chance to learn how to love books as much as you do.

Begin your mentoring slowly. Pick out a few narratives in *Speaking of Reading* you think this person might enjoy (but only a few), and talk about which ones you related to and why. Read some of them together. Remember, your friend might be a person who hasn't read an entire book since those required in high school, if ever. Read for yourself the narratives in the frustrated readers chapter to gain insight into the difficulties such readers encounter. Tread softly. Don't be overzealous. With your help and gentle encouragement, your new reading protégé may be able to develop a more positive relationship with the printed word.

Mentoring adults who are infrequent readers

There are many ways you can serve as a reading mentor to an infrequent reader. You can give him books as gifts, but be sure to choose short, clearly written books on topics you have reason to believe your protégé will enjoy. Find books with fast-moving plots and lots of dialogue, as well as books with characters that are in situations similar to those of your friend. Tell him why you are giving him the book, and why you think he will enjoy it. After a few weeks, ask if he has started the book and discuss it if he has, but don't be concerned if he hasn't even opened it; simply give more encouragement. He probably has years of resistance to overcome.

You can browse bookstores together looking for favorite authors and subjects. Choose a book to read together, then get together to talk about the book, its characters, and plot. Visit a magazine kiosk with your friend and buy magazines, and later discuss the articles you've read. Give a gift subscription to a magazine you think he will enjoy.

Once your relationship is established, consider forming a reading group with your partner by finding four to eight other people to join you. A good mix might be to include one or two other established readers who are interested in mentoring, with the remaining ones new readers. Reading groups generally meet every three to six weeks, rotating homes for each meeting. But groups can also be held in cafés or library group rooms. Some combine a meal or snacks with the discussion. Members select books according to group interest, and all may attend the group, whether or not they actually read the entire book. Some groups designate a discussion leader for each book while others are less structured. Reading groups provide opportunities to meet people with backgrounds different from your own, whom you may not otherwise have met, but with whom you may find you have a lot in common.

While mentoring an infrequent reader, remember that a person who doesn't read may have a poor self-image. Reading is very important in our culture, so those who find reading difficult often suffer embarrassment in the company of well-read peers. As a reading mentor, be aware of these potential sensitivities, and take advantage of opportunities to encourage your friend with positive comments that will enable him to develop a positive sense of himself as a reader.

Building a mentoring relationship takes time. Don't give up if your friend acts disinterested at first. It may be that the fear of failure is simply paralyzing him. Or his self-esteem may be so low that he does not understand why you want to spend your time with him. Just keep persevering, but take it slowly. Eventually you will build a mutual trust.

Modeling your comprehension strategies

If your protégé is not reading the books and articles you suggest, perhaps it's because she is frustrated in her attempts to comprehend. She most likely never learned the reading strategies that avid readers taught themselves, that you probably taught yourself without even being aware of doing so.

To develop your ability to show your protégé how you successfully read, I would like to suggest an excellent technique called Reciprocal Teaching.[23] This technique was designed to be used as a small-group activity in reading classrooms with the goal of enabling poor readers to develop better comprehension skills by learning metacognitive skills— learning to think about the text while they're reading. Reading mentors can easily adapt the Reciprocal Teaching technique for their tutoring purposes, using all or some of the following suggestions:

First, *read* a short segment of a book or article with your reading protégé. Then:

- *Ask* thoughtful questions about the reading that you both can respond to. Then invite your friend to ask her own questions.

- *Summarize* the segment briefly, then ask your partner to elaborate on your summary.

- *Clarify* any part that is not immediately clear to you, then invite her to do the same.

- *Predict* what may come next, then ask for additional predictions.

This practice enables you to model your reading strategies and encourages your protégé to focus on the text instead of drifting off when she reads. In the beginning, you may find that you ask all the questions and make all the summaries, clarifications, and predictions. With time, you will discover that your reading protégé will be able to take over while you relax. She will begin to monitor her own comprehension, relying more on herself, and less on you. She will develop self-confidence in her reading as she has successful reading experiences through Reciprocal Teaching.[24] You might want to review the discussion of metacognition and schema theories in the Introduction and reread the introduction to Chapter 8, Those Aware of Their Reading Process, in which I note some additional comprehension-monitoring strategies.

If the Reciprocal Teaching approach seems too structured, here is another approach you can try. The use of this more generalized language strategy will help to give your friend the words she needs to begin articulating her comprehension process. Sometimes an opening phrase is all she will require to begin summarizing and clarifying the text as she reads.

Have her read a short segment of a book or article with you. Then:

• Begin with one of the following openers, and complete the sentence:
  "So, in other words, . . ."
  "What I'm curious about is . . ."
  "What I'm confused about is . . ."
  "What struck me is . . ."

• Ask your friend to complete another opener about the same part of the book.

• Continue to read short segments and trade comments.

You may find it somewhat difficult when you begin modeling your reading strategies for your protégé, but very quickly you'll find a style and strategy that work for you. Both reading instructors and their students agree that modeling techniques such as Reciprocal Teaching and language strategies enable students to raise their reading abilities surprisingly quickly.

Mentoring Children

Although *Speaking of Reading* is not about children's reading, it is very much about adults who were once children. Nearly everyone I interviewed told me stories about their childhood reading. The signal was clear: The majority of those who were read to as children became readers, while those who weren't read to often became infrequent readers. Even I was amazed at just how often these generalizations were true.

Yet many parents, including those who are avid readers themselves, do not recognize the significance of reading regularly to their own children. They neglect reading in favor of other more pressing chores and let the television baby-sit their children more often than they readily admit. I am including this section on reading activities for children for those of you who might benefit from its list of ideas.

Experts agree that children who listen to lots and lots of books being read to them have the best chance of reading successfully as adults.[25] And parents who enjoy reading often produce children who also enjoy reading, particularly if these children are read to constantly from the time they are six months old through their ninth birthday. This reading is especially effective if it is done with enthusiasm and made into a fun activity, which might include acting out the stories.[26]

Parents are most often their children's first reading mentor since they are the most available adults to take on the task. But any adolescent or adult who enjoys reading and desires to develop a special bond with a particular child can easily become a reading mentor simply by making the commitment to do so.

When reading mentors read to children they open the door to the riches found within the pages of books. From books, young children can develop their imagination and creativity, as well as their intelligence and problem-solving abilities. They quickly begin to develop a love of stories and will want to read on their own to satisfy their own interests. They soon become readers themselves and their world (and perhaps the world of their own children) is forever expanded and enriched.[27]

Reading to children

There are many simple things you can do to encourage children to become successful readers. When children are infants, let them listen to the sound of language while you read very simple picture books. Look at pictures together and point to objects while saying their names. Buy plastic and cardboard books they can put in their mouths. When your children reach preschool and school age, read to them every day.

Here are some additional activities that reading mentors of children can do to enhance their reading pleasure:

- Read at a scheduled time every day and make reading a fun and rewarding activity.

- Point to the words with your finger as you read and have the child turn the pages.

- Read slowly and pause occasionally to think out loud about the story.

- Speculate on what will happen next or why a character acted in a particular manner.

- Answer the child's questions and encourage her imaginative responses.

- Try not to hurry through a story even if reading delays other activities.

- Talk about stories the day after you read them.

- Have fun and share the joy of reading together.

- Try very hard to not act like a teacher; rather, be a friend.[28]

Read to school-age children regularly until they can read more sophisticated books by themselves. It is very important not to stop reading to them when they just begin to read on their own since the interest gap between the books they have been listening to and the books they are able to read on their own is just too wide, and they can easily become bored by the more simple books.

Finding books

Find books your child will love by asking other parents to share the names of their children's favorite books. Go to the library and get your child a library card. Check out award-winning books. Ask the librarian for book ideas. Be aware of which books are best for which age level. Ask teachers and librarians for summer book lists.[29]

Children's favorite subjects

Find out what topics interest your child and then find books on those topics in your library or bookstore. Genres that children tend to enjoy include: fantasies, comics, jokes and humor, crafts, series books, adventure stories, science fiction, mysteries, biographies of heroes and heroines, science experiments, suspense, sports, teen romance, how-to books, historical fiction, supernatural, occult, trivia, and general children's and adolescent fiction. Often, children will want to read a number of related books one after the other.

Setting up a personal library

Surround your child with books and magazines. Keep an eye out for inexpensive books at flea markets, garage sales, used book stores, and children's used clothing stores. Give gift certificates for books. Subscribe to children's magazines. Once you've amassed a significant number of books and magazines, set up a small bookcase near an appropriate reading area with a reading light and designate the area as your child's reading spot. Encourage your child to arrange the books as she sees fit.[30] I know a four-year-old who is very proud of his own little chair and light right beside his own bookcase in a corner of his room. Whenever he has visitors, this is the first place he brings them.

Letting school-age children read to you

Let your school-age child read to you. Give lots of encouragement and praise and hugs, and appreciate her skills. Show excitement for her reading accomplishments, and be gentle and nonjudgmental when she has difficulties. If the reading moves very slowly, take turns reading paragraphs. Help her with difficult words or let her skip over the words to see if the sentence makes sense anyway. Supply the correct form of words she stumbles over. Remember, you are not her teacher; you are her mentor. While teachers will persuade their students to 'sound out' the words, mentors simply encourage their protégés to enjoy reading. And most importantly, show an infinite amount of patience and love.[31]

Avoiding discouragement

Even if you have read to your child diligently every evening before he goes to bed for the first six years of his life, he still may encounter reading difficulties as he reaches first or second grade. I've worked with many children, mostly boys, who began reading relatively late, in third or fourth grade, even though their well-read parents read to them when they were young. Parents, please don't become discouraged and assume your child has a reading disability, such as dyslexia, if he is only six or seven years old and still does not read. He may pick up that you think something is wrong with him from the way you act, and he may become frustrated believing that something is wrong with him and that he can't learn to read.

The son of two librarians I know still wasn't reading on his own in the third grade, which worried them tremendously as they had read to him every book imaginable. With my advice they simply continued reading sophisticated books to him, which aroused his interest. Finally, one day he came home and said, "Mommy, I can read now." And in fact, he could. A few years later the boy became an avid reader.

Try to relax with your child who seems to be a little beyond the age when you believe he should be reading naturally. Your anxiety can potentially give him a complex about his reading that could interfere even more with his reading development. If you are genuinely concerned that he has a reading problem, seek advice from a reading specialist, but do this first on your own, without involving your child. Meanwhile, continue reading to him.

Family reading times

Designate a quiet time each day or week when everyone in the family reads silently—together. Let your child pick out any type of reading material she wants for this activity. This is not a time to do homework. Relax and enjoy your quiet reading times.[32] Talk about what you read.

If you don't have time to read

Ask an aunt, uncle, cousin, neighbor, or friend who has the time and interest to become your child's reading mentor, especially if this person wants to develop a special relationship with your child. Enlist older siblings to read to the younger children. Let your child stay up a little later than usual if she is reading on her own. Consider releasing her from a chore if she is completing a book.[33] And please don't make reading a punishment or a chore.

Like many friendships, a reading mentorship is based on common interests. It is based on the two of you being engaged in a common activity—reading—which will provide you countless opportunities to discuss, analyze, critique, argue, laugh, and learn together. I think you'll enjoy this new adventure.

I cannot think of a better blessing than to die in one's own bed, without warning or discomfort, on the last page of the new book that we most wanted to read.

John Russell

◊

ENDNOTES

I want to acknowledge the many reading researchers whose studies on reading comprehension have influenced the way we define and teach reading in our classrooms today. These remarkable individuals have influenced me and my own teaching, and their theories and ideas permeated my mind while I worked on this book. In addition to the references listed below, I want to acknowledge the following leaders in the reading field for what they have added to our understanding of this complex process. They include Ann Brown, Dolores Durkin, Paolo Friere, Kenneth Goodman, Dale Johnson, Stephen Krashen, Martha Maxwell, Anne Marie Palincsar, David Pearson, Frank Smith, and L.S. Vygotsky.

1   Nicholas, Z. and M. Winglee. 1990. "Who Reads Literature?" *Future of the United States as a Nation of Readers*, Washington, D.C.: National Endowment of the Arts.

2   Commission on Reading of the National Academy of Education. 1985. *Becoming a Nation of Readers*. Springfield, IL: Phillips Brothers.

3   Brown, A.L., J.C. Campione, and J.D. Day. 1981. "Learning to Learn: On Training Students to Learn from Texts." *Educational Researcher* 10 (2).

4   Weaver, C. 1988. *Reading Process and Practice: From Socio-Psycholinguistics to Whole Language*. Portsmouth, NH: Heinemann.

5   Smith, F. 1982. *Understanding Reading*. New York: Holt, Rinehart and Winston.

6   Harste, J.C. 1986. "What It Means to Be Strategic: Good Readers as Informants." Austin, TX: Paper presented at the Annual Meeting of the 36th National Reading Conference.

7   Borko, H. 1986. "Students' Conceptions of Reading and Their Reading Experiences in School." *Elementary School Journal* 86 (5).

8   Thompson, M.E. 1987. "What Happens When Readers Do Not Read? The Problem of Reluctant Readers." Notre Dame, IN: Paper presented at the 30th North Central Reading Association.

9   Borko 1986.

10   National Assesment of Educational Progress. 1985. "Profiles of Literacy: An Assessment of Young Adults." Development Plan.

11   Moss, A. 1985. "Adult Illiteracy: A Plan for Action." Pamona, CA: California State Polytechnic University.

12   Johnson, J. 1985. "Adults in Crisis: Illiteracy in America." San Francisco, CA: Far West Lab for Educational Research and Development.

13   McGrail, J. 1984. "Adult Illiterates and Adult Literacy Programs: A Summary of Descriptive Data." San Francisco, CA: Far West Lab for Educational Research and Development.

14   Bush, B. 1983. "Why We Can't Afford Illiteracy And What We Can Do About It." *Foundation News* Jan/Feb:18.

15   Project Literacy U.S. 1988. "First Things First." An ABC/PBS Television Documentary. This statistic was noted by an interviewee during the documentary.

16   Rosenthal, N. 1987. *Teach Someone to Read*. Paramus, NJ: Globe/Fearon. A comprehension-based tutor training manual for adult literacy volunteers.

17   Mitchell, W.M. 1987. "The Workings of Working Memory." *Science* 237,4822: 1564–67.

18   De Costa, D.M. 1986. "Metacognition and Higher Order Thinking: An Interdisciplinary Approach to Critical Thinking in the Humanities." Atlanta GA: Presentation at the 15th Annual Conference of the International Society for Individualized Instruction.

19   Harste 1986.

20   Brown, A.L. 1985. "Teaching Students to Think as They Read: Implications for Curriculum Reform." Urbana, IL: University of IL, Center for the Study of Reading, Reading Education Report No. 58.

21   Brown 1985.

22   Sledge, A.C. 1984. "This Book Reminds Me of You: The Reader as Mentor." Atlanta, GA: Presented at the 29th Annual Meeting of the International Reading Association.

23   Palincsar, A.M.S. and A.L. Brown. 1988. "Teaching and Practicing Thinking Skills to Promote Comprehension in the Context of Group Problem Solving." *Remedial and Special Education Journal* Jan/Feb.

24   Palincsar and Brown 1988.

25   Binkley, M.R. and others. 1988. *Becoming a Nation of Readers.* Washington, DC: U.S. Department of Education, Office of Educational Research and Improvement.

26   Lockledge, A. and C. Matheny. 1987. "Looking Toward the Family: Case Studies of Lifelong Readers." Anaheim, CA: Presented at the 32nd Annual Meeting of the International Reading Association.

27– Cullinan, B. and B. Bagert. 1994. *Helping Your Child Learn to*
33   *Read: Activities for Children from Infancy Through Age 10.* Washington, DC: U.S. Department of Education, Office of Educational Research and Improvement. This short pamphlet is a wonderful resource for ideas. For your copy send fifty cents to the American Federation of Teachers, 558 New Jersey Avenue NW, Washington, D.C. Ask for Item #350.